Everything You Need to Know About Homeschool UNIT STUDIES

The Anyone Can How-to Guide

By Jennifer Steward

Everything You Need to Know About Homeschool UNIT STUDIES

Is published by

All Rights Reserved

Revised and expanded 2nd Edition 2005
ISBN # 0-9770444-0-8

Illustrations by Scott Borello

Steward Ship Publishing   P.O. Box 164, Garden Valley, CA 95633   530-333-0803
PRINTED IN CHINA BY PRINCO INTERNATIONAL

TABLE OF CONTENTS

FOREWARD

Unit Studies. The very words fill my mind with a myriad of favorite homeschool memories our family has shared in the 14 years we have been homeschooling our seven children.

Timelines dotted with people, events and inventions, notebooks bulging with research and discoveries, and hours spent reading excellent literature aloud are the common themes of our Unit Studies. In addition to providing a well rounded education for our children, Unit Studies have allowed our students a healthy degree of free choice as they pursue topics that tickle their individual interests.

Certainly, over the years, our family has utilized many different teaching methods. Unit Studies has been the method in which each student does not merely survive, but thrives. Unit Studies have equipped our children with the lifelong ability of knowing how to research any subject, to continue learning long after the diploma has been earned.

Jennifer Steward has been a mentor to me for many years, both as a friend and as a fellow homeschooling mother. Our family has benefited from using Steward Ship Unit Studies. Jennifer's creativity and exuberance is apparent in her products and now in this book, *Everything You Need to Know About Homeschool Unit Studies.* Her pleasant, conversational style of writing will make the reader feel like you are sitting in Jennifer's sunny kitchen sharing tea and encouragement. Any fears or questions you may have about Unit Studies will dissolve like sugar cubes in your favorite cup of steaming tea. I am confident you will find your time with Jennifer inspiring. I always do.

PeggySue Wells
Author of *Holding Down the Fort*

Thank You!

My children often refer to this book as "Mom's Book"...but it is all because of them that I could even write it. I owe so many thanks... to so many people.

First, I must thank my Lord for EVERYTHING! He has given me my wonderful husband, Jim, who let me have eight beautiful children ~ Cacey, Tyson, Whitney, Brooke, Kally, Samuel, Anna, and Laurel. Each of you are such a blessing to me. I have had the privilege to spend time with you on our homeschooling adventure and been given the bonus of getting an education, too. Thanks, you guys, for helping out so I could get this project done!

Jim, you have been patient, kind and loving - thank you!

I would like to thank you Aaron, my amazing son-in-law, (our cover designer) for ALL the things you've done to encourage and help me.

Thank you to Steve Friedrich - Mr. Computer Genius - for doing everything so willingly that I didn't know how to do which brought peace of mind to a frazzled mom! Thank you, Karen Tissue (Steve's smart sister-in-law) for coming to the rescue at the last minute!

Thanks Coie for providing the cover picture!

Thank you to my artistic brother, Scott Borello, who is a nut!

Thanks Mom - for helping me whenever I call for whatever I need!

A big "thank you" to my oldest daughter Cacey, who took the time to edit this book and make her mom sound better!

I want to thank Amy, my sweet daughter-in-law, who is always available, willing to help and does a lot of behind the scenes "stuff!"

Thanks Elaina (my granddaughter) for being so precious. I can't wait to do a unit study with you!

I'd like to thank all the parents who have taken the time to read this book. It humbles me to think that the Lord would use any of our experiences, strengths or weaknesses to encourage another. Also, thank all of you moms who have come to a workshop and then become our friends and in turn encouraged us!

Jennifer Steward

Introduction

Come with me and let's take a peek into the window of a homeschooling family. We see a familiar picture - breakfast over and the chores under control, Mom calls to her children, "It's time to start school." Then comes a familiar sound. We've all heard it - it's the sound of dragging feet and of muffled moans and groans. Does this picture represent life in your home? Well, that's exactly the way it was in our home for years... until we made some changes and switched from conventional classroom teaching methods to that of doing unit studies. The positive changes in how our children have responded to learning have been significant. So now, instead of just going through the motions and merely meeting a blanket set of predetermined standards, our children are getting a "real" education. I am excited about those changes and can't wait to share what I've learned with you.

I would like to invite you, through this book, into the life of my family to share over twenty years of varied experiences I have had educating my eight children at home. At the time of this edition, three of our children have graduated from homeschool high school. We have another daughter in the 10th grade who works independently on unit studies and then we have four in grade school. Let me see, yes - that's all eight of them. Since our children range in age from age 24 down to five, I find myself in a really great place- being able to see the fruit of our labors in the older children, while still having an active Kindergartner! This also confirms to us that home education turns out adults who are succeeding and thriving in their professions and callings. Further it has proven to us that the unit study method turns out students who are well educated!

Because of our long history in the homeschool movement, we would consider ourselves pioneers. Over the years, we have tried a variety of methods and observed countless changes in many areas:

- Available teaching resources.
- Differing methods and programs.
- Popular curriculums.
- Reasons parents choose home education and more!

OUR STORY

The great and exciting news is that we HAVE developed a true love for learning. Our kids love to learn and they love books. The interesting truth of it all is that it happened quite by accident! Here's the story of how we got started using unit studies. In the early days, we didn't have many curriculum choices so we had to purchase expensive, bulky teacher's manuals suited for whole classrooms. We spent a lot of money on test keys, workbooks, and other devices required by the curriculum for every child and every subject. We never had to worry about whether we'd miss anything, because it was ALL contained in the manuals. (That's not completely true. Because we lacked confidence and experience, we still worried!)

Since homeschooling was relatively new "back then," we didn't dare stray from the curriculum instructions. We were always concerned that others would challenge our abilities to teach (which they often did), so we played it safe by attempting to "do it all." In fact, my biggest problem in those days was running out of time to cover the material. You would find me still doing school at 8:00 pm - sound familiar? Well, meanwhile I lost my children's attention and all interest. You can picture the poor darlings bored to tears, sliding down in their chairs. Sadly, the result was that they had not truly "learned" all we had hoped they would even after all the hours of sacrificial effort I had devoted! I am certain you may have experienced this same frustration.

When the time came that I was teaching three children at once and I realized that with each passing year I would gain another student at a different grade level, I KNEW I needed an alternative. The Lord had called us to take responsibility for our children's education - we knew this for sure, so my husband and I were determined to keep going (at that point, my husband more than me! Thank God for husbands who don't get so emotional about things!) For me, switching to using unit studies was a last resort, but necessary if we wanted to survive. We attended some seminars on the unit study method and found the concept intriguing, interesting, and fun. We decided to give the unit study approach a try, and the rest is history because since then, we have used unit studies extensively and exclusively as a core for teaching.

So, let's talk about unit studies—the why and the how, the basis, the benefits, the tools, the subjects, the planning, the details, the resources, the records—let's discuss EVERYTHING you need to know about unit studies!

In the area of education, the unit study method is a first-rate choice as a powerful and effective teaching approach, and I would encourage you to carefully consider the benefits it offers.

**If we were to place an ad in a magazine
to sell the unit study approach,
it might read:**

EXTRA! ◦ EXTRA!

Exciting approach to teaching children of all ages promises to live up boring subjects! No more yawning through history lessons. No more arm twisting to get your students to pay attention in school. Students fit the learning puzzle together as topics relate. Studies are richer and more meaningful. Moms love unit studies once they understand planning and scheduling. Combine subjects and topics and have more time for creativity and fun!

Our guarantee? If your children are not entirely satisfied with this hands on, interactive, living books approach… if they do not ask when they can start school, if they do not have sparkling eyes and smiling faces… you have our permission to go back to using textbooks!

The Unit Study Method is a popluar and widely accepted teaching method, but many questions remain unanswered. Like me, many parents get excited about unit studies but knowing about the potential benefits of unit studies and yet not how the details all fit and work together is rather like purchasing a computer and getting excited about what it can do but then if you don't understand how to get it to perform all the wonderful functions you know it can perform, you are lost. So, to discover what the computer can do, you must read the manual. Likewise, you can consider this book your unit study how-to manual. I have had parents bring their tattered book to a meeting or workshop all marked up with pages folded down at the corner. They call it their Unit Study Bible! This manual will teach you the nuts and bolts of unit studies and how the method can help your children have a rich, memorable, lasting, and superior education.

While I didn't develop the unit study method, I like to think that I have "refined" it and figured out the problem areas that cause people to think the method is too complex and difficult for most people to use. This book is really the result of years of my own bumblings of trials and errors as I tried to figure unit studies out! Together with hosting and leading a monthly unit study meeting for many years and answering questions for parents, I have simplified the method by suggesting specific guidelines to follow. You might say I worked the "bugs" out.

People explore the option of the unit study approach for many reasons. Your interest in unit studies might have arisen from one or more of the following situations:

- You are embarking on the road to home education and want to know about the different teaching approaches that are available.

- You heard a positive report about unit studies from a friend.

- The dynamics of your family have changed and you need to reevaluate your current method.

- You are discouraged or confused with the method you are presently using and are ready to give up.

When I present workshops on unit studies I receive a wide range of questions and concerns connected with this approach. Many parents feel that the Lord has called them to educate their children at home but do not know how and where to begin. Just a few of the common questions about the unit study approach include the following:

"What exactly is a unit study?"

"How do you do a unit study?"

"How do I know what to teach?"

This book comes to you as a result of the many conversations I have had with moms. We've seen countless benefits from teaching by the unit study method, not just with our children, but with our whole family. Those who home educate tend to be generally more "home based" and are able to build and master various skills from home. This book is meant to assist you in gaining effective teaching skills using the unit study method. We will shed more light on this subject and help you understand *Everything You Need to Know about Unit Studies*, so that your family might benefit, too.

TO HELP YOU UNDERSTAND...

I will be offering information, tips, ideas and insights which I have gained over the years doing unit studies with my children. I will share examples from many different topics from various units in the areas of: history, science, and the arts. Doing so will help you gain a thorough understanding of how this method works.

 Throughout this book you will see little lightbulbs here and there. These are placed in areas where an important point is made or where there is a tip or idea worth remembering. You will often notice a piece of text that is highlighted. It might be a good idea to go through the book, after you have finished reading it, and write out all the important tips and ideas on one piece of paper so you can go over them and have them in one place. You'll be surprised how it will help the "lights go on" (pardon the pun!) and you will be able to see the whole unit study puzzle start to come together.

As I explain "everything" I will not only be informing you, but I will also be instructing you in a method - and offering a sort of road map or skeleton framework to follow so you can easily begin to adapt this teaching method into your family. I will refer to what I do and what I teach as The Steward Method. The most important issue and the point I will repeatedly bring forth and reiterate is that learning is exciting and that God's world is a fascinating place. It is not just some special gift or teaching ability some mothers have. ALL children CAN develop a love and hunger for learning. The unit study method is merely a vehicle - a really great vehicle - to use in accomplishing the goal. And the goal is to delight the child and lead them into real, joyful learning.

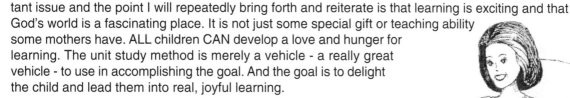

Okay, now fasten the seat belt on your recliner and get ready to be enlightened! But proceed with caution—unit studies are contagious. If you catch the bug, there's no cure. You'll tell your friends, and they will catch it, too!

Choosing a

(1)

Teaching Method

The first decision to be made concerning your children's education is where they will acquire it. If you have already decided on home education, the next step is to choose a teaching method. Choosing a teaching method to suit each child's learning style requires some work.

Your part begins as you:

- Determine your child's learning style.

- Learn about what methods are available.

- Seek the Lord's direction.

- Listen to the advice of experienced homeschooling families so you can avoid some of the stumbling blocks.

- Practice patience.

Many parents jump into home education, visit a curriculum fair or a teacher's store, pick up a truckload of books and resources, and start teaching and often find they end up with materials that don't meet their particular needs. A good number of parents start their homeschooling adventure by selecting a traditional/ conventional teaching method possibly because of the security it seems to offer, then within a few years, they become dissatisfied and start looking for an alternative... frequently turning to the unit study method.

~ Imagine a newspaper article written about veteran homeschooling families ~

DISease Strikes Homeschooling Parents

It is reported that a strange disease, doctors are calling D-I-S, has struck thousands of homeschooling parents nationwide. It continues to spread year after year in epidemic proportions. Parents are D-I-S satisfied, D-I-S couraged, and D-I-S illusioned with their present teaching methods. Doctors say there is alarming evidence that the solution lies in The Unit Study Method.

I used to be more hesitant in suggesting the unit study approach to NEW homeschoolers because I felt like it might overwhelm them. So I let them "do their thing" until they started floundering and became desperate then I'd step in and help. Then a new family moved to our community and asked for advice in getting started with homeschooling. I hesitantly invited the mother to a unit study meeting. I told her this was my area of expertise so I could show her what I know and teach. She did jump into unit studies and at the end of her first year I asked her what she was planning to do the next year. She said, "I'll do phonics for my little guy, we'll use the same math program we used last year… and unit studies for the rest." I don't know why I was so amazed. She got it. She understood!

Now my approach is teach parents right from the start. It is so important for mothers of young children to get off to the right start and lead children to delight in learning. Why should new homeschoolers have to struggle through the first few years using traditional methods which they often become dissatisfied with after two to three years, when there is information and help?

SWITCHING GEARS

If you have not started out using the unit study method and are "switching gears" you very well may have a hard time getting off on the right foot.

Sometimes families have a hard time switching gears and will stick with a program and method that does not work for them because:

- They have made a financial investment in it and don't want to "waste" money.

- They are afraid to step out and try something completely different, new or seemingly unstructured.

Stumbling blocks homeschooling parents struggle with:

• **_Looking to the public school classroom as a guideline for teaching._** Sometimes our perception of what takes place in the conventional school setting leaves us feeling threatened and intimidated. When we see a public school student who seems to "know it all," we panic and think our students are not where they should be academically. Yet imitating the typical classroom is not the most conducive environment for encouraging creative minds.

• **_Not being able to let go of tradition._** We as home educators yearn to relax and enjoy our studies. We want our students to be happy and excited about learning and our hearts tell us this is a good thing while our heads tell us we are not doing enough. We fall back into the trap of thinking "Everyone else uses traditional methods so this must be the best way."

• **_Listening to the challenges of others._** Sometimes we are challenged by relatives, friends, or neighbors who are skeptical of homeschooling. They ask, "How do you know your children are learning what they should?" and "Who watches over you, tests your children, and holds you accountable?"

Wherever you are on the road to home education, this manual will provide guidelines to help you devise a plan and set goals and requirements for your students. Before you do anything else, be sure you prayerfully seek the Lord and respond to Him in what He wants you to teach your children. Those who seek - find. He knows your children better than anyone and He is faithful to give direction to those who ask for it. Try it!

There are many ways to homeschool. If you choose to work with an Independent Study Programs (ISP), they often provide some guidance and accountability by outlining certain requirements for member home educators, but ultimately you are responsible and accountable to God for educating your children.

Attending seminars and curriculum fairs can provide you with instruction, information, and exposure to all the great things home education has to offer. But BEWARE… proceed prayerfully and carefully. Homeschool conventions are a place where you will find needed information and encouragement from experienced speakers. It is also sort of like a trade show offering almost everything you can imagine for obtaining a quality education! Homeschool conventions and curriculum fairs are also a place where you can lose your mind and your bank account. Be discerning and explore your options before making a large investment. Becoming familiar with methods and materials that are available will help you in your decision-making process for educating your children.

POPULAR TEACHING METHODS

The following are some of the most widely used teaching methods we find in home education:

- Unit Studies
- The Traditional Textbook Approach
- The Moores
- Charlotte Mason
- The Principle Approach
- Classical
- Unschooling

We will mainly focus and compare two specific methods. They are the "unit study approach" and the "traditional textbook approach." The unit study approach can be used with most of the methods listed above with the exception of the textbook approach and the principle approach. Most of the others are what we would consider more eclectic because they often incorporate a living books, literature approach.

Many methods are similar, sharing some of the same philosophies and characteristics. You don't have to ascribe to only one method and narrowly adhere to it. You can incorporate the best aspects of the methods that apply to your situation, resulting in a program that meets the specific needs of YOUR family.

THE MOORES

This is not so much a method as it is a philosophy. Raymond and Dorothy Moore have written a number of books that spell out the benefits of delayed education and promote a balance of service, study, and work. This method tends to be one that, like unit studies (and Charlotte Mason), makes use of multisensory learning.

CHARLOTTE MASON

This method focuses on Living Books and real life experiences. Basics like the 3R's (reading, 'riting, and 'rithmetic) are taught in a hands-on fashion and other subjects (like history, geography, science, and literature) are learned by using Living Books that help each subject come to life. Charlotte Mason coined the term "Living Books" to describe books that impact your life, stir you, move you, and touch your heart and mind. They are timeless.

THE PRINCIPLE APPROACH

In this approach, subjects are studied using the scriptures. Students learn to identify, apply, and understand biblical principles and how they relate in the different subject areas. This method emphasizes God's providential role in history and the need for education to return to those biblical principles.

UNSCHOOLING

Unschooling, also referred to as child-initiated learning or self-directed study, suggests that when a child is surrounded by good books, resources, and tools, that child will direct his or her own education.

CLASSICAL EDUCATION

This can be a broad term meaning different things to different people. A method of reading the ancient classical authors: Plato, Caesar, and Homer - a narrower definition would be teaching the same educational principles toward the same educational goals as the ancients - not necessarily the same literature of the ancients. This can be referred to as Applied Trivium.

TRADITIONAL TEXTBOOK APPROACH

This approach involves the use of graded textbooks with the intention of covering a subject over the course of a school year. Most who use this method like it for the structure and security it provides. Materials are prepared and completely laid out for you. Those who choose this approach tend to run their home schools like conventional classrooms. There are both advantages and disadvantages to this approach.

UNIT STUDIES

A UNIT STUDY BY ANY OTHER NAME IS STILL A UNIT STUDY

Some other terms which are used to describe what we are calling a unit study are:

- Learning Capsule
- Thematic Study
- Whole Learning
- Delight-Directed Study
- Integrated Study

> "Unit studies involve taking one topic, subject or word and building an entire curriculum around it."
>
> (Vicky Brady, *The Basic Steps to Successful Home Schooling*
> [Lafayette: Vital Issues Press, 1996], 64)

WHAT IS THE UNIT STUDY APPROACH

When we did our first unit study on Trains, all I knew about unit studies was that you chose a topic and tried to include as many of your subjects as possible. That simple explanation still stands today! The unit study approach involves exploring one topic by incorporating many subjects around the same theme. This approach appeals to many, because…

- It allows you to include children with varying ages in the same study - each working at their own level.

- Of the use of living books.

- It is hands-on and activity-oriented. (Children are often better able to remember what they learn through doing, rather than just through hearing or reading.)

UNIT STUDIES…

…tie topics together, allowing them to be seen and understood as a whole, rather than in bits and pieces. The study can be about a topic, a piece of literature, a time period, a person, or just about anything else under the sun. This natural learning process allows students to become knowledgeable about the topic through total immersion in it.

"Homeschoolers are often on the leading edge of what works in education and they don't know it. This is true in the area of unit studies. College textbooks are now extolling the virtues of the thematic approach again. State guidelines are being rewritten to include it. Teaching skills the context of activities that are enjoyable and integrating several subjects has always been effective; now it seemd to be recognized as being more practical."

(Debbie Strayer, *"Getting Your Feet Wet,"* Homeschooling Today, July/August, 1997)

BENEFITS OF THIS APPROACH

There are many benefits to the unit study approach, including the following:

- Children of all ages learn best this way because of the comprehensive and innovative ways in which the topics are covered.

- Students become somewhat of an expert on many topics since studies conducted are so thorough.

- Unit studies stimulate creativity through hands-on activities.

- Self-designed curriculums offer freedom in the learning environment.

- Unit studies provide greater flexibility for dealing with students of varying ages. (This is easier for families of any size, but essential for large families!)

- Unit studies accomplish more in less time. This helps to eliminate guilt over not "doing school" all day.

- Assignments are of academic value - not just busywork!

- As the core method, most subjects are covered and included.

- A more natural and delightful approach to teaching - students don't even realize they are doing subjects or even "school" for that matter!

- Because so many topics are studied over time, students build a mental timeline.

- Unit studies can be more cost effective if you use the library and collect resources in advance at used bookstores, etc.

- Unit studies provide a wide range of experiences so children enjoy their studies.

- Students learn and retain more of what they study.

- Unit studies unify the whole family because they are interactive.

Each of the benefits listed are discussed in detail later in this chapter.

ADVANTAGES TO USING TEXTBOOKS:

- Parents are familiar with textbooks from their own schooling experiences so using something conventional makes parents feel secure.

- They are relatively easy to use, because everything is laid out for you lesson by lesson.

- The highly structured format makes them attractive for those just starting out in home education because parents lack the confidence for knowing what to teach next. Textbooks help them stay on track since the scope and sequence is provided.

- Page numbers and assignments make work easier to grade and simplifies record keeping for parents.

- They are sometimes geared for visual learners.

- Parents like the security of feeling that if the materials are all there, they won't miss something important. They also find them convenient and accepted,

DISADVANTAGES OF USING TEXTBOOKS:

- Generally, textbooks are boring because they are full of dates and facts and designed for a classroom to be completed in one year.

- Learning and retention is limited as kids don't retain what they didn't learn.

- They do not work well for active, kinesthetic, and auditory learners.

- They are expensive.

- They are designed for only one age or grade.

During our early years of homeschooling we used textbooks for teaching. Today many homeschoolers choose to be somewhat eclectic - using textbooks for some but not all subjects. But when we started out we purchased all our materials/curriculum from one company, so we had an English workbook and a reading program that included a reader and a workbook. Each child also had a math book, a history textbook and workbook, a science textbook and sometimes a workbook, and also a spelling workbook. We began our day with Bible and moved into reading, spelling, math and so on doing six to seven separate subjects each day. All the subjects were unrelated to each other. Nothing was combined to make it cohesive for the teacher or the student. It didn't take long to see that my children did not enjoy or delight in their studies. They were just going through the motions, and often we would still be "doing school" at 4:00 o' clock in the afternoon. As soon as we finished, it would be time for me to start dinner! It also didn't take long before I was desperate… about four years… which is generally how long people last before they are at our doorstep asking for help and alternatives!

"One way to understand the difference between the unit study approach and the textbook approach would be to think of each subject as a spool of thread, each color representing a different subject in the textbook approach. The red spool for History, the green for Science, and the blue spool stands for Literature. Each spool is separateand unrelated to the other spools. With the Unit Study approach, we take those spools of thread and weave them together, making each spool of thread more meaningful as we begin to see them woven together into a beautiful tapestry. As you look upon that tapestry it is delightful to the eyes—likewise, as you look upon separate spools of colored thread, it is not delightful."

(Gregg Harris, Noble Institute)

COMPARE THE METHODS

And furthermore...

~ Textbooks condense rather than expand information and only offer a small portion of subject matter. When you expand a study, you are able to enjoy it by exploring the topic thoroughly. ~

Textbooks are only a fraction of the way we learn. In homeschool, don't rely on them as your main source of information. Why not? There are many reasons. Especially on the elementary level, textbooks skim the subject area.

(Gayle Graham, *How to Home School*, [Hawthorne: Common Sense Press, 1992], 125)

Textbooks often present difficult material in a highly condensed fashion. New vocabulary words are met only a few times, but retention is expected. On the other hand, if information is given in what I call a real book - a library book - that same vocabulary may be met over and over again.

Why do we even have textbooks then, if they are so inefficient in presenting subject matter? Why were they even designed? They were designed for convenience in teaching a large group at once. (ibid., 127)

...we must not only teach our children facts, but how to find and use them. Not only do they retain information but more importantly, how do they learn to reason..., to think..., and do something with all that information? (ibid, 122)

~ Unit studies encourage thinking rather than memorization. ~

...we must not only teach our children facts, but how to find and use them. Textbooks are commonly used to meet the needs of a class room which must operate under certain limitations homeschoolers don't have.

By the way, figuring it out takes more time than just memorizing and regurgitating answers. That's okay... we have the time. As you've noticed by now, we are not limited by time constraints. (ibid., 130)

Now, some kids thrive on textbooks but this is the exception and not the rule. I have had more people than I can count come and tell me that their kids hate school and are dying on the vine using textbooks. My whole point in this comparison is to show that to get an education, kids need to LEARN and not just fill in the blanks. However, they will not learn if it is not interesting. Parents and students are quite willing to skip over real learning in order to "get done" and feel that they have met the requirements. I will share my story later about how I went through school, got good grades and did not get an education!

OUT OF THE COMFORT ZONE!

To teach effectively, we must be ready to extend beyond what may be the traditional teaching method and involve more senses. We must NOT do merely what is comfortable, but what is beneficial!

How God designed us to learn:

Hearing .... Retention 10%

Seeing .... Retention 50%

BUT if you add...

Touching, smelling, tasting .... Retention 90%

DEVELOPING YOUR PHILOSOPHY OF EDUCATION?

You have begun to learn about some of the philosophies and characteristics of the unit study approach. As a homeschooler, it is vital that you evaluate what YOU think it takes to give your child a good, solid education. We will call the product of this evaluation process your "Philosophy of Education." Evaluating your ideas and goals for education is an important step because if you are not sure about your foundation before you take a plunge into unit studies, you can easily become confused and frustrated. Sometimes I see parents wavering, losing the heart and the strength to carry out their commitment to home education, because this foundation hasn't been laid. When you have a bad day or begin to compare your child to another, you will be tempted (and might threaten) to send your child to a REAL school!

It has taken years for our family to fine-tune a solid philosophy of what we believe about education. Our philosophy of education developed both by trial and error and through gaining experience in teaching over time. An important aspect is being sure of the Lord's direction for our family. We know WHY we are homeschooling. We know we would continue to home educate our children even if all our friends stopped. To us, homeschooling is about more than teaching our children academic skills.

Don't be surprised if your philosophy needs to be revised as time goes by and you gain experience. Your philosophy could even change before you finish this book! You must start somewhere, so sit down with your spouse and jot down your ideas and goals for education. Taking the time to compile your thoughts will help you clarify your convictions about education and set specific goals for your family. It will also give you something to refer to when you need to reaffirm your decisions. As you begin, consider each child's strengths, weaknesses, and interests.

There are some good resources which might help solidify your resolve:

Educating the Wholehearted Child by Clay and Sally Clarkson

The Ultimate Guide to Homeschooling by Debra Bell

The Christian Home School by Gregg Harris

Dr. Ruth Beechick's books and articles (Homeschooling Today magazine)

How to Home School by Gayle Graham

For the Children's Sake by Susan Schaeffer McCaulay

Ignite the Fire by Terri Camp

Other things which can help you formulate your philosophy would be:

- Attend homeschool seminars and listen to those speaking on topics that relate to your child's heart.

- Visit vendor booths at homeschool seminars to see what is available and how materials might fit with your philosophy and goals.

- Read some articles in home education magazines and catalogs. Read reviews.

- Observe the outcome of home educated students. Listen to and read testimonials from experienced parents.

- The time and experience in teaching your own children and observing the way others teach.

Your philosophy of education may develop from many sources:

- Your present teaching experiences and observations.

- Your own experiences while attending school.

- Your ideas about college and higher education.

OUR PHILOSOPHY OF EDUCATION

We believe the most important thing you can teach your children
is to love the Lord with all their heart, all their soul,
all their mind, and all their strength,
and to help develop godly character in each of them.

We believe we were put here for God's glory
and He desires for His children to serve Him
and work to advance His kingdom.

We believe acquiring an education is important so each person
can be prepared to be used for God's purpose in their lives.
Children need to learn to read well so they can read the Bible
where all of life's answers can be found. Education is not something
that occurs during a specific and limited time
during one's life. We feel education is, and should be,
an ongoing process. We'd like our children to have the attitude
that they are never DONE with learning. It is our desire
that our children excel instead of merely fulfilling a status quo.

The greater part of learning should be devoted to the years
of preparation, which is infancy to young adulthood.
Those years of preparation should be spent in maturing
and equipping oneself to be able to become a husband or wife,
and to develop skills that would enable them to fulfill that role well.

A wife should be able to help her husband so he can succeed
in his task, which is to provide for his family and to provide
leadership in the community and the local church.

We believe the best way to equip our children
for this task is to lead them into a love for learning.
Fostering this atmosphere requires more than doing "school."

We should not attempt to fit our children into molds
that tell them what they must learn and when.
We believe children learn best in a pleasant environment
which is not dominated by peer pressure
a proven deterrent to learning. The better they understand this world,
the more effective they will be for Christ's cause.

Jim and Jennifer Steward

You will ask yourself as you evaluate your philosophy of education, "What is best for my child?"

Over time, we have learned some priceless principles that have helped us evaluate and develop our philosophy:

- Time is precious and passes quickly.

- Educational standards are not always best.

- It may ALL be there, but your child may not get it all.

- Academics aren't everything!

TIME IS PRECIOUS

In the early years of our homeschooling, we wasted a great deal of time "covering" material I felt I was "supposed" to cover. Now I keep an eye on my children to see if they are really tuned in. If they aren't, I am wasting my time and theirs. If they are not tuned in, I need to determine why.

To determine this, I evaluate:

- They way material is being presented.

- How important the material is to cover.

- Whether my children are just trying to get out of something.

- Whether we could do something different and more interesting in order to acquire the skill or knowledge.

TIME PASSES QUICKLY

When we started homeschooling, I thought I had forever to teach my kids all those great and wonderful things I wanted to do and places and topics I wanted explore with them. Well, guess what? I don't have forever. Time flies by all too quickly when it comes to my children. Three of my children have graduated and two are married! I look at the rest of my teens who could be leaving home in a few short years (where did they come from and how did they get here so fast?) and I want to make the most of our time together. Don't wait to talk to them. Don't wait to read aloud. I don't want to try to "finish" a bunch of textbooks just to meet an established standard requirement. My goal is to do my best to delight and inspire in my children a love for learning that will continue throughout their lives and you know what? It's working and I am thrilled!

To achieve this goal, I look at the following:

- The bigger picture of life and the choices we have before us.

- Goals spelled out in our Philosophy of Education.

Public school standards may not be what is best for homeschoolers. Classroom teaching has many downfalls as they are suited for the needs of the whole and not the individual. We don't need to necessarily study topics according to state standards. In our school system in California, it is recommended that you study our state's history when students are in the fourth grade; however, our whole family did a unit study on California History when Cacey was in ninth grade, Ty was in eighth, Whitney was in fifth, and Brooke was in first. Each child worked at his or her own ability and skill level, and it was great! We studied this topic when it fit into our schedule. We did not follow educational standards.

We don't have the dynamics at home as to that of the classroom, so we don't need to follow the same pattern. It would NOT be possible to teach a class of thirty according to readiness or interest, but you CAN teach the small numbers in your household this way. Some subjects like phonics and reading, if taught or forced on a child when they are not ready just because standards say this is the right time, could kill their budding joy and desire to learn… maybe for good! When my fifth child was six years old, we had been "doing school" all year and she had struggled a great deal with phonics sounds. I became frustrated and began yelling at her for not learning. The Lord knocked loudly on my brain saying, "Lay off!" I realized that I was intimidated by the fact that if she didn't learn this, I would have to hold her back because, after all what others would think? I should have known better since I had taught four other children before her, but I gave into my worse enemy of comparing my children to others or to standards! Even though she was slow to read, she has always been able to participate in our unit studies, learning at her own unique level of ability. We continued to work on phonics passively and over time she became a good reader.

To evaluate educational standards according to the needs of MY family, I look at:

- The dynamics of our family, including the children's ages and our schedule.
- Whether the child is ready.

IT MAY ALL BE THERE, BUT YOUR CHILD MAY NOT GET IT ALL

Here's a big question. I have parents tell me constantly that they are afraid their children will miss something important if they use the unit study method. Let me assure you that just because the curriculum includes "all" the information, this does not mean that your child will necessarily learn it all. There is a certain amount of security for parents knowing that the information in a particular curriculum is comprehensive and complete but the truth is that children do not generally remember a list of facts, names, and dates because the text is not interesting to them. Unless they get into it and learn it… not just cover it, the information doesn't stick. Most likely it didn't really go in. I hope you get this important point.

Remember to ask yourself the following questions regarding why you want your children to get an education:

- Is it because you're supposed to give them one?
- Is it because you want them to get good grades so you will look good. OUCH!
- Is it so your children can get an education because you know it is through understanding God's world that they will be most effective in impacting their generation and this world for Christ?
- Is it so they can get good jobs and make it in this world?

I cannot stress enough that instruction and training, building and developing godly character AND glorifying God must be the priority.

In order to keep this perspective, I have to constantly look at:

- The end result—the life goal.

- How we can encourage our children to love learning.

- How we can provide the resources and experiences that will make for a rich, memorable, and lasting education.

ACADEMICS AREN'T EVERYTHING!

Every homeschooler becomes aware of the fact that there is much more to learn than academics. Walking alongside our children over the years in this longtime homeschooling adventure, we have definitely seen the value of teaching and emphasizing valuable life skills. Deuteronomy 6:6-9 instructs parents to teach God's ways to their children. Homeschooling allows us the time we need to do this because of the time element afforded them. We live in perilous and uncertain times so we must consider the importance of teaching life skills equipping them both spiritually and physically! If you will let go of worry and allow your children to develop a love for great literature and enjoy history through reading, they will be exposed to skills generally lost in our push button, fast food society and have the opportunity to experience them first hand - as part of a unit study experience.

Children need to learn traditional living skills like:

- To be selfless in doing chores and sharing in household duties.

- To understand soil, plants and gardening, animal care and husbandry.

- Homemaking skills - cooking, preserving food, and sewing.

- To do without modern conveniences - T.V., electricity, computers, etc.

- To work with their hands - yard work, woodworking, building.

All men are like grass, and their glory is like
the flowers of the field; the grass withers and the flowers fall,
but the word of the Lord stands forever.

I Peter 1: 24 (NIV)

It is apparent our society has placed education on a pedestal - making it an idol or a god. We see this because we work so closely with homeschoolers and education. It is of great concern to us that this drive toward what we refer to as "academia", is so prevalent in the homeschooling movement. We have seen many changes in the homeschooling movement since we first became part of it. Part of the reason we see a large emphasis on academics and a real push for the most "superior" education a child can have, is due to the fact that there are so many people homeschooling now, which gives way to a wider variety of views.

I don't want anyone to get the idea that I am not in favor of excellence. I am just stressing that we need to follow our heart when it comes to our children and be careful not to get "sucked" into the wave of society. What we are experiencing now reminds me of the Renaissance when scholars became interested in the works of ancient Greek men such as Plato, Cicero, and Aristotle. The study of this culture was known as humanism and they considered themselves universal men who had a broad knowledge of all subjects. This is not a bad thing unless we begin to get puffed up with knowledge. Read I Corinthians 1:18-29. We must strive toward real learning and never allow our education to become an idol.

You might be as surprised as I was the first time I heard that some people think the unit study approach is for lazy people who like to do crafts. Some have formed the opinion that this method is inferior and not a good choice for those who are interested in going on to higher education! I must say I believe this is far from the truth. All the people I know who do unit studies, do such an impressive and serious job of providing a superior education for their children.

To sum it up - a child's education should not be confined to textbooks, to a specific time slot or period such as 9:00 a.m. to 3:00 p.m., Monday through Friday, kindergarten through twelfth grade, September through June. A child's education should not be confined or dictated by standards set up by others. Education is a living experience. For this reason, the motto in our home has become "LIFE IS SCHOOL."

Today, business executives are telling us they don't need

graduates filled with facts. Instead, they're asking for graduates with

skill to retrieve and organize information so it can be used.

What does our society need? Individuals who can creatively develop

new ways of doing things - people who can take information

which is readily available, and do something with it from start to finish.

As one educator put it, "If we don't help people learn how to think,

then the information that goes in may never come back out."

I'd add we need graduates that have the determination to finish a task

that takes a period of time to do. We need students who have inquisitiveness,

courage to stand alone, honesty, diligence… so they can

do something with the information they have access to.

(Gayle Graham, *How to Home School*, Hawthorne: Common Sense Press, 1992], 122)

WHY CHOOSE UNIT STUDIES?

The popularity of the unit study method is growing quickly. Many homeschooling families are choosing to teach by this method. Why is this so? Because it works well to achieve true and joyous learning.

"Children enjoy the variety of learning methods employed in a unit study
and parents appreciate the reinforcement resulting from integrated study activities."

(Clay and Sally Clarkson, *Educating the Wholehearted Child*
[Walnut Springs: Whole Heart Ministries, 1996], 115)

LET'S GET DOWN TO DETAILS

We have listed briefly several benefits of the unit study method, but let's go into more detail starting with...

KIDS OF ALL AGES LEARN BEST THIS WAY

The first time we ever did a unit study we decided to study Trains and it only took one study for me to see how positively my children responded and learned. I saw the "lights go on" and it was so exciting for me to see their minds click into gear. We learned about the different types of train cars, the history of the railroad, the invention of the steam engine and the industrial revolution. We read about historical events and famous people connected with the railroad. We took a field trip to the Sacramento Railroad Museum where we could walk inside railroad cars and learned about the "guage" or size of track and how it is laid. Our last activity was to each choose a train car to draw. When everyone was finished we joined our train together and hung it on the wall. Our kids still talk about it today - which is true about all our studies!

What do you think would happen if you gave your child two choices for learning about nutrition. Read the ideas below and decide which option they would prefer.

OPTION #1

Read a chapter or two on nutrition from a science textbook and answer questions.

OPTION #2

Do a unit study which would involve the following:

Read aloud time	Make a food resources map
Do research on the computer	Learn about vitamin rich food
Take a field trip to a grocery store, farm, or food factory	Compile a notebook
Plan a healthy menu - do some cooking	Learn about Louis Pastuer
Write about pesticides vs. organically grown food	Make a food groups poster

I'm pretty sure I know which option most children would choose, but what is more important is to see which one would bring the most benefit toward lasting knowledge and understanding of the content. Children are more willing to study if they have something to DO and it's the doing part they love. When they get their hands into it—reading, writing, mapping, touching, hearing, drawing and so on. As we have discussed, these are the components that make learning stick!

There is an old saying that goes something like this:

> ## Tell me and I'll forget it.
> ## Show me and I'll understand it.
> ## Let me do it and I'll remember it.

Student Hails Benefits of NEW Teaching Method

No More Boring Textbooks –Unit Studies Are Fun!
Students Even Do Extra Work—It's A Miracle!

I came across a letter in a magazine a student had written to the editor, who was also the publisher of unit study materials. In her letter she thanked the editor for the curriculum, noting how fun it was to be DOING things instead of sitting over textbooks. She wrote, "I'm even doing extra work!"

UNIT STUDIES STIMULATE CREATIVITY

Children learn best when their senses are stimulated. Textbooks are geared toward visual learners so we find students "inhaling" more than they "exhale." With unit studies they have more opportunities to express themselves, explore learning and get their hands into their work. We all have a creative flare, at least to some extent! Who knows what hidden talents might surface if a child is given the chance to let their creative juices flow!

Children who just can't sit still are known as kinesthetic learners. The ones who want to get their hands into the action are known as tactile learners. Auditory learners learn best by speaking their lessons aloud to themselves, while visual learners prefer to see visual aids. All of us have a little of each mode mixed together and so unit studies work great for most people because as you proceed through your studies, you will most likely engage students in all these different ways.

HOUSES FILLED WITH DIFFERENT AGES

Unit studies are great for home educators because they often have students of varied ages. Many people with large families choose to use unit studies simply in order to survive—that's why we started! So I started out merely as a means of survival, but once I discovered how much freedom they brought to teaching, school life and our entire household, there was no other option! Let me stress though that whether you have one child or ten, unit studies are extremely family friendly and an excellent choice, but I believe unit studies are the only practical solution for those with large families.

To conduct a unit study with different ages, choose a study topic and then devise your plans with your children's ages in mind. You can choose your spelling and vocabulary words according to each level. Most everything including silent reading titles, writing assignments, and all other activities are selected to suit each child's level. We have included some sample assignment sheets in the Appendix to help you see how you might plan for different ages. I think it will help you see how you CAN do the same study with different ages.

There have been a couple of questions and concerns about teaching children when there is a large gap between grade levels. I think there does come a point when the age span might be too broad. Probably Kindergarten and 7th or 8th grade. For one thing, topics your 8th grader might be learning (like Slavery) might not be interesting or appropriate for a young child. Also, your 8th grader might feel that Mom is making things too juvenile in their effort to include the little one. Now, if you have K up to 8th and have other children in between - this is quite a different story!

Here is an example of a 6th grader and a Kindergarten child both studying Medieval Times. We had just read (during Information Time) about how the monks had access to books and they copied manuscripts. Their beautiful large initial letters seemed to almost light up so they were called illuminations. After reading about this, Brooke (the 6th grader) wrote a couple of paragraphs about illumination. Anna, who couldn't read yet, just copied the word twice after I wrote it and I told her what it said. They each decorated their own illuminated initial letter and you can see that their work is appropriate for their age and skill levels. Both listened to me read the same information, but the outpouring of their work shows their respective levels.

Anna
Kindergarten

Brooke
6th Grade

Unit Studies Allow You to Get More Done in Less Time

You can get more done in less time by integrating most subjects into your topic. Many moms feel like they are drowning under the weight of teaching so many subjects to so many children. Teaching is a huge job and quite challenging. In our case, trying to teach eight subjects to each of eight children—well, you can count! In reality, I've never had eight children in school at the same time - but it is still a big job no matter how many. I've found unit studies to be THE answer to this challenge as it truly minimizes the work load both in planning and teaching which is another reason it is delightful for students - they don't get bogged down or burdened either! You are covering more material and the children are learning more, too.

You can test this to see if it is true. Choose a topic and start by reading from a textbook then ask your child some questions to see what he learned and remembered. Then conduct a mini unit study on the same topic and let the results speak for themselves. I wanted to study The Alamo and I had about five or six books on the topic and I didn't want to spend alot of time on it so we took one week and did a quick study. We made a flapbook instead of a notebook and put maps, information and pictures into it. I know I could have read about The Alamo from a history textbook, but by reading a few, short books and "doing" something - my kids know ALL about The Alamo, Davy Crockett and his Tennessee boys, Jim Bowie, General Santa Ana, War with Mexico, the Texas Republic, other battles connected with gaining their independence, and Sam Houston! What's really neat is that before that "I" didn't really know anything about it - but, now I do!

You'll be surprised at how many "subjects" you can "check off" at the end of a week. The purpose of this next section is to demonstrate how many "academics" you can accomplish through unit studies, in a short period of time and show what "A Day in the Life of a Unit Study" might look like. Of course, our "schedule" varies according to the unit topic and changes from year to year, but here's an example of what we might do in our home:

7:00 a.m. ~ Rise and shine! Dress, breakfast, morning chores.

8:30 a.m. ~ Short Bible time at the breakfast table. During our study I often choose a verse from the Bible for the children to use for handwriting practice (subject #1). *They will get other handwriting practice from unit study activities, poems, and dictation.*

9:15 a.m. ~ Read aloud time. I usually read one or two chapters from our read aloud title. A few times each week I give the children vocabulary words drawn from this book. Older students will look these up later in the day. (Dictionary skills - subject #2)

10:00 a.m. ~ At least twice a week I either copy text on the wipe clean board or I dictate a paragraph from the same book. I have the children mark misspelled words and correct them by looking at the paragraph in the book. (Writing practice - subject #3)

10:15 a.m. ~ The next hour is Information time when I present information about our topic from nonfiction books touching on a different aspects of the topic. Nonfiction books are "source books" which contain the information for teaching. Sometimes I've read a portion ahead of time, then I can sort of "lecture" or tell them about it. When we are starting a study, I always begin by teaching geography so we can understand "where in the world we are." We'll usually do some work on the map at that time. (Geography - subject #4) Once geography has been introduced, other days we will do some other "connecting activity" in some other type of subject area - writing, art, research, diagrams, etc.

These activities usually take us up to...

12:00 p.m. ~ Lunch - After lunch, the children work mostly on their own.

This is usually the extent of my involvement with the children. The rest of their day will be devoted to working independently, (for those who can), on assignments listed on their assignment sheet, silent reading (subject #5), math (subject #6) and other loose ends. By the end of a one month study, our children have a notebook FULL of their school work divided into different subjects! Did you notice that we covered at least six subjects painlessly and only took a few hours. Are you surprised by this? Remember, unit studies simplify schooling. These daily activities usually keep me busy until lunchtime. Keep in mind as needed, I take breaks throughout to deal with a toddler who is supposed to be napping, change a diaper, or answer the phone. (NOTE: at the time of the revision of this book... I no longer have toddlers, but I keep this in here to help moms who do understand that "I've been there" and I understand the challenge little ones present to THE PERFECT DAY or... never having a perfect day!

I just described an ideal day which we hardly ever have! We do try to stay on some sort of schedule, but if something comes up (and something always does!), we can at least feel that we have accomplished these basics. When we do have interruptions, the kids can grab their math, reading, or other assignments and work independently.

To further help you understand what kind of "activities" might take place and academics which can be accomplished during this time, see example below.

EXAMPLE of information taught during "Information Time" ~ **BIRDS**

We would learn about: homes, food, habitats, wings and flight, aerodynamics, feet, beaks, the structure of a feather, species, bird watching, eggs, birds of prey, birds that are helpful and harmful and so on. There is enough material to keep us busy and enthused about BIRDS for about four weeks.

During this time, the younger children lay on the floor and color a picture of a bird from an educational colorbook or just look through the pictures in nonfiction books. I do ask them to "look up" whenever I show a picture of what I am talking about. Younger children can play nearby. Most days we end this learning time with a group activity, which is usually a way to somehow fulfill a subject/learning and keep and organize the information. For example, if I read about how a bird's wings are like the wings on an airplane designed to give lift, we might try to make a diagram comparing the two and we would label the parts of the wings. A short caption can be included (writing).

Some days I help get the younger children start on an assignment listed on their "Assignment Sheet," (which usually includes assignments in subjects like: writing, research, art, handwriting, or geography). I will pull the youngest student aside and work on phonics, writing letters and numbers. This usually takes about one half hour. The rest of the day, the children will do their daily basics like: studying spelling words (once or twice a week - oral test given on Friday), look up any new vocabulary words, silent /independent reading (one hour each day reading from a novel related to our topic at their skill level) or reading out loud to me. They also work on their math (unrelated to the unit study).

EXAMPLE of group activities ~ **BIRDS**

Depending on the activity, I might have all the children doing the same thing, but if there is writing involved I usually have the younger ones copy a short piece from the wipe clean board. The six year old would make her own bird picture and glue feathers on a piece of construction paper writing a couple of words to describe something. The nine year old has colored a picture of a bird and carefully labels body parts. She also writes a paragraph about the bird she chose. The thirteen year old is drawing her own picture of the bird she chose and hers is more like a mini report consisting of a few pages. The sixteen year old is in high school and is not really doing the full study with us, but since she has never studied birds, she is studying (as a sideline unit study along with some other "things") working more independently using an assignment sheet. Her work is more complete, contains lots of research and writing and is more impressive at the upper grade level.

The children might be working at the dining room table chatting as they work, or I might take some time to read from a book about Ornithology, showing pictures. There are always so many good books I want to get through, so I might read the biography of *James Audubon* (this is aside from our read aloud time). This type of interactive study promotes togetherness and unity.

The next day, our unit study activity might center around a Bible concordance as we look for scriptures that refer to birds or to flying. These verses can be used for handwriting practice.

For those times when we are not working together, I have worked out a schedule or assignment sheet the children can follow that lists other things they can do on their own. This list applies if they are finished, if I am busy with another child and they don't know what to do, or just to keep them on track with unit study activities they can do themselves. You can see how you can save time by teaching different age groups.

No Excuses

Children shouldn't have any excuses like "I don't know what to do" because there are always plenty of "loose ends" to work on outside the unit of study.

Some of these might include the following:

- Practice typing using a computer instructional program.
- Do personal Bible reading and study.
- Sew or cook. Have children help by making lunch!
- Work on an ongoing study like U.S. Geography (where the children research a new state once or twice a week decorating maps with mountains, rivers, state capital).

• Have dictionary races.	• Review math fact flash cards.
• Write thank-you notes.	• Write letters to pen pals or missionaries.
• Play an educational board game.	• Play an educational computer game.
• Work with a younger child.	• Read aloud to younger child.

If your children end up with papers as a result of working in some areas outside the unit study, these things can be placed in an "All School" binder, or notebook. A child should never need to be at a loss for things to do or skills to build!

Age integrated studies are not without their challenges. Like dealing with little ones. I wish I had some easy answer for what to do with those busy little people. I would just say be patient, enjoy them and don't have high expectations for having a perfect day! They do grow up fast even if it doesn't seem like it today!

Plan to provide ways for the younger ones who can't sit still very long to participate, too. The frequent use of hands-on activities naturally provides opportunities for preschoolers to feel part of the school day as they also, for example, color and press feathers on a pre-glued construction paper bird. If you plan fifteen minutes of "school" for your preschooler and teach them first, they will be happy and more willing to be quiet later. Make sure you get books in your topic for the litte ones from the library, from the JE (Juvenile) section. Pull them up next to you on the sofa and read, read, read!

Unit Studies Allow You to Explore Topics More Thoroughly

I always tell people, "You always do a more thorough job with unit studies." This is because you are using lots of great books and exploring your topic from many angles. There is evidence that when children see how the things they are learning about are related, they learn a lot more.

Q: One mother expressed: I'm worried that my daughter's first-grade class isn't teaching academics.

My first-grader tells me that she's learning about penguins in her math class. I know she's being taught through "thematic units," in which various subjects are tied to a common theme, but I'm skeptical. I like penguins as much as the next person, but is my daughter wasting time that should be spent on academics?

A: Rest assured: Your daughter's education isn't going to the birds. Kids who are taught through thematic units learn the same academic subjects - reading, writing, arithmetic, social studies, and so on. The information is just organized in a different way. What distinguishes this approach is that a central theme ties together what kids learn. In this case, penguins. They might be used to teach addition (adding penguin eggs together), spelling (learning words such as "bird" and "cold"), science (learning how water freezes), and social studies (discussing why penguins aren't pets, but dogs and cats are). Projects such as building penguin habitats or drawing maps of Antarctica help students demonstrate what they've learned. (By the way, the penguins your daughter is studying now are most likely part of a larger theme, perhaps "animal families," that she'll be working on for much of the year.)

"Thematic units show kids the connection between different subjects," says Cathy Shevey, director of elementary education for the Montclair, New Jersey, public school system, which has been using the units for more than ten years. "Learning math, for example, isn't isolated from the ways in which these skills are useful when studying science. This approach also helps kids make connections between what they do in the classroom and what goes on in their day-to-day lives." Far from taking time away from academics, classes structured around thematic units actually provide more reinforcement of basic skills. Kids are evaluated for their spelling in science class and for their science composition in social studies.

...to see if thematic units are working for your daughter, ask her to give you a demonstration of what she's been learning. You'll probably find the results very reassuring.

("Answers to Your Questions About Your Child's First Years at School,"
Parents Magazine, September, 1997)

Because you are doing such a thorough job, topics may only need to be taught once, instead of a little every year - as in textbooks. I have been known to say, "Teach it once and teach it right!" The question of having to repeat teaching topics/units often arises. Parents ask, "Won't I have to teach some units again at a deeper level?" The answer is yes, some units will need to be taught again, but probably only twice and not until several years have passed. Many times, it will NOT be necessary to teach a unit topic again.

Please don't let this idea deter you from unit studies and, in fact, if we are truly developing a love for learning, we should look forward to teaching a topic again because we KNOW about the topic now and we enjoyed learning about it. It will be all the more rich the next time.

If you have used textbooks, you know they present the same material year after year adding more information at a higher level with each grade. With unit studies, I have found that as you teach different units you will see how topics begin to cross and relate as the whole puzzle comes together. For example the following American History topics occur in the same time periods so your students will come upon similar and familiar information as they study different topics: Westward Movement, Cowboys, The California Gold Rush, Pony Express, The Transcontinental Railroad, The Industrial Revolution, The Civil War, etc.

Teaching a unit more than once is good because:

- It will be easier for you to teach since you know what you're doing.

- Students will be older so the study will be more in depth.

- You'll have more/different books you WANT to use.

I find that I do a better job the second time I teach a unit study than I did the first time. This is because I know about the topic and am excited about it. I tease my children who are grown saying "I feel sorry for you - I'm such a better teacher now than when you were in school!" Notebooks are more complete because I am always finding some new teaching tip or ideas to use to keep things interesting! Being a bookaholic, I continue to find and add books to our home library so I have more neat books to use!

One question moms have is whether their child would use the same notebook since they are doing the topic a second time and just add to it. I definitely would NOT recommend that because your 8th grader is not going to want to add their advanced work to their 2nd grade notebook! They are really two different studies since the skill level changes so much over time.

You will see what a thorough job you are doing as you look back over the month/study. One tip that will help you know how to be thorough is to "teach to the older children" and let the younger ones glean information at their own level. What the younger children are going to really remember are "the basics," so it is more important to teach to those who can comprehend. And remember that it is not just your goal that your children learn "information," but you are also trying to accomplish academic skills. See the sample assignment sheets for Pony Express (in the Appendix) prepared for three age levels. When writing an assignment sheet, begin your plans "teaching to the older child" and simplify your ideas for younger students.

UNIT STUDIES ARE COST EFFECTIVE

Unit studies can be more cost effective. This area can either work for or against you—the wealth of resources that is available can be enticing… and expensive. You have to train yourself not to think that you have to have every book and resource available on a topic. The library is a great FREE source of books. In a later chapter, we will spend more time talking about libraries—both taking advantage of the public library system and building your very own home library.

You can actually save money doing unit studies as compared to other curriculums. In the first place, you can use many of the same books over and over (if you own them) with your other children. You can also use many of the same books for all your children during the course of a unit. For example, publishers like Usborne and Dorling Kindersly books all have great pictures accompanied by text. The older children can appreciate the text and use them for research while the younger children enjoy the pictures, either by looking through them on their own or following along as you read and point out details.

Unit study enthusiasts look at life as "One Big Unit Study!" If you can put together any kind of long term plan for topics you might be studying, you will be able to keep your eyes peeled for items that will fit with those topics. One time while on vacation, we went through historic Virginia City. I picked up a postcard with pictures of Indian symbols on it because I knew we would be studying American Indians in the future. Another time I planned a Butterflies study for the spring, so I collected stickers and goodies for my kindergarten child all year! I pick up inexpensive items like this all the time at museum gift shops, yard sales, thrift stores, and used book stores.

UNIT STUDIES PROVIDE A WIDER RANGE OF EXPERIENCES

Unit studies provide such a wide range of things to do and that's just what children enjoy - the "doing" part and these memorable experiences are what help them retain what they learn. So when you study the people of the United States colonies, a child's learning could be reinforced by making and flying kites as Ben Franklin did. Allow their handwriting exercises that week to be done with a quill and ink as they did when they penned the Constitution. Don't just read about—DO it!

"Quick, name your favorite textbook from school.

How about your favorite worksheet? Drawing a blank? Why am I not surprised?

Well, how about your favorite books from childhood?

(*Little Women, Huckleberry Finn, To Kill a Mockingbird*... what's on your list?)

Or your favorite project? (A short story in fourth, my leaf collection in fifth,

a relief map of Egypt in seventh.) If you can't even remember

the textbooks and worksheets of childhood, how much better

can we remember what we learned from them?"

(Debra Bell, *The Ultimate Guide to Homeschooling* [Nashville: Thomas Nelson, Inc., 1997],74)

UNIT STUDIES UNIFY THE WHOLE FAMILY

Unit studies unitfy the whole family because they are interactive. There will be times when kids complete assignments on their own, but unit studies generally have the distinction of being interactive. I believe interaction is really the KEY to why unit studies work so well for developing a love for learning. The time I spend with my kids exploring learning together is rich. If you do something similar to what we do (The Steward Method!), you will be spending time reading aloud and incorporating vocabulary, dictation, and narration. There will be times when you offer instruction by reading to your kids from nonfiction books, initiate projects, give assignments, and do activities and these are all times spent together.

By combining subjects and having all the students learning the same information, I find myself on the saving time side of the equation. There will be a difference between the interaction found with unit studies as compared to your previous program, but stick to it because it will be refreshing for everyone involved. The benefits of unity, capitalizing on meaningful discussions, and seizing teachable moments far outweigh anything you could imagine. After all, this is what teaching is all about—this is WHY you are homeschooling!

Parents need to evaluate their priorities. They need to consider why they respond

"We wouldn't have time to read a book together every day.

We don't have time to hike/camp/paint/talk with our children."

What is really important?

(Susan Schaeffer Macaulay, *For the Children's Sake*, [Wheaton: Crossway Books, 1984], 10)

The educational benefits when everyone is studying the same thing, listening to the same book, meeting the same people and visiting the same places cannot be measured. The shared experience becomes dear to all who listen. When sitting around the dinner table eveyone can jump into the converstation because the experiences have been shared by all who listen and learned together. These experiences become part of your children's precious memories.

Recently, we had dinner with a group of friends. One person suggested an activity where each person tell what they liked best about their childhood. What was so enlightening about this exercise was that every single person shared about the times they spent with their family, talking, fishing, visiting Grandma, climbing trees, being home, and building forts. No one said anything about a trip to an amusement park, watching TV, or hanging out with their friends. I hope my children will look back and recall their best times as those we shared at home.

Other countless benefits include:

- They encourage children to think and reason.
- They help children discover their own interests and talents.
- They introduce children to people, places, time periods, and cultures.
- They help children develop a lifelong love for learning.
- They help children appreciate their Creator.
- They provide children with a well-rounded education.
- They introduce and make wide use of good literature.
- They help with personal growth.
- They allow for spontaneity.
- They promote lots of reading which broadens their scope of learning.
- They appeal to the many different learning styles— there is something for everyone!

WHAT UNIT STUDIES ARE NOT

We have spent a lot of time talking about what unit studies ARE but I feel I should address briefly some concerns parents have about unit studies. At a recent curriculum fair a skeptical mother who was obviously intrigued and interested in unit studies said to me, "So, are YOU surviving unit studies?" At first I was puzzled by her question but realized she had the idea that teaching by the unit study method was a BIG, insurmountable task. My reply surprised her as I said, "I am surviving homeschooling because of unit studies!" Then, I was able to explain.

People drum up visions of what they think a unit study "must be" from something they have heard. Some FEARS associated with unit studies are actually based on the misconception that unit studies are too much work, requiring too much planning and too many activities and projects.

Unit studies really are whatever you make them. They can be as involved or as simple as you want them to be. We are trying to give some basic guidelines you can follow which will help you figure out what will work for you. Unfortunately, many of the qualities that make them so appealing can also make them intimidating if you don't keep a good balance to your plans.

<u>Here's the KEY</u>: *Unit studies should make your life and schooling easier, simpler, save you time and energy AND end up providing a richer education in the meantime!*

The number one rule to remember with unit studies is... THERE ARE NO RULES! You get to decide what you want to do. It belongs to you. Can you develop and teach a unit study? The answer is a resounding YES!

COMMON CONCERNS ABOUT UNIT STUDIES

WHAT IF I'M NOT CREATIVE?

Many mothers think they are not creative enough to do unit studies. There's good news! You don't have to be creative and come up with the ideas yourself because all the help in the world is available to you. Unit study guides and curriculum provide all kinds of ideas. The upcoming chapter on planning will walk you through that step.

If you decide to create your own unit studies from scratch, the books you choose will help you think of projects and assignments. Like prepared curriculum, if you are using a prepared guide, they too are full of ideas. And if you are using a prepared curriculum, your biggest problem will be in deciding what NOT to do!

Start small, use a prepared guide, and do a unit study on a topic you know something about. Or find another experienced mom and do a unit study co-op together. Once you do two or three studies, you will see that it is not all that much work and doesn't require a lot of creativity.

DO I HAVE TO PLAN AND DO ALL THOSE ACTIVITIES?

Unit studies have a reputation for being BIG on activities. Parents are afraid academics will suffer as the balance swings toward a heavy emphasis on the activities which they know their kids would enjoy. To understand more clearly what part they play in unit studies we need to define activities.

<u>Activities</u>: Anything educational you DO in any subject area - these are not just models and crafts. For example: studying spelling or vocabulary words, researching a subject, making maps or timelines, alphabetizing lists, silent reading, writing assignments, drawing and other forms of art, building models and so on. (Many of the "smaller" activities are compiled into your notebook project.)

Whether you use a unit study curriculum, a topical guide, or plan your own from scratch, ultimately you will be designing your own curriculum since you will be deciding what to study. YOU get to choose how much you will do. As you use your topical unit study guides, curriculum, or source books to choose activities, include a balanced menu that fits with your schedule and goals. Some activities are more FUN than others, but even the more "academic" activities, when tied into your topic of study, can be interesting.

WILL I MISS SOMETHING TRADITIONAL CURRICULUMS PROVIDE?

If you are concerned about using unit studies because you are afraid of missing something your child would otherwise "get" if you used traditional methods, all I can say is you must give it a try and see for yourself how much your children respond and how much they learn. Remember that we need not be fearful if we are seeking the Lord. We also need to remember that though we feel secure in textbooks because they are inclusive, this doesn't mean your child WILL learn it all.

I gave a little presentation to demonstrate this truth at a recent unit study meeting. I went to my bookshelf and pulled off a textbook just to see how much it contained on the topic of Ancient Greece. I found a total of eight pages - that's all. Then I pulled ALL the books I owned on Greece which was a stack of about ten consisting of: an educational coloring book, Plato's writings, Greek Mythology, an Eyewitness nonfiction book, a novel about the Trojan War and many others. At the meeting I showed the textbook, in one hand, and the whole stack of books in my other hand. Now, how could anyone say you could miss something the textbook might provide? What's more impressive is holding up a notebook from a one month unit study on Greece and seeing how full it is… so many subjects covered and the kids learned so much and loved the study!

It was fairly easy for me to break away from workbooks and textbooks when we started doing unit studies because of the unsatisfactory results and frustration I felt with school. I have to admit there was still a nagging, little voice inside saying, "What if you misssomething important? What if your child doesn't measure up to THEIR standards?" (I've lived with this illusive "they" hanging over me and I don't even know who THEY are!)

Whenever I find myself struggling, I try to remind myself of this story a friend relayed to me - it always helps me keep my educational priorities straight!

A Christian couple who raised their two children in the 1940's could see their children would not thrive in public school and decided to teach them at home. Of course, at that time home education was not a known alternative nor was it part of the movement we see today. My friend asked this woman, "What did you teach them? What did you use for curriculum? Did you teach them all about the 50 states and capitals, the presidents in order, and the Periodic Tables?" The mother replied, "I taught them to read from the Bible, because they needed to be able to read the Word of God. I also taught them math, and that's it. You see, I knew once they learned to read, they could learn about anything, but more importantly I knew when my children got to college, if they came upon an area where they found themselves lacking scholastically, they could quickly take any classes they would need. But the one class they could not take was one where they could learn how to have godly character." Their two children grew up, both attended college, and became professionals— one was a doctor and the other a missionary nurse.

I am not suggesting that you reduce your teaching to Bible reading and math, but I hope this inspiring story will help you get the right perspective so you might attain your goals.

With unit studies we cover a lot of material and the truly great thing is that the content in the material we cover is really learned and retained. If you have fears, remember this important point—life's most important lessons cannot be learned by filling in blanks on workbook pages while sitting at a desk.

"…life does not afford us enough time to fill in the possible gaps.

The only gap to be concerned with is any void in your child's life

that can only befilled by the Holy Spirit.

Remember, academics aren't everything."

(Valerie Bendt, *How to Create Your Own Unit Study* [Hawthorne: Common Sense Press, 1990], 6)

TESTING

How will I know my children are learning what they should? I know testing is an area where people often have strong opinions, however, I have a few guidelines I follow in this area. I have my own opinions and I'll keep most of them to myself, but I will say "Who decides what your children need to learn? I would like to give my readers the vision to see themselves as the teacher/parent and responsible party for everything connected with their child's education.

Because unit studies are interactive, you will be spending time in close contact with your students. You will be able to tell what your child is learning and how much he is comprehending.

Testing is an area where using a scope and sequence guide like *A Typical Course of Study* can help because you can map out your educational goals for each child when you make your annual school plans or, if you teach by the unit study method exclusively, use the Big Picture Unit Study Plan (in the Appendix). This way, once you have decided what you are going to teach, you can watch your child to see that he is learning.

Some test for the sake of testing and have a hard time letting go of tradition. I would encourage you to ask yourself what you are trying to accomplish by testing. If you are just looking for a number or a test score, but the student hasn't really learned, is it a true assessment? When I do test, the results I am looking for is to be sure my children have learned the material. Often I allow them to use their unit study notebooks to answer questions they are unsure of. I never say "Too bad, you failed." Instead I say, "Let's find out and make sure you understand."

There is a danger in thinking a subject has been covered if a textbook

has been read and test passed. When I did annual achievement testing

of homeschooled children, I saw too many children who had studied

under a workbook approach to history or science who could not apply

what they had learned on standardized tests. Material was memorized and

soon forgotten.Their parents would tell me the children read the workbooks,

answered all the questions and did wonderfully on chapter tests. (What happened between the time the subject was studied and the yearly achievement test was given? Could it be that the information was meaningless to the child and discarded along the way?)

(Gayle Graham, *How to Home School*, [Hawthorne: Common Sense Press, 1992], 127)

I always give my children a quiz or test at the end of every unit study. It was difficult for the younger children to take the test because they couldn't write the answers. Recently, I discovered that if we take the test together it is less stressful. My goal is, again, to use it as a review and to reinforce the information we covered. **Here's what I do:** I type up a quiz on the computer and get around thirty questions on one sheet. I can do this easily because I taught my children the material and I learned along with them. So I can use our books and their notebooks to recall the material and within fifteen minutes, I can have it ready. It works really well if I ask a question and let the kids arrive at an answer they all agree on and then I write the number of the question and just the answer by the number on the wipe clean board. This is something all my school age children (except the five year old) can do.

How would I grade a test like this? I probably wouldn't or if I did I would have to give all the kids an "A" because all the answers would be right!

> World Geography Quiz
> 1. How many continents are there? Seven - Africa, No. & So.America, Europe, Asia, Antarctica, Australia
> 2. How many oceans? Four - Pacific, Atlantic, Indian, Arctic
> 3. What is a map maker called? A cartographer
> 4. What is the imaginary line around the middle of the earth? The Equator
>
> *Four questions - this is just a sample*

We write unit study guides and sell materials to homeschoolers. Most of our guides are planning guides to help moms plan unit studies on many different topics. We often get phone calls from moms who wonder why we have not included a test. A few of our guides do include a sample test and in these cases, we get calls from moms wondering why we don't provide the answers. The reasons we don't usually provide tests is because the study you conduct, the books you use, and the information you decide to cover will probably be different from our study. The test should be geared to help you answer questions about things you studied. We don't provide answers because we are not encouraging a "fill in the blanks" mentality." If you did the study, you should know the answers. I've had people say "I can't find the answer to this question." So are we looking for information or for answers? Do we know how to research? Do you see what is wrong with this picture? Too many home educators still want to fill in the blanks and check off the boxes to say they have "done it." What we're after and trying to encourage others to want as well, is REAL learning not just doing what THEY say you're supposed to do!

Likewise, we make a product giving information and ideas for how to make flapbooks. Still, people ask us to just make them a packet with pictures to glue in and words to paste on for specific topics they might study. We could probably make a lot of money providing such a product, but we want you to put together something that will reflect what you learned If you studied Oceans, we could give some fish to paste on and it would "look" good, but it wouldn't be YOUR work! Test if you must and if it is your desire to do so, but please test for real learning and accurate assessment.

I do think it is good for students to take tests occasionally. This sort of challenge will sharpen theirthinking skills and also help you (and them) to see what they know and don't know. Be careful though, some things are not that important to know! Let's enjoy learning and not get caught up in the what ifs and the have tos.

Remember

- Pray for wisdom and direction when you are trying to gain a true assessment of each child.

- If the test does not give you a true assessment, it is a waste of time.

- Refer to your Philosophy of Education when you are trying to determine how testing helps meet your educational goals.

Remember also that the student's collection of notebooks is a compilation of reports and can serve as an impressive portfolio, a far richer record of your child's academic progress than a grade point average ever could be. (See the section on notebooks.)

MOM IS GETTING AN EDUCATION

When I teach workshops, or talk to moms, about the unit study method, I often use examples of things we've learned during different studies. They look at me with a blank look and even say, "You're so smart!" No, that's not it! I've learned so much by reading and studying with my kids. I'm so excited and interested that I remember what I've learned and can relay it enthusiastically. I am finally getting an education and this is something that can happen to each of us - another convincing reason to choose interactive teaching!

THE THREE X'S

There are three words which will help cement the concept of this method. They are the three "X's" ~ **Explore, Expand, Excite**. As we *explore* an area of interest, we find we can *expand* our knowledge until our desire to know is satisfied. The result of our *exploration* is *excitement* about what we've learned. And... don't forget to add Enjoy!

I challenge you, friend, if this isn't happening in your educational process, then you are probably stuck somewhere going through the motions just "doing school." By taking hold of a few simple principles you CAN all enjoy your studies and time together and that's why we've devoted a whole chapter demonsrating why you SHOULD choose unit studies!

Get on your mark...

② Get set... Go!

Now that you've decided to give unit studies a try, what's next? The heart of this approach is to help make learning desirable and something children anticipate. Learning should be a delightful, lifelong experience... and get ready... even fun!

Start with these guidelines:

- Get excited! Get excited about books!

- Involve your children in your plans.

- Find out what topics interest them.

- Make your first unit easy, short, and fun.

- Begin to develop a love for learning - this starts with Mom!

- Prove that learning is exciting.

- Teach interactively - it's the KEY!

- Foster good attitudes and an environment toward learning.

- Be enthusiastic - it's catching!

Sound a bit idealistic? It really isn't. Conducting successful unit studies truly is attainable, something within us all. We just need to have the right tools and know *how* to use them.

STOCK YOUR TOOLBOX

DEVELOP A LOVE FOR LEARNING

Since we've established that inspiring your children to love learning is at the heart of unit studies, you must help them to see the importance of books and reading. Although a great deal of learning will be gained through experiences, books play an equally vital role in a child's education. We're not talking about just any books, however; we're talking about books that have value.

When children are encouraged to explore their own interests through books, and can do research utilizing good books and other resources, they are able to find their own answers. In this way they begin to learn "how" to think rather than "what" to think. The more they think for themselves, the more confidence they build. You will begin to observe a learning cycle that looks something like this: as children build confidence in themselves, the sense of satisfaction

31

which is gained, further encourages more love for learning as well as an eagerness to learn. Confidence equals more interest which equals eagerness which equals more confidence which equals a love for learning!

We decided to do a unit study on insects (yuck!), so I brought out all the books I had on that topic. I had books on bees, ants, and all kinds of bugs! My eleven year old son, Samuel, grabbed the ant books and I found him hours later in his room reading about ants. I couldn't get him to go to bed! The next day he went out in the yard and collected some dirt in a jar and found some ants, and spent lots of time observing them. I went right down to the store and bought him an ant farm. When we got together with another family to do a co-op, he already knew everything one could know about ants. It was sort of embarrassing because he sounded like a know-it-all, but it actually thrilled me. You see, he had an interest (which came about through exciting books) and he was eager to learn.

Some ways you can encourage a love for books in your home Is to:

- Start acquiring good books and build a home library.
- Arrange books so children can easily find them and reach them.
- Spend time reading as a family. Read aloud, inflect your voice, show pictures.
- Make visiting the library part of your life.

WHAT AM I SUPPOSED TO TEACH?

I want to give you permission to not need or have to get permission! I hope you'll catch the vision for owning this teaching and parenting task and begin to think "outside the box." We need to change our robotic mentality and stop saying, "What am I SUPPOSED to teach?" There are certain things your child needs to learn, but how and when is up to you! And who's to say they need to learn it? We will NOT be able to develop a love for learning as long as we are jumping through someone else's hoops. Parents need to catch the vision and have the desire to make their own hoops!

PROVE THAT LEARNING IS EXCITING

One BIG thing you are going to have to do - and this takes time, is prove that learning if fun and that it is a good thing. See, we need to switch from SCHOOL to LEARNING! The way to do this is to FOSTER an atmosphere and attitude that invites delight. Let's face it, when you tell most children it's time to start school, the sound parents usually hear is "Ugh!" Although they might still be a bit skeptical, your children will probably perk up when you tell them you are going to do something different and fun. When you embark on your first unit study choose a topic that will allow you to prove that learning can be fun. It is not necessary to stand on your head to provide a "Disneyland" experience for your first unit, but try to include different activities and whatever you do, keep it light. Go on a field trip, do some art, read lots of colorful books and so on. If you are genuinely enthused, your children will be excited, too! You have to be the "love for learning leader!"

FOSTER GOOD ATTITUDES TOWARD LEARNING

There's that word again... Foster. I guess I am using that particular word to mean, we must create, allow and encourage this love, and we can only do this by demonstrating it and leading our children into it. If you are running around the house all stressed out over time crunches and getting subjects done... you will not be "fostering" this attitude. So get a cup of coffee (read your Philosophy of Education!) and sit down and look at books with your kids.

How can you develop an attitude in children that says "I Love to Learn?" Relay the message that the learning process continues throughout their life, not just for a set period of time. You might choose to teach year round, possibly devising a weeks-on, weeks-off schedule. Instead of calling it school, you could call it "our official learning adventure time!" They will see that "school" is not from 9:00 a.m. to 3:00 p.m., Monday through Friday, but that you "school" on the way to town in the car, at church, and even at the grocery store. We school all the time because life IS school!

Our schooling schedule is more relaxed and over the past few years we've decided to continue along with some of our studies throughout the summer. This approach helps us avoid the feeling of wanting to get done. We also take longer breaks here and there so we can feel refreshed. In this way we feel more relaxed (fostering an atmosphere of delight) all the time instead of pushing to get done by a certain date. This way, depending on our schedule, we will be learning all the time, but if we need to take a week off because our workshop schedule demands that we have to travel and be away, we don't stress about it.

If you're a mom who can't wait until summer to have that well-deserved and much-needed break, why not try to let go of "tradition" and try something different - you might really like it! Find the schedule that fits your family, a schedule that serves you rather than one that you serve.

Year-round teaching provides benefits like:

- Less time is needed for review.

- The relaxed pace affords you more freedom.

- A good attitude toward lifelong learning is cultivated.

Since you don't have to plod through a determined amount of material in a set period of time, learning can be approached from the standpoint of being "delightful." If YOU demonstrate delight, your children will not dread education as something they "have to do."

GET INVOLVED - INTERACTION IS THE KEY!

We've already established that unit studies are interactive in nature and provide more interaction between:

- Teacher and students

- Each other - students and students

Often other teaching methods isolate students, sending them off into their own corners to work over a stack of books. One of the best ways to relate enthusiasm for learning is to get involved with your students. It's awfully hard to be enthused about what your children are learning if you don't know WHAT they are learning! Before unit studies, I felt like Mother Rabbit, hopping all over the house helping my children figure out the directions for what they were supposed to be doing for each subject. Now, I don't want to insult anyone, but this is NOT teaching. It's more like being an available resource person. I so much more prefer teaching and learning, to just filling in the blanks.

FINE TUNING • WORKING THE BUGS OUT • SOLVING PROBLEM AREAS

Okay, we've been homeschooling for twenty one years now. We started out using traditional methods (because that was what was available to us). After a few years we started using unit studies and though we loved the method, things didn't always go well, but we did hang in there. I also host a local unit study meeting, speak at homeschool conventions, and teach workshops on unit studies. Over the years, these combined and varied experiences have helped me to find what I call the "problem areas" with unit studies.

Sometimes people ask if I developed "The Unit Study Method" and while I did NOT, I believe I have found out some tips and tricks to help people understand the methods and not feel that it is so insurmountable. I think unit studies have gained a bad reputation and I would like to stand up and wave a flag in their defense! As I mentioned before, some of the things people believe about unit studies is that moms need to be the creative type, have loads of energy, spend lots of time on planning and know how to make costumes! I've said it before so I'll say it again - a unit study can be anything you want it to be.

The next couple of pages outline what we do in our home and what we feel are the keys to success with unit studies. These are the guidelines which, when followed and implemented, will enable parents to succeed with this method using any unit study guide or currciulum - or none at all. I refer to this list of guidelines as a Prescription for Success and I would like to use the visual example of building a skyscraper using steel beams which provides a solid framework. With unit studies we desire a relaxed and delightful atmosphere but if we get too relaxed, everything falls apart. When we started out, I floundered alot because I didn't know quite what to do. So what we need is something we can adhere to - a concrete or solid framework to build on or stick to. The list of guidelines are the things we do the same with every single unit study. We are able to just "slide" the new topic and new books into this framework. This works so well because my kids know what to expect and I know what to do!

RX - PRESCRIPTION FOR SUCCESS

- Read aloud from a piece of good literature.
- Build a unit study notebook.
- Give students a spelling list of words in topic.
- Give vocabulary words from spelling list AND from read aloud title.
- Look for pertinent scripture to shed the light of God's Word on your topic (which may be used for handwriting practice).
- Write up an assignment sheet (listing activities students can do on their own).
- Spend approximately four weeks on each unit topic.
- Help students choose a book for their silent reading - in topic.
- Stick to a daily schedule (outlined later).
- Concentrate on history OR science - not both in one month.
- It's really the BOOKS that MAKE the study.

THE TWO KEY ELEMENTS OF A UNIT STUDY

In the Steward Method, I teach that there are two key elements to unit studies. They are:

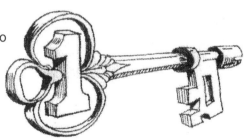

The Read Aloud Title is the piece of literature you choose to read out loud to your students duringa study. When you are gathering information and resources for a unit study, look for a novel or piece of classic literature of value. Since the read-aloud element is what you focus around and build from, it will be a main part of each day and the center of your study. Besides Bible time, it is the MOST important subject of the day. Read aloud equals a story or novel.

The Notebook Project is the hands-on portion of the study. It is the central project for each unit. The notebook is a folder or binder students create during the course of any study. This binder/notebook is di-

vided into sections which are ultimately the students subjects - in most cases each student will have their own. Using notebooks for our studies has changed everything. Our kids love their notebooks! The notebook is not merely a place to file papers away, but it truly is a project so if you never do any other "projects" during your study, the notebook stands alone as a very cool project.

READING ALOUD

We'll devote the next several pages on Reading Aloud and then we'll talk about Notebooks. I am a strong advocate of reading aloud and family reading because of the favorable results I've seen. It's hard to explain, but something important occurs through family reading time. Making read aloud time a consistent part of every school day, enables you to relay the message and place importance on the fact that spending time together, reading and building a tie that binds, is what counts.

This read aloud time should be considered a school "subject" - and not only that, but one of the most valuable subjects of the day. I believe we accomplish more "teaching" during this time than at any other time, so if you're in a hurry, scrimp on other subjects... but not on read aloud time! Some homeschoolers put reading aloud on the backburner and will get around to it if they have time in the day but I would propose that you bring up it to the front of the line.

When you read to young children every day, they begin to experience each book's excitement and pleasures. These reading experiences spark their interest and fuel their creativity.

Reading aloud to your children:

- Provides a great source of enjoyment.
- Affords opportunity for discussion.
- Improves and broadens child's vocabulary and language skills.
- Develops listening and comprehension skills.
- Promotes unity and togetherness.
- Becomes a shared experience.
- Makes good use of time (i.e. reading together, instead of spending time watching television).
- Awakens the child's imagination and enables them to develop a love for good literature.

Children of all ages enjoy having someone read to them, even "grown-up children" - like my husband! Many times he comes home for lunch and gets so wrapped up in our story and then it's hard for him to get back to work! Be sure to allow younger children to be in on read-aloud times also.

Children absorb a lot of learning by osmosis just by being nearby. I remember when I was teaching our daughter how to write her letters. A few minutes later my preschooler came running up to me with a whole page covered with the letter "H." She said "Look Mommy, I draw 'H'!"

There have been times when I have allowed the younger children to go play elsewhere because I thought the author was too wordy, or the content too advanced for them to understand. However, I am usually surprised how much the younger ones can comprehend. While we don't want to "dumb them down" we also need to be careful that we don't kill learning by making them sit in on a book that is too hard to understand. Two or three chapters of a book like *Great Expectations* are probably too much for little ears. If you proceed with material that is too deep for your audience, your listeners will become frustrated and lose interest. Then you are wasting everyone's time.

During a study on Ancient Egypt, I was reading aloud *The Cat of Bubastes* by G.A. Henty. If you've read any books by this author, you know his books are truly great (from a Christian worldview) but he can be wordy. My fourteen year old daughter and eleven year old son, loved this book and understood most of what was going on, but my nine year old daughter, would often say, "I don't know what is happening." Instead of dismissing her, we would just explain and help get her over this little bump in the reading road!

Reading aloud affords great times of discussion and offers an abundant supply of teachable moments. Reading aloud allows opportunities for me, the teacher, to stop and ask questions. I will ask questions such as: "Why do you think he said that?", or "What do you think that means?" I'll ask a question to spark their memory: "Did that happen before or after the time of Columbus?" to determine if they can relate current incidents to units covered in the past. I am constantly stopping to comment or ask questions - it's part of teaching.

By asking questions, I can determine:

- If my children are listening.
- How much they are comprehending.
- That they can reason things out.
- If they see how things relate in the subject.

I know my children DO listen because they can answer my questions and tell me what I just read. Most days I start our read aloud time by asking, "What happened yesterday in our story?" This helps us remember and review, but sometimes I can't remember so this little exercise is really for Mom!

Something that has helped our children become better listeners and comprehenders is to use the wonderful tool called narration. Narration means "to relate, to tell in detail or describe." Simply have the child retell the events of a chapter. As the child begins to narrate the story, he must put it into his own words which enables him to learn to think for himself. Neither the parent nor the other children are allowed to make comments or judgments by saying, "No, that's not how it went!"

Susan Schaeffer Macaulay, has this to say about narration:

**Read the child a good tale, full of interest. Then say to him, "Can you tell me the story?"
As he puts it into words, he has to think for himself. He uses his memory,
and he is attending deeply. But his own reactions and expressions are involved.
It is a total human activity. You don't need to reduce the child's appreciation to elementary
"true/false" tests. The child has acquired knowledge, and having expressed it creatively
in his own words, he will be able to remember what he has learned.**

(Susan Schaeffer Macaulay, *For the Children's Sake* [Wheaton: Crossway Books, 1984], 29]

Read aloud time is a priority in our home. It is one of the first things we do to start off our day. Family reading is a wonderful habit every home should develop. Usually when I refer to reading aloud time I mean the time you spend reading a novel (in your unit study topic) during your school time. We also try to have a family reading time and this would be a completely different book (not necessarily related to our unit study) that we read at night as a family - when Dad is home.

When we studied Immigration, I read a biography on the life of Robert Louis Stevenson, who emigrated to America to be with his sweetheart. Our interest in this famous author sparked an enthusiasm to read the book *Treasure Island*, which we read together as a family in the evening, so in this case we were not reading a book related to our topic.

We frequently use narration around the dinner table giving the children opportunities to narrate the details of the read aloud story as they remember them. The children can't wait to tell their father about what we read during the day. They get so excited when they tell him about the story. We have to tell them to slow down and take turns so he can understand what they are saying. Other times, I see the children following Jim around the house as he takes off his shoes and washes up after work, telling him all about a certain character or part of a story. Without even knowing it, they are using these beneficial skills which I didn't even assign them to do!

Reading aloud is a great family hobby. These shared experiences will be something your kids will remember, treasure and talk about for years. Together you visited different countries and time periods, met fascinating people and learned about other customs and cultures. Since not many families get to travel the world together, you can do it through books! This will also give family members a huge number of experiences to relate back to. I so enjoy it when I see the children's eyes sparkle when they can take part in conversations because they "know" something - something usually gleaned from our shared reading and study times together. This is especially exciting for the children and such instances serve to renew, once again, their enthusiasm for learning. One example would be when we went to San Francisco to visit family to learn about our family history. In the course of conversation, my cousin, who is from Italy, happened to mention the Celts, the Irish potato famine and a few other things as he talked about other countries and their history.

Our daughter Whitney, who was twelve years old at the time, picked up on it. She was so excited that she knew what he was talking about - because she had read about them. Teachers - it's like getting a paycheck for all your hard work when you see your kids excited and enthused about learning.

USING THE READ-ALOUD TIME TO ITS FULLEST POTENTIAL

I would now like to invite you into our living room to share our read aloud time so you can see how to use a single piece of literature to its fullest potential. I will be reading excerpts from two chapters from Jules Verne in *A Journey to the Center of the Earth*, an abridged version of the book which we used during a unit study on volcanoes. (I usually don't prefer abridged versions, but I did choose this one because of the length of time I had set aside for the study and the age of the children I was teaching.)

Through this exercise you will see how to use this time to include:

- Vocabulary words
- Dictation
- Math concepts
- Discussion
- Material previously learned
- Geography
- The author's ability to paint a picture with words

All are incorporated quite naturally! Comments made to my children will be in bold italics; those to my readers will be in caps. (There are parts I will skip over to make my points as brief as possible.)

Used for Study on Volcanoes

A Journey to the Center of the Earth

by Jules Verne

(Playmore Inc., NY, NY 1987)

Chapter 1: The Great Discovery

Looking back at all that has happened to me since that eventful day, I am hardly able to believe that my adventures were real. They were so wonderful that, even now, I am amazed when I think about them.

I was living with my uncle, a German, who was a professor of philosophy, chemistry, geology, mineralogy, and many other "ologies." (p. 7)

If his uncle was a German, what country was he from? Can you point to it on the globe?

Professor Hardwigg, my uncle, had invited me to study under him, for I was greatly interested in learning as much as I could about the Earth and what lies under its surface.

Although my uncle was a most learned man, and could speak with the great scientific world in almost any language, and could classify six hundred different geological specimens by their weight, hardness, sound, taste, and smell, he did not at all look the part. (p. 8)

Before I describe what he looks like, why don't you get out your pen and doodle a picture of the author's description.

He was fifty years old, tall, thin, and wiry. Large glasses hid his vast, round, bulging eyes. His nose was thin like a file and was constantly being attracted to tobacco. When he walked, he stepped a yard at a time, clenched his fists as if he were going to hit you, and then walked on. At most times, he was far from a pleasant companion. (p. 8)

Can you recall what a yard is? Who wants to show what he looked like when he walked a yard at a time with fists clenched?

But Professor Hardwigg is by no means a bad sort of man. However, to live with him means to obey him... (p. 8)

SKIP AHEAD - AS THE STORY CONTINUES, THE PROFESSOR FINDS A BOOK CONTAINING SOMETHING OF INTEREST TO HIM - A PIECE OF PAPER UPON WHICH A SECRET CODE HAS BEEN WRITTEN.

On the inside cover, my uncle found what at first looked like an ink stain, but on close inspection, it proved to be a line of writing almost rubbed away by time. My uncle studied the letters.

"Arne Saknussemm!" my uncle cried in triumph. "He owned this book. He was a brilliant Icelandic professor and chemist of the sixteenth century. It was he who wrote the mysterious words on the parchment - perhaps some astounding discovery of his." (p. 20)

What block of years comprised the sixteenth century? Now, for vocabulary write down "parchment." P-A-R-C-H-M-E-N-T

THE TWO OF THEM WORKED FOR HOURS TRYING TO DECIPHER THE CODE. WHILE THE UNCLE WAS OUT OF THE ROOM...

I sat down for a while, relaxing and smoking. Then my mind returned to the parchment, and I picked it up and began studying it again. I found a few scattered Latin words, an English word, and several French words. It was enough to drive a man mad!

The heat in the closed room was too much to bear, and I began to fan myself with the parchment. For the first time, I saw both the front and back of it.

Imagine my surprise when, glancing at the back of the parchment, I saw that the ink had gone through, revealing the Latin words craterem, "crater" and terrestre, "earth." I had discovered the secret! All I had to do to read the parchment was to look at it backwards. (p. 23, 24)

Isn't it interesting how many of the words we use today come from Latin roots?

My eyes were dazzled and my hands trembled with excitement as I began to read. But what horror and shock possessed me as I discovered the terrible secret! It had really been accomplished! A man had actually dared to do - what?

I immediately made a decision - no living being should know the parchment's secret. (p. 24)

THE YOUNG MAN DECIDED NOT TO REVEAL THE SECRET, KNOWING HIS UNCLE WOULD BE CRAZY ENOUGH TO ATTEMPT SUCH A TRIP. HOWEVER, PROFESSOR HARDWIGG SOON DISCOVERED THE SECRET OF THE BACKWARDS CODE HIMSELF.

"Backwards!" he cried. "It is backwards. Oh, how cunning Saknussemm was!" Then he began to translate the parchment:

"Descend into the crater of Yocul of Sneffels, which the shade of Scartaris caresses, before the kalends of July, audacious traveler, and you will reach the center of the earth. I did it. Arne Saknussemm" (p. 28)

Needless to say, the uncle was determined to find out more!

Chapter 2: Starting the Journey

It didn't take long for my uncle to take a book of maps from the shelf in order to explain Saknussemm's message to me. "You see, the whole island is composed of volcanoes," he said as he pointed to a map of Iceland. "And they all bear the name of Yocul, which means glacier in Icelandic." (p. 31)

Whitney, would you get our world atlas and look up Iceland.

"But what does the word Sneffels mean?" I asked.

"I knew you would ask," my uncle answered. "Follow my finger to the western coast, past Iceland's capital, Reykjavik."

I followed his finger. (p. 32)

Let's do the same girls. Who can find, Reykjavik?

"There," he continued, "that peninsula shaped like a thighbone with a mountain in the center. Do you see it?" (p. 32)

Okay, let's write down "peninsula" for vocabulary. P-E-N-I-N-S-U-L-A.

AS THE STORY CONTINUES, HARRY DECIDES TO TELL THE GIRL HE HOPES TO MARRY ABOUT THE MESSAGE. HE THOUGHT SHE WOULD OPPOSE THE IDEA. INSTEAD HE GETS HER COMPLETE AND ENVIOUS BLESSING TO GO.

"We are really going then?" I asked, hoping he would give the journey some more thought.

"We leave the day after tomorrow at daybreak," he answered.

We went by train from Hamburg, Germany, to Copenhagen, Denmark, and from schooner to Reykjavik, Iceland. The trip was a hard one, the seas rough and wild. (p. 36)

Point out Hamburg and Copenhagen. Using the map key, quickly estimate the distance from Hamburg to Reykjavik. Now, jot down "schooner" for vocabulary. S-C-H-O-O-N-E-R.

(ALTHOUGH I DON'T ADVISE DOING THE SUBJECTS MATH OR BIBLE WITH YOUR UNIT STUDIES, YOU CAN SEE HERE HOW THESE OPPORTUNITIES CAN BE USED TO REINFORCE MATH CONCEPTS.) AS THEY EMBARK ON THEIR JOURNEY, THEY ARE PUT IN CONTACT WITH A MAN WILLING TO GUIDE THEM TO MT. SNEFFELS FOR A SCIENTIFIC INVESTIGATION.

Later that night, we had dinner with a Mr. Fridriksson, one of Iceland's most learned scientists. We told him nothing of our planned journey, explaining only that we were here as tourists. However, we did learn from him more of the story of Arne Saknussemm. And what we learned made the reason for the coded parchment clear at last.

My uncle had asked Fridriksson if the library in Reykjavik had any books written by Saknussemm.

"You will not find any such books here in Iceland, nor anywhere else," the scientist said.

"Why not?" asked my uncle.

"Because Saknussemm was accused of heresy, of opposing the beliefs of the church and in 1573 his books were all publicly burned… But to turn to a more pleasant subject…" (p. 38, 40)

WE'LL USE THIS PARAGRAPH (BECAUSE OF ITS CONTENT) FOR OUR DICTATION. I REPEAT IT EXACTLY AS IT APPEARS, ADVISING MY STUDENTS OF THE QUOTATION MARKS, CAPITAL LETTERS, PUNCTUATION, ETC. THIS TIME PROVIDES A PRIME SPOT TO STOP AND DISCUSS WHAT WE ALREADY KNOW ABOUT THIS PERIOD OF HISTORY.

Who else was accused by the church (what church?) of heresy?

THE STORY GOES ON TO TELL OF THE BEGINNING OF THEIR JOURNEY TO THE CENTER OF THE EARTH. A LIST OF ITEMS BROUGHT ON THEIR JOURNEY IS INCLUDED WHICH I WOULD HAVE MY CHILDREN COPY DOWN AND ALPHABETIZE. ITEMS LIKE THIS LIST AND THE PICTURE OF PROFESSOR HARDWIGG WOULD BE LABELED AND INCLUDED IN EACH CHILD'S NOTEBOOK UNDER THE MISCELLANEOUS SECTION OR POSSIBLY A SECTION FOR ASSIGNMENTS AND PAPERS DONE DURING THE READ ALOUD.

Because a great amount of educational material today is prepared in a literature-based fashion, this demonstration shows various worthwhile and meaningful opportunities you can take advantage of during a read-aloud session. Though you might have noticed other places in the chapter which could have been discussed, be careful not to stop at every other word, chopping up the story for "teachable moments." Doing so will take the enjoyment out of the story.

Reading Aloud and Choosing Good Books

Strive to choose classic literature for it will build godly character in your children and inspire and encourage them. Read about noble people and their noble deeds. Talk with your children about the lives of the people characterized in these books by discussing their attributes and the choices these characters made whether good or bad. Children will be taught valuable lessons about how those choices affected the lives of the characters and those around them. The people who demonstrate good character become heroes, mentors and role models to their readers. Through reading we are introduced to real people who displayed character, extolled the virtues of righteous living, stood up for what was right, and acted with honesty and integrity. Though not always laced with peaches-and-cream story lines, good books cause readers to weigh the consequences people face with the choices they made in real-life situations. When you share living examples from the lives of others, your children will also learn to discern good from evil. These discussions offer priceless opportunities to show your children WHY you believe the way you do. Therefore, instead of saying "Do it because the Bible says to," you can explain, "This is the very reason the Lord instructs us to tell the truth. See what kind of trouble came to this man because he lied?"

Historical fiction books are usually based on real people and places and include true facts revealing realistic events throughout the course of an enjoyable story. During our unit on World Explorers, each child chose a biography or novel to read about an explorer (at appropriate levels). We chose to read aloud a book by Louise Andrews Kent entitled *He Went with Marco Polo*. This book told the story of a boy who worked as a gondolier in Venice, where he met Marco Polo. The two became friends and eventually journeyed to Cathay together. Many facts were laced into the story and we learned so much about Marco Polo, people and places like Venice and Asia, and that particular time period.

The following excerpt is a warm example showing the value of friendship. Pietro, a young man traveling with the two boys, was accused of stealing.

> **"My Lord," said Marco hastily, "I have heard that such offenses can be paid for. Whatever Pietro has done, let me pay for it."... The affair was finally settled by Marco's paying the owner of the arrows ten times their value. Pietro, who had never even moaned during the whipping, burst into tears when he saw the sulky-looking Tartar carrying off Marco's best knives, strings of Venetian beads, and scarlet cloth... "Oh the thief!" Barka Khan said. "Take him by all means. We can do without him very well!" Messer Nicolo smiled. "A friend by your side can keep you warmer than the richest furs, my Lord," he said.**

(Louise Andrews Kent, *He Went With Marco Polo*, [Cambridge: The Riverside Press, 1935], 94, 96)

Older books are always better and *He Went With Marco Polo* was published in 1935. Although it is not known as a classic, we include this book on our family's list of classics.

If your child is a slow starter easily discouraged in his efforts to read, be sure to spend a lot of time reading aloud to him. He will learn to love stories and be inspired to read them for himself. If your stubborn reader ever says, "What's so great about reading?" help him to get excited about books by choosing something really adventurous to read. Find out what interests him and let him choose some books at the library for you to read to him. Make sure the books and pictures are colorful and interesting.

The key to success in selling your product is to advertise it over and over, again and again, singing new praises, extolling new tastes, announcing new products.

(Jim Trelease, *The Read-Aloud Handbook* [New York: Penguin Books 1983], 24)

To encourage good oral reading skills, give children opportunities to read aloud to the family, even if they aren't very fluent yet. Just have them start by reading a small portion - it makes them feel important. Make sure your other (more advanced) readers are patient and kind. Reading helps them learn proper voice inflection, develop good speech patterns, and build confidence in speaking before others.

If you find that your children don't enjoy this read aloud time consider his/her maturity level. Two of my children (who were ages seven and nine years old at the time), weren't interested in our read aloud time, no matter what I read. The next year, however, they began to love it immensely. I believe it was because they both matured enough in a year's time to appreciate, understand, and enjoy it.

Another thing to consider is possibly changing books. Sometimes the book is too long, too boring, or too technical for the child's aptitude. You have permission to quit the book and choose another even in mid-stream. Always treat your child as an individual. Some children simply are not auditory learners so listening to a story being read aloud may not be their strength. However, I would encourage you to continue to try and develop a love for family reading time with them. Experiment with many different kinds of books to see if you can spark their interest. Historical fiction and adventure type books can be more interesting than some biographies.

The question often arises, "How do you find good books to read aloud?" We will go into more detail concerning this in a later section, but one helpful hint is to prepare an "annual unit study plan" which will give you a good idea about what you are going to teach in the upcoming months. If you will do this, you will have plenty of time to look for and ask others for recommendations of good books on your topics.

Reading, reading out loud, and the world of books should become an exciting part of your home and is KEY to any unit study. It is also the foundation for sparking an early interest and love for learning.

Why Read Good Books?

Immorality and humanistic thinking and attitudes are everywhere and are constantly being rained down on us. We may avoid watching television but society cannot be "turned off." The tabloids are in full view as you stand in line at the grocery store. Driving through town, you see the breakdown of values on all sides. In contrast, a good book can provide a breath of fresh air. Parents can help provide stability and virtue for their children by exposing them to good literature.

You can even safely 'stop school' for a few years and feast on good books and right living! This could give childhood a lot more zest and vigor! Your child wouldn't lose out, by the way.

(From the foreword written by Susan Schaeffer Macaulay, *Books Children Love* [Westchester: Crossway Books, 1987], xiii)

Discussions that occur while reading good books help children see that historical people, events and works of art are related and not just isolated bits of information. These were people who lived, and worked, and were acquainted with each other. For example, during the study on the lives of famous explorers we learned that Amerigo Vespucci's wife modeled for the famous Italian painter, Sandro Boticelli. The children - who find it exciting when they are able to relate new information with material previously learned - remembered Boticelli, his work and the time period in which he lived from our art history unit.

Share good books with the children. It is a magic door of contact between the child and some of the most interesting and creative people our culture has enjoyed.

(Susan Schaeffer Macaulay, *For the Children's Sake* [Wheaton: Crossway Books, 1984], 84)

Tips:

- Try playing the part of the characters in your stories - changing your voice where appropriate. When I read *Treasure Island*, I would often change my voice to that of the gruff pirate, Long John Silver. The children loved it!

- Allow students to occupy themselves while you read by doodling, hand sewing, coloring, whittling or working on notebooks (as long as they listen quietly).

- If younger children don't sit quietly during your read aloud time, satisfy their need for "their time" by reading to them from a picture story book for fifteen minutes. Then you can send them to play in another area nearby while you read aloud to the older children.

Read Aloud Resources:

The Read Aloud Handbook - by Jim Trelease

Storytime With Your Children - Insights and suggestions for reading aloud with your children plus a listing of books for young children - by Edie Lauckner

 # THE NOTEBOOK PROJECT

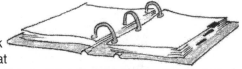

Building a notebook is a hands-on project and not only adds fun to the unit study but should be considered a vital part. There's something about students getting their hands involved in their work that helps them enjoy their studies and remember and retain what they've learned. It is a work of art, the student's own creation, and something for which they can be proud. Therefore, this notebook or three-ringed binder is much more than just a place to stash papers (but it certainly IS that also!).

WHY NOTEBOOKS?

Notebooks are important because they:

Are loved by the students

This notebook becomes a key part to the study and students look forward to working on them. My children frequently pull their unit study notebooks out and talk about the times where they collected a postcard, went on a field trip, or did the research for a paper they wrote. Notebooks help us to recall the great times we have had learning about different things over the years.

Provide a place for students to compile their work
and to keep each unit study more organized

Since it can be very frustrating to waste time searching for misplaced assignments and papers, students who prepare a notebook during the course of their study will have a place to keep all their work. Section dividers provide a place for each subject in the unit study. Assignment sheets are usually organized by subjects so if students are following an assignment sheet, it will be easy for them to know which section to place their finished work into.

Serve as a record of the amount of work, effort, and quality that has gone into a particular study

A project notebook is a valid record of different areas and the extent students have explored and studied. Apart from this type of record, often the only evidence to show what material has been covered is a few wrinkled papers stuffed into a desk, lost around the house, or merely written in Mother's record-keeping book.

This notebook will also serve as an overall report for the topic and will include completed assignments, spelling lists, quizzes, writing, artwork, diagrams, visual aids, and research. The notebook might contain forms listing books read and used during the course of each study as well as book reports, pictures and postcards from field trips.

We recently attended a homeschool graduation/promotions program. Each family prepared a table where they displayed the student's work for that year. Out of ten or so tables, only a few stood out as exciting. Most tables contained stacks of textbooks and just a few workbook pages! Since we've been doing notebooks as a project for our unit studies, I do not suffer the frustration of feeling like, "I know we've done more than this, but we don't have anything to show for our time and effort."

One time I called HSLDA to ask what kind of records I should be keeping for requirements in my state. They told me if we were ever called to account for teaching, that courts would not be looking for teacher's records which show page numbers from different books/subjects or by looking at the teacher's planning or record book. Instead, what they would be looking for is that we can show "reasonable progress" and the way to do this is to produce samples for each student, in each subject area from September, January and June. Wow! Notebooks are the answer to this huge stress! I mark the topic, student's name and grade on the spine of each notebook so I can pull notebooks from the shelf for studies we did all year. This has been such a big relief for me!

Allow students ownership - something to call their own - which encourages students to take pride in their work

Students become excited about something they can call their very own. I've noticed that, my children are enthused about having their own notebook for each study, so they tend to "do more" because they want to expand and work on their notebooks and take pride in their work. This motivation is great for building better research and thinking skills.

Stimulate creativity

The first thing we do when we begin a unit study is to design a cover and get our notebooks set up. Students are encouraged to be creative since they design their own covers and section dividers and their notebook can become whatever they want it to be. As they study they are able to come up with different assignments and visual aids to enhance each study.

Give students something to DO - a hands-on experience

If building a notebook during the course of a study is the only project you require your children to do, it is an easy one.

Are an "easy" and worthwhile project to focus or center the study around

The notebook offers something concrete to connect with and come back to.

Serve as future reference and teaching tools to be used by yourself or others for reteaching the same topic

The time spent in research and putting together information into interesting assignments and visual aids can be saved and used again to benefit younger siblings or future grand children when your students get married and desire to teach their own children. Why do all that work again when you can save it? Does this seem like a far off possibility? We already have one granddaughter who will be starting school (at home) in five years!

Can be expanded and added to as the years go by

Many times we stumble upon something interesting we'd like to add to a study notebook. You can keep adding to them as time goes on. If you are home educating for the long haul, you will end up teaching some units more than once because your students have advanced to a higher learning level. Sometimes the span between studying the same topic is several years, so your student would want to make a new notebook.

Become an educational keepsake

When your child has completed his formal education, he will have shelves full of wonderful educational keepsakes and he will be so proud. Have you ever found a report or project you put together in your school days? What a joy it is! Imagine what a wonderful collection of memories your students will have if you encourage them to compile each study into a notebook.

Most of the time we take pictures of many keepsakes that don't fit into notebooks. Field trips, plays and projects that crumble and fall to pieces can be preserved through pictures! Our whole family made a wonderful coat of arms which we laminated during our unit study on Medieval Times. It is fun to pull it out from time to time to admire!

For all the times you've thought something your child did was so cute or a paper you were so proud of and you wished you had a place to keep them - now you can keep ALL your child's work!

Offer a place to duplicate and include vital information gained during a study

Often our children have seen something interesting in a book and wish to somehow keep the information. You can't very well put the book into your notebook, but you can duplicate the information by creating and drawing your own, copying (where permitted) or by tracing the picture. When Cacey studied Shakespeare, she wanted to include a timeline she had seen in a book. She just created her own sheet for her notebook. She also did the same when she wanted to keep information about types of plays. When studying birds, the children drew their own diagrams (ideas taken from books) of beaks, feet, wings, feathers, wing shapes. If copyright is not an issue, you can scan pictures from books and use for assignments.

Helps you conclude your unit study as it gives you a reason to "wrap things up"
When you have concluded your unit, your students should finish all papers, assignments, and projects so you can tuck your notebook away on the shelf. Spend a little time at the end of your study to pull it all together and make sure the notebook is organized and assignments are finished. When it's all done - it goes on the shelf.

As already mentioned, all papers unrelated to a unit study topic go into an "All School Binder." Our children begin each school year with an "All School Binder" complete with dividers. (You can buy section dividers or make your own from colored cardstock.)

Papers to include in this type of binder would be:

- Assignments done outside the unit study
- Papers from grammar skills
- Correspondence
- Miscellaneous artwork
- Scripture memory verses or Bible work
- Math worksheets

SUPPLIES NEEDED FOR YOUR NOTEBOOK PROJECT

Here are some of the items you will need to get started on your notebook:

- Folder or three ringed binder (preferably with slip sheet/view front cover)
- Tabbed section dividers or stick on tabs to place on colored cardstock
- Vocabulary Sheets
- Section divider designs
- Sheet protectors (clear slip covers)
- Student's Planning/Record Sheet
- A three-hole punch
- Copies of other sheets which are pertinent to the particular study

There are a variety of folders and binders available for making notebooks. Our personal preference is to use three ringed binders with slip-sheet fronts which are 1/2" to 1" in size. Slip-front binders allow students to easily design and create their own cover, then slip it into the front of the binder. These can be purchased fairly inexpensively at office supply stores or bulk shopping membership warehouse stores. Slip-front binders come in several colors including the standard white and black. You might choose one binder style and stick with it so your notebook collection will have continuity.

Another option is spiral or "comb" binding if you are using one binder for each unit study. If you plan to spiral bind a notebook, keep the student's work in a file folder for the duration of the study and don't three hole punch any papers. Then at the end of the study, take all papers, dividers, etc. for the notebook to a copy center and have it bound (cost is usually around $1-$2).

ORGANIZING YOUR NOTEBOOK

Notebooks will differ because of the type of study (science, history, literature, etc.), the age of the student, the student's creativity, and the topic. For example, a study on nutrition would include items much different from a study about state history. You will have to decide what size binder you need. You will need a big (2 1/2" binder) for a full year study on your State History, but you'd only need a 1/2" binder for a mini study on Ants.

Organize your notebooks by purchasing inexpensive ready made tabbed dividers, or make your own. It is cost effective to make the section dividers by using colorful sheets of cardstock (65 - 80 pound), which can be purchased for just a few cents per sheet at many print shops. You could also buy a whole ream of one color stock, which is 250 sheets, from a office supply store. If you go in together with a friend, you can buy a few colors and split up your reams and each have a nice supply of cardstock. You can ask at the business service centers In office supply stores to see if they will sell you single sheets. Cut your own tabs along one edge, adjusting your cut up or down so tabs on each divider are different. OR purchase packages of stick on tabs to stick onto the regular cardstock. One other option to inquire about is an item called "Repro Tabs." These are pre-cut sheets which can be run through a copy machine.

Most notebooks will include sections like, but are not limited to:

- A Miscellaneous Section - things that don't fit anywhere else: record sheet, assignment sheet, menus, programs from a presentation night, tests and quizzes, pictures of activities, field trips, and projects.

- Spelling & Vocabulary/Terms to Know

- Writing /Handwriting - poetry, compositions (dictation)

- Worksheets and General Information

- Geography, Maps, Diagrams

- Bible

- Art, Activities and Worksheets

- Reference Information

People have asked if you could do one notebook for the whole family. This option does not seem workable to me - only space saving. If all your child's work is going into the notebook (and it will if you are using this method as your core of teaching) then each student NEEDS their own.

We've also had people ask whether it would work to put more than one study into a notebook. You'd need a pretty "fat" binder but you might be able to do it. It would certainly work for younger students who don't do that much "paper work" and writing. Big binders are cumbersome and the pages are hard to flip. You'll have to experiment. We find our notebook projects for each study are too large to fit all units for a school year, thus we prefer one binder per study.

Please take the time to have your children work on a notebook for every study and put forth the effort to guide and motivate your students. After just one study, you will all be able to witness the value notebooks hold. If we reduce "school" to filling in the answer boxes and avoid putting the effort into quality education, we are missing the point - which is delightful learning. In order to get your children excited about learning, you must not skip over the "stuff in the middle." Let them learn about areas they are interested in and they will get even more excited. At the end, you will see how proud they are to "show off" their work. Each person, whether they are creative, talented or not, has the potential to create a unique and personal notebook. Give them your help and ideas by spending a little time with them to get their project started. The "pay off" will be amazing!

When we're in the daily grind sometimes it is hard to appreciate how blessed we are to have the opportunities with our children that home education affords - especially when we are having a "rough" day. We should truly count it a privilege to have this time with our children. If it wasn't for home education, our family would have missed out on so much. Only now am I painfully aware of how quickly children grow up. Knowing this should help us all to make the most of this time. Notebooks become the educational keepsakes which will serve to remind us of the worthwhile investment of time.

It is quite difficult for me to limit this section on notebooks. I am only able to give you a glimpse of what they are, how they work, and the many positive educational benefits they provide. In order to fully understand notebooks, check out our Notebook Package described below. In fact, this book (you are holding in your hand) and the Notebook Package are the two main resources and helps we try to put in people's hands first to get them going on understanding unit studies and notebooks!

Notebook Resource:

Everything You Need to Build a Unit Study Notebook is an instructional manual chock full of packet also includes 50+ masters to copy and use in notebooks. (It is available in our STEWARD SHIP Unit for assignments to use for any unit and any age, plus tons of information about working with notebooks. The generic ideas Study Supplies catalog 1-888-4R-UNITS.)

THE DAILY SCHEDULE

Now that you understand the two key elements of a unit study I would like to share our daily schedule with you. I did this briefly in the last chapter but it was for the sake of showing how many subjects you can accomplish in one day. Now you may not be able to fully adopt our suggested schedule, but adhering to this schedule has helped me SO MUCH to stay on track and to know what my day will be like.

7:00 a.m. ~ Rise and shine! Dress, breakfast, morning chores.

8:30 a.m. ~ Short Bible time at the breakfast table. I read from the Bible, a daily devotional which gives a "thought or character trait for the day." This gives me something to recall throughout the day when a child needs correction. I also read from old books like "Moral Lessons from Yesteryear." (Mantle Ministries). I don't like to do some BIG Bible program pasting on Bible figures because we do hands-on activities in the unit study so we want to keep Bible time more simple. I also try to do something that is good for all the ages in my home.

9:15 a.m. ~ Read aloud time. We usually do school in the living room so we assemble there and I read one or two chapters from our read aloud title. A few times each week I give the children vocabulary words drawn from this book. My children usually color or draw while I am reading. They do tire of this, so more and more I am trying to "prepare" something educational that is connected with what we are learning that day, which they can do while I read. This takes a bit of planning but is not hard. I will share a couple ideas at the end of this schedule.

10:00 - 10:15 a.m. ~ The next hour is Information Time when I present information about our topic from nonfiction books touching on a different aspects of the topic. Non-fiction books are "source books" which contain the information for teaching. Almost every day I have either planned a simple connecting activity or one comes up while I am reading. These connecting activities fall into some subject area and are not just busy-work, but involve valuable learning and make use of skills.

These activities usually take us up to...

12:00 p.m. ~ Lunch - After lunch, the children work mostly on their own. They still have one hour of independent reading, math, some days they need to look up vocabulary words or write definitions for terminology. They also have assignments listed on an assignment sheet which they can work at independently.

Along with the subjects we cover through our unit study, my children also have what I call their "basics" and these consist of: Phonics (for my younger readers who are still developing skills), Reading (I require one hour a day), and Math. My children also have a spelling book and a grammar book we work from, spending about one hour a week on each. If I am not ready to get started with my chidlren, in the morning, if I see them "wandering" about I ask them if they've done their basics yet.

SEE WHAT WORKS FOR YOU

I have had the opportunity to listen to a well known speaker who publishes unit study materials. This lady is very experienced and I have a great respect for her... however, I found out that we disagree completely on our approach to scheduling unit studies into our day.

Her advice is to accomplish what she calls the Three R's during the morning hours as these are the subjects necessary for one to be equipped for taking SAT tests. Then she does the unit study part in the afternoon.

I think the main difference for me is that I don't really schedule unit studies into my day... they ARE my day. We are using the unit study method almost completely as our core of teaching - EVERYTHING with little left out. So in everything I do, I am doing it with the goal of trying to incorporate as many subjects and skills as I can. So, with my schedule, I am almost done by noon and I am FREE - FREE - FREE! Besides... I am ready for a nap in the afternoon - I can't imagine having the energy to get started on the "doing" stuff after lunch!

I do realize that many feel certain subjects like Math must be done in the morning while students are fresh and awake... before they start to wilt. If this is the case you might try a different approach. Many times kids drag their feet because they don't like math. They spend an hour staring at the wall, drop their pencil, hit their sister (well, MY kids don't do that but yours might!). You could tell your kids if they get up and get busy and don't fool around, you could get started on the unit study! This might give them some incentive to get math done!

Whatever your circumstances, you will have to figure out what kind of schedule works for you. I know that having a schedule has revolutionized unit studies for me. I have my basket of books right by my chair so I am able to grab different books and read bits and pieces from them. I have found if I give my kids this three hours each day, we get so much done! At the end of one month our notebooks are full of schoolwork covering many different academic skills in many different subject areas and it is so rewarding (and it is painless and I find myself content and guilt free).

SOMETHING TANGIBLE

How do our notebooks get so full of "schoolwork?" I try, whenever possible, to have my kids "do" some sort of connecting activity. These assignments and papers are always the result of what we just learned and reflect some subject area. We could read about lots of things but unless we "make" or "do" something which is tangible and something we have to show for what we learned, it does not really imprint or stick as well. When we were studying Medieval Times, we read about architecture, building cathedrals and stained glass windows. For a connecting activity, we did a stained glass window activity by tearing paper and placing it inside an arch we drew. On the same paper, the older ones wrote a paragraph about cathedral building while my kindergartner wrote the word "cathedral" on a strip of broken line paper.

THE BIG SECRET

Okay, it's time to let you in on "The Big Secret." Now, this is just between you and me. Whatever you do, don't ever tell your children this secret! My goal with this unit study and with this topic is not only to delight my children with the exploration of the topic and to become familiar with the subject BUT it is to slip in or accomplish as many academic subjects as I can. So, I always have an ulterior motive and they don't know it - so let's keep it that way, okay?

In this way, YOU get your kids to accomplish what you know they need academically and they get to learn and love it and they don't even know the work they are doing are "subjects!" It's so cool and everybody wins.

Let's not forget the BIG picture though. I want to constantly reiterate the goal for education and that is so we turn out truly educated, well rounded, kids who love the Lord and are ready to be used for whatever purpose He has called them to. It might be a homemaker raising warriors, a rocket scientist, math teacher/tutor, a landscape designer, a hairdresser, a computer technician, or a thousand other things! If we train our kids to follow a biblical model and mandate and educate them responsibility - how can we lose and what do we have to fear?

Okay, I'll step back down from my soap box and do what I promised and that is to show you what kinds of things I might prepare for my kids to do during read aloud time.

SOMETHING TO DO DURING READ ALOUD TIME

One day during our study on Astronomy, I finished Information Time but before I closed the book I noticed that the next page had information about "The Five Stages of the Moon." I prepared a sheet with five circles with lines next to them to write on. The next morning before I started reading aloud, I read a short bit of information about the stages of the moon and then the children copied the pictures from the books using their own artwork. I had written the information about each moon on the wipe clean board so the children could copy it down on the lines. If you had a worksheet related to your topic, you could use that, but if not, you can easily create your own.

INCORPORATING SUBJECTS INTO STUDIES

Now that you understand the two key elements of a unit study, let's talk about which subjects to incorporate. Most but not all subjects can work into unit studies.

SUBJECTS THAT FIT WELL

- History
- Science
- Geography
- Art
- Music
- Reading and Literature
- Language Arts (Spelling/Vocabulary, Writing, Grammar, Reading, Handwriting)

SUBJECTS THAT DO NOT FIT INTO UNIT STUDIES

- Math
- Bible
- Phonics (for those learning to read)

NOTE: An important fact to note is that much of the stress associated with planning unit studies is due to the difficulty required with trying to incorporate subjects and don't fit. We recommend that you let subjects like Math, Bible and Phonics stand alone and carry them out separately.

Consider these guidelines when planning which subjects to work into your studies:

Keep it simple

Unit studies should make teaching easier for you - not more difficult. Take the daily academic exercises you need to practice and fit them into some area of your unit study. We can put grammar skills into application when we edit our writing assignments. We practice writing by writing or reporting on some area connected with our topic. We have opportunities to learn geography in most units by using or making maps. We study spelling words by topic and they are reinforced by the frequent use of words through reading and writing, and I also issue vocabulary words from reading aloud. These are just some of the ways you can easily teach and fit necessary skills and subjects into a unit study.

Keep your focus on your goal in education and don't force subjects to fit into your study for the sake of covering every subject

If you were doing a history unit such as "The Life of Columbus," geography, reading, writing, spelling, reading aloud, art and possibly science could be included. A unit study on weather is an obvious science unit.

Concentrate on the key parts of the study - the parts which will reap the most educational benefits

Some of the unit study guides I have used strive to provide activities for every subject. Such an approach is referred to as "whole learning." If your children are "scratching their heads" wondering, "What does this have to do with what we're studying?" you might consider skipping it.

Remember — It is not necessary to cover every subject every day

Make an effort to balance each subject area throughout your studies but don't worry if you do not cover each subject every day - most likely you won't. The nature of this method allows you to explore more thoroughly so much is accomplished. While it is important to be consistent, keep in mind that you are trying to accomplish what is valuable and that you are not doing things "just because."

If you begin to use unit studies exclusively, be sure to devise an annual unit study plan which includes choosing a balanced number of history, science and literature-based units to provide studies in each subject area. Use the Big Picture Plan sheet in the Appendix which has a chart to help you see at a glance what kinds of topics you've chosen.

ABOUT EACH SUBJECT

READING AND LITERATURE

Reading is a major part in all unit studies because it is so important for learning therefore we need to help our kids to learn to read well. I am convinced that a child can obtain their whole "education" just by reading! Students can read novels and biographies that fit with your unit topic and also peruse the pages of "educational" source books which contain great pictures and diagrams with corresponding text and help bring the information to life.

Learning to read well is important as it is the basis for every other educational function. A good foundation must be laid in order for children to gain the confidence needed for success. I feel very strongly about reading because I personally did not get a good foundation in reading which proved to be detrimental to me throughout my education.

TESTIMONIAL

When I was in the second grade we used the SRA reading program to test for comprehension in which we were timed as we read a story segment. Because our desks were arranged in groups, I was intimidated by the fact that others might finish before me. To avoid looking dumb, I skimmed the story then recorded a "good" time.

The two obvious problems were:

- I was lying (that's what peer and academic pressure can lead to).
- I never comprehended what I had read.
- I never learned to enjoy reading.

My little scheme continued for the whole school year without attracting the teacher's attention. Since I couldn't read and comprehend well, I believe this experience was the beginning of my inability to obtain a quality education. I never did become a good reader in school. In fact, believe it or not, I never read ONE book until I was an adult. I didn't enjoy reading and was left out of the literary circles. My sister, an avid reader, was always talking about the exciting things she had read which I knew nothing about and could not be part of. Although I could read well enough to get by, and throughout the years I was a good student, did my work and even got straight A's, I didn't get much of an education and I didn't enjoy learning. Imagine how excited I am now to finally be getting an education and learning things I never even heard about in school.

I've often wondered how my husband Jim knows so much about things that were not taught in school and asked him, "Why didn't I ever learn about the Roman Empire or Joan of Arc and other important "things?" Did I miss out on that much in school?" The answer is that Jim is well read. Even now he will pick up a book, any book, and get involved in it right away. I have to remind him that the children are climbing the curtains and they need some fatherly attention—right NOW!

Each of my children are unique, with different interests. Some like mysteries or adventure stories while others love history and biographies. We encourage our children to read different types of books which helps them to discover their own interests. It was a surprise to me when our twelve-year-old daughter expressed an interest in reading poetry. We may not have discovered this had she not been exposed to it. She is now our third homeschool graduate and still has a love for poetry and is a collector of great quotations!

It is so important to listen to your children and consider the areas in which they either excel or struggle. One day one of my daughters told me that she was more comfortable reading books with larger type. I hadn't even considered the size of the type when I pulled out some books for her to read. She has since moved on to longer books with smaller print. I'm glad she pointed that out to me - if I had insisted that she read my selections - it may have caused further struggles for her. Be prepared to offer the challenge when they can handle it but allow them to be comfortable at their level as long as they are enjoying reading.

Because books relating to our units keep us reading full time, we don't ordinarily use textbook or basal type readers. Even when we take a break from a unit, the children prefer to read Living Books instead of readers. We do keep some readers on hand, though, and use them on occasion. One benefit I have found with literature textbooks (for upper grades) is they offer a variety of short pieces of literature including poems and plays. Our oldest daughter uses a literature text from time to time to sample excerpts from different authors. Often she is inspired to look up and read one of their complete works. You might find it beneficial to use a reading program for a time until your child becomes fluent. Gayle Graham, author of How to Home School says:

A reading instruction program should be used to get him to the point of fluency so that he can get on with learning... give him the luxury of time to read, read, read, to build fluency.

(Gayle Graham, *How to Home School* [Hawthorne: Common Sense Press, 1992], 73, 75)

If you have a late-blooming child who struggles with reading, try not to worry too much. Our son never really bloomed in this area until he was about 12 years old. Before that we had some knock-down, drag-out, tearful sessions in my effort to make him read. I decided to act upon the counsel of other mothers who convinced me that everything would be okay if given some time. We just kept encouraging him, having him read at his level. It was difficult to listen whenever it was his turn to read scripture during our Bible time or when he was called on to read publicly. We had to be very patient with him. But one day it just "clicked." This is our son Tyson, and I will tell you "Tyson's Story" later! Stay tuned!

Put your effort into working on basic skills, giving your child plenty of enjoyable reading at his level. Forcing the issue may only serve to kill the joy that is beginning to build—even though it is building slow-w-wl-l-ly! I guarantee that if you keep reading aloud to them and keep working on phonics they WILL get it in time. Jim Trelease, in his book The *Read-Aloud Handbook* says,

We parents have a product to sell and that product is reading.

How do most salesmen get you to buy?

It's communicated by their enthusiasm over the product.

You can communicate your love of books and learning

to your children by the passion you feel for it.

They can see it in your eyes, in your tone of voice.

(Jim Trelease, *The Read-Aloud Handbook*, [New York: Penguin Books, 1983]

Mr. Trelease asserts that "readers aren't born, they're made." How can you tell if your children are enjoying themselves? If they follow you around the house telling you about a book they've read… that's how.

Kally, who is now fourteen and fifth in the line-up of our children, really struggled with learning phonics sounds and reading. She is the first to display any learning problems and though it has been challenging at times, it has reaffirmed what I know and believe about learning. I had to keep reminding myself that "she is where she is." She is improving more and more and reading very well now (in the eighth grade). I followed The Moores - better late than early - approach but by the time she was in the fifth grade I started to worry. I asked a retired teacher/friend if she could give her an assessment test, and what she found was that Kally just need lots of reinforcing exercises in phonics. Once I knew what kind of help she needed, she was able to advance more quickly.

My experiences with Kally have also helped me to help people who are in the same boat. The beautiful thing is that though she couldn't read and therefore couldn't be self directed and do lessons or assignments on her own because she couldn't read and understand well enough to do that, she WAS able to learn and was very bright because I taught interactively through unit studies.

Reading Resources:

For the Love of Reading by Valerie Bendt

LANGUAGE ARTS

Grammar is the study of how words combine to form sentences and serves as a guide to help people communicate effectively. A question people frequently ask me is, "What about grammar?" I don't do much beyond teaching the basics to my elementary grade children. Once my kids are in high school and writing more, then they are able to understand and put grammar to use. Until then we spend about one hour a week using a grammar program in a light manner.

Grammar is an important part of our daily life. Through unit studies we want to master the following skills:

- The mechanics of writing and composition
- The proper use of capitalization, punctuation, contractions, synonyms, homonyms, antonyms
- Learning how to use the dictionary and thesaurus
- Learning how to alphabetize words
- Learning the parts of speech
- Journaling, essays, reports, outlines, rough drafts, editing

Introduce the basics as the children learn to read. Many of the necessary grammar skills are learned by frequent and fluent reading, and also through writing practice. Build on the skills listed above as time goes on. With unit studies we work together in close contact as opposed to isolating children to work by themselves with a grammar workbook. In this way, I am able to explain the mechanics immediately and the children gain an understanding in context. I call this "Living Grammar!"

There are a few grammar helps we've enjoyed and believe have helped our children. One of these books entitled, *The Great Editing Adventure* is a nonconsumable text divided into three sections, each containing fun stories for students ages 10-13. You can write a paragraph on the board from one of the stories. This paragraph contains a few errors which you can number so they can spot the problems. Other words are underlined indicating the need to find a synonym and vocabulary words are circled. As they search for the errors, the children feel like Sherlock Holmes. Our children enjoy this grammar exercise, they don't even grumble. Their skills have improved noticeably using this text.

Simply Grammar follows along closely with the Charlotte Mason approach and is also referred to as "Living Grammar." This book is recommended for 4th-8th grades but is also good to use for high schoolers. Each lesson teaches a grammar rule clearly and simply.

Other invaluable resources for language arts are:

- *Writer's Express*, for elementary grades
- *The Write Source 2000*, for middle grades
- *Writer's Inc.*, for high school (all from *Great Source Publications*)

These handbooks are a wonderful resource full of helpful and needed information. Not only do they contain information about such things as the paragraph, poetry, punctuation, spelling, capitalization and more, but other sections cover speaking, thinking, writing, book review, and literary terms. They also contain a measurement table, periodic tables and other reference tools.

This company offers skillsbooks, sourcebooks and handbooks. You don't necessarily need them all but if you can view them at a curriculum fair, you can decide what you want according to the ages of your children. I find these books user friendly and especially like the "workbooks" from this publisher.

Though we DO need to teach the mechanics of writing and grammar rules, I think I've seen the real value in learning grammar mostly through our writing because this gives us a place to apply what we learn.

You can point out many things as you read aloud and teach. One time during our Pirate study, I noticed while reading to the children that we kept coming across other words that mean "Pirate" (like Swashbuckler, Privateer and so on). These are called synonyms. As we found more synonyms, we divided notebook paper into three sections, labeled it Synonyms and each time we found a new one through our reading, we added it to our list. Another time while reading *The Golden Goblet* by Eloise Jarvis McGaw (for an Ancient Egypt study), a character named Hequet used idioms like "I thought I heard a voice, the cow remarked as he stood on the leopard's tail." We really enjoyed these and wrote them down each time we came across another one. This way children receive real-life examples of grammar rules and word usage within the context of a story.

In the following passage, Ralph Moody, author of *Mary Emma and Company*, explains how he got into trouble at school while daydreaming about a carpentry project he was working on for his mother. During our read aloud time I took this opportunity to show the children how the author painted a vivid picture with words—in this case using similies.

"That day I was thinking about wanting to get out in a hurry, and about what I was going to say to the lumberman, and I sort of forgot about marking time until I heard Mr. Jackman call out, "Feet high, children! One, two, three, four; one, two, three, four," as he came down our line toward me. He was almost to me before I noticed that I wasn't lifting my feet, and I didn't want to give him any excuse for scolding me, so I started lifting them in a hurry, but I started a little bit too hard. My knee bumped the girl in front of me when Mr. Jackman was right beside her.

She squealed and jumped about a foot high, and Mr. Jackman <u>pounced on me like a coyote on a prairie dog</u>. He jerked me out of line and <u>shook me till my teeth rattled like stones in a tin can</u>. Then he told me that he wouldn't tolerate any smart aleck boy getting fresh with the girls in Franklin School, and that if he ever caught me at it again he'd expel me altogether. He wouldn't believe me when I told him that I didn't do it on purpose, and made me stand marking time until the very last line had marched out of the schoolhouse."

(Ralph Moody, *Mary Emma and Company*
[Lincoln & London: University of Nebraska Press, 1961], 163)

In our home I have taught basic grammar including: parts of speech, punctuation and capitalization, contractions, synonyms, antonyms, homonyms, spelling rules and so on. Our children have learned that each paragraph needs a topic sentence to follow, and how to organize and outline their thoughts, but I have not taught daily grammar skills so much as a subject. I used to, but my children didn't understand and weren't able to apply what they were learning. Unit studies gives us a reason for writing and provides a forum for editing writing. They are experiencing "living grammar" and what they learn sticks better than practicing rote skills in a workbook. As children begin to write more (this is not usually until around age nine or ten), they have a reason to know such things as mentioned above. I can explain to my child that baseball is a compound word - putting two "base" words together to form another word. Now they need to know what a contraction is because they are using them in their writing!

Teaching children to write well and communicate thoughts is one main purpose for teaching grammar. Our goal for teaching grammar is to equip our children with what they need in order to write well. My daughter came to me during her last year in high school and asked, "Why didn't you teach me grammar?" I pointed out the fact to her that she is both an avid reader and a wonderful writer. I could see at that point that she had the need and desire to fine tune her grammar skills. I was quite encouraged by her motivation to learn something she thought needful and useful. They learn so much faster when they have a reason to use the skills they are learning. Why go through years of struggling and fighting when some areas can be mastered in a short time when the student is ready?

WRITING

In order for students to become comfortable and adept at writing, they have to write so it should be practiced and exercised often! The problem is children seem to have a universal reluctance to write. I don't know about your children, but when my children would try writing, it would take so long to write one paper, they dreaded the next time. We must relay to our children the message that learning to write is important because communication skills are of vital importance if we are to be useful in society and in our families. It is a good idea to show students the extent to which our founding fathers wrote - writing was sort of like breathing - necessary and important and is also the reason we know so much about history - people kept journals and wrote everyday. As I remember, George Washington wrote something like ten letters a day.

Well, I figured out why my children were reluctant to write. I noticed that it wasn't because they didn't want to or know what to write about, it was for fear of doing something wrong. They weren't sure about the spelling or punctuation, so they were hesitant to get started. What we have done for the sake of encouraging their creative juices to flow is to allow them to spell incorrectly on their rough drafts.

- Incorrect spelling = inventive spelling   • Correct spelling = conventional spelling

Educators have differing views and some adamantly disagree with this practice because they believe once you allow the child to spell incorrectly it will become ingrained. This has not become a problem because we always go over the rough draft to review and correct the spelling and grammatical mistakes.

My children write a lot more now because many aspects of the study can involve writing. You shouldn't have to go outside your unit to look for other writing assignments because unit studies provide endless opportunities for incorporating writing and, in fact, give students a reason to write. Sometimes we think of writing assignments as essays or creative writing pieces, but there are many ways you can incorporate writing.

Writing assignments for the topic MUSICAL INSTRUMENTS:

- Watch the video "Orchestra" (found at the library) and take notes while watching.
- Classify instruments into groups.
- Listen to a musical selection and describe the different instruments you can identify and what sounds they make (i.e. kettledrums = thunder, piccolo = bird singing).
- Read several articles written from a Christian perspective on discernment and evaluation of music. Form your own opinion, based on scripture, and write a paper explaining your views.
- Write a story somehow connected to music, the orchestra, or an instrument.
- Write a book report on your read aloud or silent reading title.
- Write a biographical sketch about a composer.

Ideas for writing assignments for the topic WESTWARD MOVEMENT:

- Write a list of provisions one would take in a wagon.

- Keep a diary or journal of a child's trip West.

- Describe how to build a log cabin.

- Write a paper, as if you were a Native American, and tell how you felt about the changes brought to you because of the Westward expansion and progress.

- Describe the many aspects of pioneer life: chores, preserving food, planting, hunting, defending themselves, hospitality and entertainment.

Lists:

- List the reasons one would want to leave their home and move West.

- List the many ways Native Americans used the different parts of the buffalo in their daily lives.

- List all the states west of the Mississippi River.

We have run across the problem where our kids don't really want their rough draft, complete with red correction marks, to be seen in their notebooks. The notebook is not just a showpiece but should be representative of all of our children's work - even the "not so great stuff." To solve this dilemma, we place the corrected piece in a sheet protector with the rough draft hidden behind it. This satisfies both mom and the student.

A POSITIVE ATTITUDE HELPS

I was blessed by a recent experience my children had in a writing class. The teacher, a retired missionary "grandma" in our area, truly taught the children to love writing. I asked myself, "What's different between her class and mine?" I noticed that she was very positive and encouraging with the group and there was never a wrong answer. She gave assignments, instructions and suggestions, but she also helped the students realize that writing is part of life and an important way to express one's self. She presented writing not as a drudgery but as a joy.

Use your read aloud time to point out:

- An author's style and choice of words

- How an author can paint a picture with words

- Each paragraph adheres to one idea

- The power of written language

Notice how the author of *He Went With Marco Polo* uses words to paint a vivid picture in this excerpt:

Just then his eyes fell on a man who was standing a little outside the noisy group, a <u>short, round-faced man with a mustache the color of straw drooping over a thin, straw colored beard</u>. He was looking at the laughing men out of a pair of <u>gentle, pale blue eyes</u>. No one was paying attention to him. He was <u>shabbily dressed in faded blue cloth, stained with sea-water and patched with squares of various colors here and there</u>. He had a <u>queer straw hat on his lanky, straw-colored hair</u>. On his <u>feet were scarlet leather boots, much too big for him, and pulled over blue hose</u> as ragged as Tonio's. <u>The boots were splendidly stamped with the gold patterns of vines and flowers</u>. They were so gay that they made the rest of the man's costume look all the dingier. <u>Beside him was a big bag made of a cow's hide with the hair still on</u>.

(Louise Andrews Lemt, *He Went With Marco Polo*,
[Cambridge: The Riverside Press, 1935], 10)

As I read over this part to my children, I had my children draw a picture of what they thought this man looked like according to the author's description. Since this character became a key person in our story, the children titled the picture and placed it in their notebook.

The following "general" list shows how writing can involve many fun and interesting activities:

- Report on an event by writing a newspaper article.
- Write from observations in nature.
- Compile data and research incorporating charts and diagrams.
- Read a book and write a report.
- Write instructions or directions for conducting experiments.
- Describe pieces of art.
- Obtain documentation.
- Write a composition or report.
- Compose an essay.
- Send thank-you notes and letters (to friends, missionaries or politicians).
- Create cartoons with dialogue.

Another way to encourage writing is to have the child keep a personal, or bible study journal. Journals are usually private giving children the freedom to write knowing nobody will see their mistakes.

If a child is continuously exposed to well written material, whether by reading, copying, dictating or listening, he will be influenced in a positive way, much more so than by filling in worksheet after worksheet.

Valerie Bendt, *How to Create Your Own Unit Study*
[Hawthorne: Common Sense Press, 1990], 36)

Budding young writers should be familiar with how to use tools such as a thesaurus, typewriter, and computer. Desktop publishing programs designed for children can be purchased inexpensively. Computers are especially efficient because they provide a means to cut and erase mistakes easily. All four of our older children use the computer for their schoolwork and they have painlessly learned computer skills.

DICTATION AND COPYING

Dictation is a great tool to help improve a child's listening and writing skills. Sharpen your child's abilities by using dictation two to three times a week by reading a paragraph from a novel to them and ask them to write down what they hear. This might be difficult for your children at first, but you can watch to see how they do. If students are not old enough to take dictation, they can start by copying the paragraph. You can either let them copy directly from the book, or you can write it on their paper or the chalkboard. Though dictation might seem boring initially, it is helpful in building writing skills. You will see noticeable improvements within a relatively short period of time.

As I am reading aloud, I look for paragraphs of substance to use for dictation, those which have some sort of lesson or something warm and moving. I will make a mental note when I've read a paragraph I'd like to use for dictation, and use it when I am finished reading. Then I dictate a selection slowly, pointing out punctuation, capitalization and quotation marks which appear in the paragraph. After hearing the selection the second time, the children write it out. When done, they place this in their notebooks under the Writing section. I have them write the book and page number where the selection was taken from along with the date. After my children grow accustomed to taking dictation, I no longer give them the grammar tips pointing out punctuation, etc. Students should try to use good penmanship as this exercise can also serve as hand-writing practice.

SPELLING

Subjects such as spelling and handwriting which require repetition for mastery must be practiced more frequently. Unit studies naturally provide a list of spelling words and if your currciulum or guide doesn't provide some for you, you can come up with your own list by looking through the glossary of nonfiction books. For each unit prepare a list of words that suit each of your children's abilities which they will in turn study for a weekly oral or written test. I can have my child sit at the  kitchen counter and bring me their spelling list from their notebook. I can cut up veggies for dinner and dictate words they've studied, as a spelling test. Word lists and tests go into their notebooks under the

Spelling/Vocabulary section. Although I find most spelling words pertinent to our study, lists may include words from stories used during your read aloud time. You may also wish to develop a list of frequently used but non-related words from a spelling resource since children spell with other than topical words. My recommendation is that you use a spelling program in a "light manner" which means work on it an hour a week instead of an hour a day!

It makes much more sense to study words that go along with a unit study topic than to merely pick a list of unrelated words from a workbook. By using topic related words, students will become familiar with them from the repeated exposure through reading, writing, and other assignments.

Here are some ideas to add variety to spelling lists:

- Alphabetize the words on the list (key: blue indicates words to alphabetize, green marks a verb, etc.).

- Have students dictate words to siblings.

- Hold a spelling bee.

VOCABULARY

Unit studies are also an extremely practical way to increase a child's word bank. As with spelling, learning the meaning of words from the context of a story makes more sense than having a separate vocabulary workbook containing hundreds of unrelated words.

To expand your child's vocabulary with unit studies select words your child doesn't know from your read-aloud time or other topic-related books and choose some spelling words which can also be used as vocabulary words.

Here's why:

- It gives students practice in using the dictionary.

- It saves time.

- Learning words in context makes sense.

- Information is retained for a longer period of time.

When I am reading aloud, I give my children vocabulary words when I come upon words I think my children don't know. The children keep their notebooks handy and add new words to their vocabulary list. When we finish reading they search the dictionary for the definition that applies to the context of our story. You can choose several new words for your children to learn each week from your read aloud book. They can really increase their word bank this way. This helps spelling as well as learning the meaning of some new words. Words you choose from reading aloud will probably not be "thematic" words so I also include vocabulary words on the spelling list, marking words I wish to double as spelling AND vocabulary with a "V."

An example of a vocabulary word taken from reading aloud would be something like this sentence: *The king leaned forward and on bended knee, his crimson robe flowed over his back.* I would ask the children, "Does anyone know what crimson means?" One might offer an answer but if it is not correct, I spell it out so they can add it to their vocabulary sheet. "C-R-I-M-S-O-N." Because they will remember the color of the king's robe, they will be able to remember that crimson means deep red.

One good way to build dictionary skills is to conduct dictionary races. To do this each child gets a dictionary and opens it to the first letter of the word which you dictate and spell for them (so there is no unfair advantage). Recite the word and say "GO." Students race to see who can find the word first. Since the dictionary, thesaurus, and other reference books will be needed for the future, it is important that your children become familiar with these tools and not be afraid to use them. We've enjoyed using a computer program for our upper level students, called *Wordsmart*.

SOCIAL STUDIES

HISTORY

Whoever said history is boring? It is my favorie subject! I have heard people say that history is only appealing to college professors and historians. I enjoy history studies so much I have to be careful to include other types of unit studies! Remember me? I am the "A" student who didn't get an education. I remember some high school history classes where I fell asleep because we had to read texbooks full of dry lists of dates and facts.

LIVING HISTORY OR TEXTBOOK HISTORY?

Let's look at the difference between learning about the Revolutionary War by reading a Living Book as compared to a textbook on the same subject by comparing the two excerpts below. Would your students enjoy and learn most from using a high school United States history textbook or by reading a wonderful living history novel like *Carry on, Mr. Bowditch* by Jean Latham?

U. S. History textbook

> **On March 5, 1770 (a date to remember), a large crowd gathered in Boston around a detachment of the 29th British Regiment (a fact to remember). The crowd yelled insults and threw snowballs. Such outbursts had occurred many times before. But by this time matters got out of hand. As the mob pressed closer against the soldiers, someone gave an order to fire. Three civilians were killed and two others were mortally wounded. The city went wild with anger. A "massacre," the people called the affair, and demanded that the British withdraw all troops from the city.**

> **Later, when passions had cooled somewhat, the soldiers were tried for murder. They were defended by Josiah Quincy, Jr., and John Adams, who later became the second President of the United States (names to remember). Neither of these men had any sympathy for the British, but they insisted that every individual was entitled to a fair trial. All except two of the soldiers were acquitted. These two were convicted of manslaughter, but were soon released.**

> **The gap between Great Britain and the American colonies was wide indeed when Lord Frederick North (a name to remember) became prime minister of Great Britain in 1770 (a fact and date to remember). The new prime minister urged Parliament to repeal the Townsend Acts (an Act to remember). As he pointed out, the nonimportation agreements were once again ruining the business of many British merchants, and the cost of enforcing the law was proving to be much too heavy.**

> (*Rise of the American Nation*, [NY: Harcourt, Brace & World, Inc., 1966], 103)

History textbooks can be very boring, but history itself can be exciting to study if you explore it with living books.

Carry On, Mr. Bowditch

Nat pointed to the ship where men were mounting guns. "Are you sailing on that privateer?"

"Not that one, Mate. I'm sailing on the Pilgrim, out of Beverly."
He motioned with his thumb. "Beverly's just across the water from here."

"Is the Pilgrim a good privateer?"

"Best privateer that ever raked a Britisher with a broadside!
You want to buy expectations from me?"

Nat's heart pounded so hard he could not talk, but he nodded.

The big man took off his flat black hat and fished a paper from the crown.
"Just got one left. For ten percent of my expectations. What'll you give me for it?"

"All my money!" Nat laid the shilling in the big man's hand.

The big man stared at the shilling. "Well, I'll be a copper-bottomed, bevel-edged...
Most money you ever had, eh?"

"Yes, sir!"

"And you come from a long line of sea captains? Who are you?"

"Nat Bowditch."

"Captain Bowditch's boy, eh? I remember when the Polly went aground.
Same day the war started. April 19, 1775."

"Granny said 'took the tuck' out of Father." Nat told the big man about his good-luck
spell that he was going to work, only the nor'easter came, and hid the moon.

The big man rubbed his bristling chin. He looked at the shilling. "It's a bargain, Mate.
But keep it a secret! Don't even tell any man that Tom Perry sold a tenth of his expectations
for a shilling! They'll stow me in the brig. What's worse, they'd put me on the binnacle list!"

(Jean Latham, *Carry On, Mr. Bowditch* [NY:Scholastic, 1992], 12, 13)

History unit studies also provide opportunities to delve into areas like geograpy. As you travel around the world through history, you learn about different people in different time periods as well as exploring customs, traditions, food, clothing, government, architecture, technology and advancement and religious beliefs of the people from those periods. You will also discover how the hand of Providence directed events throughout time. Investigate key personalities of the era like artists and how their work influenced their contemporaries. History provides many opportunities for fun activities to bring the studies alive. I vote history studies the most fun units of all!

GEOGRAPHY

And now for the next dry, boring subject! Unit studies make teaching geography easy and interesting, too. Geography is not an intimidating subject for our children because they have grown up using maps and globes. I can't think of a unit we've done where we didn't have the globe or the maps out. Our study on ants took us to the jungles of the world where we discovered how the ant population moves tons of soil in jungles every year. We used our world atlas to find the jungles. When we studied weather, we learned about the areas most prone to tornadoes and hurricanes. When we studied the pilgrims, we learned a lot about England, Holland and the New World. Then studying ancient Egypt, I read *The Golden Goblet* - a story rich in geographical references to the City of the Dead, the River Nile, Cairo and the Great Pyramid.

In our studies we are constantly using maps and atlases to learn about the regions, climate, mountains, rivers, and so on. As we track who did what and where, geography just occurs. Take advantage of every opportunity to include geography into your studies.

We studied world geography as a unit study one year, but our goal was to learn more than names and places. We took the whole school year and worked on it one day a week learning about the animals, food, religion, dress, homes, money, trade, missionaries etc. on each continent. At the same time we continued to do other units. We did some "around the world" cooking, and read novels set in different countries - it was a colorful and fun study.

SCIENCE

You may wonder what the premise is behind teaching science? I admit science is not my favorite subject. I can handle the basic principles of science but when you get into all those atoms and protons, and the speed of light, sound waves and all that technical stuff, I'm history (pun intended!). Boys seem to be naturally interested in science as they love space, bugs, inventions, and reptiles - many girls love science, too!

Why teach science? So the child can enjoy and understand his relationship with the world and universe he lives in. So that he can say "I feel at home here, I belong, I understand, I appreciate, I know."

(Susan Schaffer Macaulay, *For the Children's Sake*, [Wheaton: Crossway Books, 1984], 133)

Even though I have an aversion to science, I have begun to really enjoy it because I've discovered that unit studies help make it understandable. We studied the Human Body and were in awe at the amazing body machine. The more we learned, the more we wondered how anyone could NOT believe in God. Looking at nature - insects, birds, plant life, the life cycle and the way everything works together in such harmony, we marveled at the loving God who designed it all! He made the beautiful flowers for us to enjoy then to top it off, we get to enjoy the beautiful butterflies that drink nectar from the flowers! When we studied birds we were fascinated by the way God had given each species the instinct to build their nests, migrate, and feed their young. God gave each kind of bird a beak specially designed for the type of food it eats.

It is definitely more difficult to find read aloud books for science units. You can always read biographies about a scientist or naturalist but it's also nice to have a novel or classic to read during your unit.

A few examples of novels that fit science topics are:

- Books about Luther Burbank and John Muir

- *Girl of the Limberlost* by Jean Stratton Porter

- *The Far Frontier* by William O'Steele

- *A Cricket in Times Square* by George Selden

- *20,000 Leagues Under the Sea* and *Journey to the Center of the Earth* by Jules Verne

If you cannot find a suitable read aloud title for every topic, choose a book which you think might relate to your topic. For example, one mom shared how they chose *Little House in the Big Woods* by Laura Ingalls Wilder as their read aloud for a Human Body unit study—a book you wouldn't typically classify as a science title but they keyed in on these parts: Pa had to go down to a well with a candle and was robbed of oxygen. Another time Charley got into a yellow jacket nest and was stung repeatedly causing an allergic reaction. When we studied Weather we read *Around the World in Eighty Days* by Jules Verne because we figured they would encounter "weather" on their journey.

It is the glory of God to conceal a matter;
It is the glory of man to search it out.

Proverbs 25:2 (NIV)

I see a parallel between Sir Francis Bacon's Scientific Method and The Unit Study Method:

The Scientific Method	Unit Study Method
Ask a question or state the problem	What do you want to know?
Gather information	What should you use for study/research?
Make a hypothesis	Take what you learned & discuss
Experiment	DO something
Analyze data	Record your findings (charts, maps, essays)
State a conclusion	What did you learn (reports)?

Science units are especially fun because you get to do alot of experiments - there's the "doing" part kids enjoy! It's nice to add little extras like games, posters, music CDs or videos. We utilize tapes during many of studies like Lyrical Life Science songs which put important science information to song. The lyrics to the song titled "The Scientific Method" is sung to the tune of "Dixie."

"Oh, what do you think a scientist does to solve a problem found
because many scientists are scientists 'cause they're great… problem solvers.
There is a systematic way they go about 'most every day.'
It's methodical and it's logical. The scientific method."

Text and lyrics by Doug Eldon

Catchy songs for all subjects help children remember information. All these "extras" really add to any study. Where do I get these? Remember, when you are a unit study/learning enthusiast, all of a sudden you SEE things all over the place that would make your studies more interesting and fun. Most of all, learning about science helps us appreciate our Creator and the creation.

Fairest Lord Jesus

Fairest Lord Jesus, Ruler of all nature
Thou of God and man the Son
Thee will I cherish, Thee will I honor
Thou my soul's glory, joy, and crown.

Fair are the meadows, Fairer still the woodlands,
Robed in the blooming garb of spring,
Jesus is fairer, Jesus is purer,
Who makes the woeful heart to sing.

Fair is the sunshine, Fairer still the moonlight,
And all the twinkling starry host
Jesus shines brighter, Jesus shines purer
Than all the angels heaven can boast.

(*From Munster Gresagbuch* • 1677)

Glory to God Our Creator

"Blessed is the king who comes
in the name of the Lord!"

"Peace in heaven and glory in
the highest!"

Some of the Pharisees in the crowd
said to Jesus, "Teacher, rebuke
your disciples!"

"I tell you," he replied, "if they keep
quiet, the stones will cry out."

Luke 19:4-38-40

The Bible is a great science book, especially the Psalms.
Try reading Psalm 104 to appreciate the Creator!

ART

Children love art and because it offers opportunities for them to express their creativity, art should be a part of all your unit studies. As they are exposed to the different works and modes of art, children begin to appreciate it and notice God's artistic flare in the world around them. They enjoy using their hands and creating their own "works of art."

In the course of your activities and projects, teach your students about technique, color, shapes, and perspective.

Allow them to experiment with different modes of art including:

- Painting (watercolors, oils, finger, etc.)   • Sketching   • Sculpting   • Drawing

Children love art. They love to make things. They love to paint... especially the little ones! I never used to take time to include art because I always saw it as a seperate subject and we just didn't have time for it. Since we've used unit studies, we always do art - it fits in so well for most topics and the kids love it. When my first daughter was approaching high school, I realized that you're "supposed" to study art history but I didn't have a clue how to go about it. I found a simple book that laid out the different periods of art so I decided to tackle it. That unit study turned out to be one of our all time favorites and it is one of the topics I have taught a second time - it was even more fun and rich the second time around. The great thing about art history is that you get to experiment with many different tools and modes of art. Through the course, I began to see the value of appreciating and understanding art. You can start by showing young children pictures of great works of art and prints.

Point out these different aspects of the artwork:

- Light, shadows, color, effect
- Style—impressionist, sketching
- Religious or secular
- Names of artists
- Medium (oils, charcoal, pencil, etc.)

Make it a point to study Art History as soon as you think your children are ready because the information will become valuable throughout the elementary years because it is History! You will be amazed how often things you learned will come up in relation to other studies and in society in general. When we studied Ancient Greece, we learned all about the culture including scenes of daily life painted on vases. We had learned about this during our study of Art History. I never noticed a Greek vase before, but now I see them all the time in books. We visited Hearst Castle in California and Mr. Hearst had a collection of antique Greek vases in his library!

The famous painting called *School of Athens* by Raphael depicts a gathering of Greek philosophers at a university - through other studies on ancient history, we had learned about many of the people named in the painting. The best part is when you see your children get excited and light up when they make the "I know this" connection. "I learned this!"

Art awakens the senses. Soon you'll notice things you never noticed before and, as you drive along in the car, you can point out things in nature, for our Lord and Creator is the Master artist! You begin to see things in a new light, appreciating sculptures, statues, and the architecture of buildings. One tool which you can use to sharpen art skills and incorporate drawing into your units is using an instructional program called *Draw Write Now*. These guides are arranged and each include three themes per book. Sometimes I have my children draw a picture while I read aloud or present information. During our unit study on Farm Animals I propped the book open so all the children could see the picture and each day they would draw a different animal. They drew their pictures on white cardstock paper and decided they like them so well, they used them for section dividers in their notebooks! Our children enjoy using these guides because the instruction is presented in a step-by-step fashion which helps them gain confidence as they build art skills.

Art Resources

Draw Write Now by Mary Hablitzel and Kim Stitzer

Taking the Mystery Out of Studying Art History unit study guide (STEWARD SHIP)

Annotated Art: a beautiful, large format, full color book on art. Published by Dorling Kindersly

How Great Thou Art books by Barry Stebbing

MUSIC

Like art, children love music, and there are many ways to add a lively bit of toe tappin' fun to your studies. In this case, I'm not necessarily talking about adding music as a subject here as much as just in corporating excellent music literature wherever possible to enhance your studies. When making plans and looking for resources, include audio casettes and CDs as well as songbooks to go along with your topic. We got a cassette for our Nutrition study which had characters playing the parts of junk food and nutritious food. I dug out a cassette of songbirds singing which was fun to use during our Birds unit study. Likewise, I had a tape with train sounds that we used during a unit on Trains.

Here are some ideas of what you can listen to, learn about or sing:

- World Geography—*Wee Sing Around the World*, also *Round the World Songbook* (by Usborne)
- Birds—songbirds singing.
- Civil War—learn "I Wish I Were in Dixie" and other civil war songs.
- Revolutionary War—learn "Yankee Doodle" and other patriotic songs.
- Cowboys—learn "Home on the Range" and other cowboy songs.
- Tall Tales—learn folk songs like "John Henry."
- Ancient History—acquire music played on ancient instruments (lyre, etc.).
- Classical music—readings featuring specific composers or time periods.

If you are interested in studying music, you could conduct whole unit studies on topics like:

- The history and development of instruments.
- Biblical instruments
- Composers
- The history of music
- Music in different cultures, past and present.
- Famous singers and songwriters.
- Hymns and their origins.
- The types of music (folk songs, jazz, blues, classical, etc.).

Music Resources:

Basic Library of the World's Greatest Music by Lee Lambert

Music Education in the Christian Home by Dr. Mary Ann Froehlich

Treasury of Great Hymns and Their Stories by Guye Johnson

TEACHING PHONICS, MATH, AND BIBLE

These three subjects should be carried out separately and not be incorporated into your unit study. There are, however, various times and opportunities to apply math concepts to an area of study or to shed the light of thescripture to your topic. And almost everyday I am able to point out spelling and phonics rules with one of my younger children. A child might ask, "Mom, how do you spell sight?" I remind them, "Remember, you're using three letter 'i' for that word." Three letter "i" in our phonics program is the phonogram "igh" so they know what I am referring to. Incorporating subjects in this way is quite different than incorporating them as whole subjects.

For example:

Using a Math concept
During a literature study on "Tall Tales,"one exaggerated tale said the distance between Babe, the Blue Ox's horns was 42 axe handles long. Our children enjoyed calculating the distance by measuring our axe handle and multiplying by 42.

Using Scripture
During the same study, one of the "Tall Tales" was about Brer Rabbit and Brer Fox. The two of them spent much of their time gossiping, scheming, outsmarting and tricking each other. We used the scriptures to seek instruction regarding this kind of behavior.

PHONICS

Phonics is part of early language arts and is best taught as a basic daily skill and is a necessary first phase to teach children to read. This subject needs to be taught APART from your unit study. It doesn't tie in to your unit study topic. Since there are several different programs you could use to teach phonics be sure to research which one is the most teacher-friendly for you. Once you get a few of these basics out of the way each day, you can roll up your sleeves and concentrate on the topic you are studying.

It might not seem possible, but children can delight even in this basic skill if you approach it correctly they will learn to love reading. Don't press your little student too hard or you might kill this budding excitement. Since we believe in teaching phonics as compared to sight reading, we have used *The Writing Road to*

Reading/Teaching Reading at Home by Wanda Sanseri. I should let you know that I don't use this program to the fullest way it is recommended to be taught. The program is quite involved and takes time to learn, plus I have had good results using the phonogram cards, teaching the sounds in the correct order, along with the rules that are printed on the back of each card. Another program people tell me they like is *Teach Your Child to Read in 100 Easy Lessons*.

Each time I embark on the task of teaching another child to read, I have to remind myself how rewarding it is when all the hard work and patience brings them to the point of reading. If you are frustrated with the task of teaching a child to read, take heart because once "the lights go on" and you can see your child is really starting to read, it WILL be exciting. A whole new world will be opened up to him and you will be able to breathe a sigh of relief!

Sometimes it is difficult for children to see the big picture since they can't understand that practicing their sounds will eventually enable them to read. When Brooke was nine and learning to read, she just wanted to read and would get impatient with daily phonics. She thought I was withholding something by teaching her "boring phonics"—punishing her! When the "lights went on" and she could finally see how sounds form words and words form sentences, it was thrilling for both of us!

MATH

Math needs to be carried out in a repetitive, straightforward, consistent, and organized manner. Since math generally requires some rote memory work, it is good to do it separately from the unit study. The answer to how frequently you should work at rote subjects might differ from child to child.

We have used different math programs over the years. Two programs we like and recommend are: *Saxon Math* and *Math-U-See*. *Saxon Math* is a textbook program and *Math-U-See* combines the methods of *Mortensens* Math and the structure of *Saxon* into a manipulative-based program. *Math-U-See* includes a video featuring an instructor who explains the concepts clearly. We appreciate the fact that we can rewind and play the tape over and over again, to fully grasp a concept. This program helps children not only know how to work the problems and find the solutions, but to really understand the concept behind it. This way the student understands the HOW and the WHY. I also really like *Abeka* math workbooks for my children in the lower grades because they continue to practice concepts after they've been introduced. However, the program is accelerated so my children are not usually in the book they are "supposed" to be in for their grade.

Using textbooks is a different story where math is concerned. With *Saxon*, the children can work through their assignments on a daily basis easily without too much help from mom or dad. If they came across something they are unfamiliar with, they can go back over the material and find where the concept had been taught earlier. Though these textbooks are somewhat expensive, we have been pleased with how the program worked for us.

Occasionally you might need to make a change to meet your children's needs. When I noticed mine were struggling and starting to complain, I tried another program. One thing to determine is whether your kids are complaining about the program or whether they just don't like math!

Hands-on is good for math, too, and younger children especially benefit from this. Look for books that offers activities for teaching beginning math skills, shapes, sizes, classification, money, measuring, counting, telling time, and working with the calendar. Playing educational games is also a great tool to use for teaching math. Games are great because children don't realize they are learning as they play—ah ha!... the same with the unit study approach.

BIBLE

Bible time should also be accomplished OUTSIDE the unit study. Though we apply the scriptures to each study topic to shine the light of God's Word for a biblical perspective, we also work through our usual Bible time everyday using a combination of resources along with the Bible.

"...but his delight is in the law of the Lord,
and on His law he meditates day and night."

Psalm 1:1 (NIV)

Studies should be approached from a biblical standpoint. Daily, consistent biblical instruction will help your children to delight in God's righteous ways and to learn to worship Him with their lives. Regular Bible study has become a model for our children and they learn that God's Word applies to their lives and walking according to God's Word should be a priority. Having family Bible time together creates opportunities for discussions and encourages closeness and unity. Don't just sprinkle your children in the scriptures - soak them!

We use our Bible memory work as handwriting/penmanship practice at least once or twice a week to ensure regular practice and improvement. In the same way, older children can use memory verses for typing exercises. The children can save their best work for their notebooks and use the Bible verses for reference.

Bible/Character Resources

Developing Godly Character in Children—a Character Unit Study Guide by Caruso

Bible Truths for School Subjects by Ruth C. Haycock - a reference book which offers Scripture pertaining to areas of study.

Pearable Publishers and Doorpost Publishers both have some great resources for use during Bible time.

Your unit study tool box is overflowing. But when you're

building for learning, you use only the tools you need.

If a study tool doesn't really fit the unit and has to be

"forced" in, your children will know it and resist that study area.

(Clay and Sally Clarkson, *Educating the WholeHearted Child.*
[Walnut Springs: Whole Heart Ministries, 1996], 115)

Planning
③ *Unit Studies*

Now it's time to "roll up your sleeves" and get to work planning a unit study. The great part about planning your study is that it allows you to design something just right for your children. There is no perfect curriculum because as soon as you find something you like, inevitably, the ever changing needs of your family will outgrow it and then you end up back in the same place - adapting and shaping the curriculum to suit your needs! Don't be discouraged by this as it is just part of teaching.

The very word planning makes most moms start to shake in their boots. I want to offer some guidelines to help you plan a unit study but I would first like to stress that I am not a real organized or strict planner. Part of this is due to my personality and part of it owes to having many years of experience. The longer you do something, the more comfortable you become with it and the easier it gets. My plans are more general and not so specific. In other words, I would make a rough plan and get an idea of what I'm going to do but my plans would not be so detailed: Monday… do thus and so. Tuesday do this other thus and so! However, I will admit that the better I plan, organize and prepare - the smoother the study goes!

In this chapter I will first point out the curriculum options open to you as a homeschool parent. The next section will aim to answer some of the most common questions a parent might have about unit study planning. And finally, the chapter will conclude with the information you need to actually plan your unit studies.

As this material is discussed, I will answer questions like:

- How do I choose materials and other resources?
- How long should a unit study be?
- How do I plan a unit study?
- How long does it take to do your planning?
- How do you know what to study and in what order?

After reading this chapter, your "toolbox" will be stocked with enough information for you to construct any unit study you choose to take on and study.

OPTIONS TO CONSIDER - THREE CATEGORIES TO CHOOSE FROM

Although there are many different types of unit studies, there are essentially three options or catagories:

- Purchasing an already complete unit study curriculum
- Using a prepared, topical guide
- Creating your own from scratch

PURCHASING A COMPLETE UNIT STUDY CURRICULUM

There are several companies who provide complete unit study curriculum. Most of them are designed for you to start at one cover and work through so you may have enough material for a year or more. If you will be teaching a number of children for a long period of time and would like to spend less time on preparation, a purchased curriculum could be the best investment for you. This will require spending more money at the onset, since it will provide the plans, ideas, and sometimes even the text or information. Unit study curriculum usually include several topics but do not contain all of your other books. If you haven't seen a unit study curriculum, borrow one from a friend or support group library before you make the investment to see if you like their approach. Many of these complete curriculum offer a sample unit so you can actually try it before making a purchase.

The main drawback to a prepared unit study curriculum is that it can seem overwhelming for those who feel they must do everything. If you don't let the fact that there is so much material included intimidate you, you will have a wealth of information at your disposal. I often refer to this type of curriculum as "a brain on your shelf!"

Most published unit study curriculums are noted for their heavy emphasis on projects. Their contention is that children learn best by doing. While this is generally true, most mothers burn out trying to organize all these activities. These hands-on projects are nice once in a while and add a change of pace to your unit studies, but a steady diet only leads to frustration for Mom.

(Valerie Bendt, *How to Create Your Own Unit Study* [Hawthorne: Common Sense, 1990], 39)

One unit study curriculum company I like is Konos; however, I have heard many moms say they gave up unit studies completely because they couldn't do it "all." Now, I'm positive that the Konos people would not want you to do that! You must realize that YOU are in charge of your study - from planning to concluding - so I would encourage you to use what you think is valuable and don't ever feel like you must do it all. (You will get better at deciding what is "valuable" as you gain experience.) I find that I am my own worst enemy in this area. I begin to look at all that I could do and feel if I don't do it all, then my children will miss something!

What I've learned over the years is that **children don't need to learn everything there is to know about the topic**, but rather to give them a good overview of it. Realizing this has given me the freedom to enjoy the study and not feel like I have to do it all! Also, you may not wish to study the topics in the order presented in the curriculum. You may jump around, skip topics or leave them out altogether and you don't need to FEAR your child will miss something important! You're the teacher!

REMEMBER:

- **Pray about your curriculum purchases** and don't make them too quickly. When visiting a vendor booth or publisher of materials you are thinking of purchasing, spend some time talking with the representative. Ask them questions then go home and pray about it. If you are at the convention for the weekend, go back to your room to pray and contemplate your decisions. Sometimes the more you think and look, the more confusing it gets. Often we are motivated to make a purchase because there may be a "show special" or savings on shipping costs. These are really mininimal compared to the money you will spend on something you end up not using.

- **The curriculum or book is YOUR tool.** Let it work for you to give direction, guidelines and ideas. As you plan your study, pick and choose and leave the remainder of the information In the book and don't feel guilty about not using it!

- **YOU are the teacher!** The study outline, which tells you how much you should accomplish in one year, is only a guide and you do not need to strictly adhere to it. Be wise with your tools and let them work for you. Allow yourself the freedom to be flexible even though the curriculum is laid out to be used a certain way and for a specified period of time. Many parents like the security found in a unit study curriculum; however, don't let it box you in.

- **To set parameters.** If possible, set your own parameters and limits so you are not enticed into feeling you must "do it all." If you become overwhelmed and feel guilty, you could have a negative experience with the unit study method… and give up altogether!

USING A PREPARED TOPICAL UNIT STUDY GUIDE

A prepared topical unit study guide usually offers an outline or plan, book and resource lists, reproducible sheets, ideas for activities and projects, writing assignments, spelling and vocabulary lists plus more. They allow you to do one unit study at a time, give you the framework to follow, and are generally inexpensive (usually around $10.00 each). They provide many of the same features as a unit study curriculum, but only concentrate on one topic allowing you to take one bite at a time. The main drawback to this choice is that you may not be able to find a guide for your topic, depending on how specific or uncommon it is. We had one gal who shared a unit study spotlight of a study her family had conducted on "SHOES!" We all giggled at first but then as she showed us what they learned, it was amazing. It is unlikely that you would be able to find a topical teachers guide on Shoes.

If this choice appeals to you, understand you still have some work to do. After purchasing your guide, selecting activities, and gathering your materials, proceed with your study for about four weeks (the usual period of time we recommend for most studies). **It is important to note that if this is your first unit study, choose a topic you know something about. If you pick something to study that is completely foreign to you, you may flounder. If you are stronger in history… then do a history topic**. When you are done, go on to another topic.

Unit Study Guide... or Study Guide?

There is a difference between a unit study guide and a study guide. There are a number of companies that offer study guides that come in the form of literature guides, history guides, etc. Study guides generally ask questions and sometimes suggest various projects or assignments connected with the area of study. They can be beneficial to unit studies if they relate to what you are studying and make sense. But they ARE different from a topical unit study guide. A topical unit study guide focuses all its attention around the study topic and will include several subjects so all of the suggested lessons and activities will revolve around subjects like reading, writing, spelling and vocabulary, geography, art, research and so on.

Creating Your Own Study

If creating your own unit study from scratch is more your style, you can expect to save money; however, it will require more of your time, effort, and a certain amount of creativity. Most prepared unit study guides and curricula outline how you should study, but they usually need to be adapted to your particular needs. But when you design your own studies, you can tailor each unit study topic to fit your family. If you choose this avenue you will be using books - lots of them...

- To learn about the topic.
- To discover the topic content and how the study might unfold and be organized.
- To give you ideas for activities and assignments you could do in your study.
- To get inspired and excited about the study.

A word to the creative and noncreative. Generally people choose this avenue because it's just "them." They are creative. People who choose this avenue, like this sort of thing and it comes more naturally to them. They tend to be the more spontaneous "fly by the seat of your pants" type of person! I wouldn't suggest choosing this avenue, because you need to save money and can't afford a topical guide.However, once you've done a few unit studies, you'll start to become more comfortable with the method and find yourself planning your own studies or at least adding your own ideas into the program you're using.

An Encouraging Word

At this point, a word of encouragement might be needed because sometimes parents become frustrated and dissatisfied with using ONE of these three unit study avenues. Instead of evaluating the problem and finding a solution by modifying their plan, they often give up altogether on the idea of using unit studies.

It helps to keep in mind the possible drawbacks of each method:

- A complete unit study curriculum can be overwhelming and too fast-paced.
- Publishers or companies of topical guides may offer materials that do not suit you individual needs. Also you may not find a guide for your topic.
- When creating your own unit studies, you might lack structure and guidelines that would help you succeed.

During a curriculum fair, my husband and I talked to a lady who told us about one particular curriculum that just didn't work for her. She seemed to know what she didn't want, but didn't quite know what she DID want! Parents often avoid the structured outline a complete curriculum may offer, yet they feel insecure about the freedom and looseness of creating their own study. There is no magic formula that will give just the right amount of information, balanced activities, study outlines, resource lists, and provide information about books that are just right for your situation. Unfortunately, when it comes to the uniqueness of each and every family and child, no curriculum can provide exactly what is needed. Additionally, the needs of growing children are always changing, so finding such a curriculum is outright impossible! Realistically, you are going to have to do some adapting of materials so if you understand this concept from the start, you will be much more satisfied with your program (whatever it is) in the long run.

You are probably thinking of investing in a Cadillac because

you don't want to have to think - "Just give me everything I need" you say.

Sorry, ma'am. A curriculum that can read your child's mind has not

and never will be written. You alone are your child's teacher.

A curriculum is a tool.

(Gayle Graham, *How to Home School* [Hawthorne: Common Sense Press, 1992], 67)

By using this delightful method, you will find what works best for you. I can personally testify to this and have also heard many people say how much easier it gets the more you do it! The nice thing about unit studies, again, is that **THERE ARE NO RULES**. Follow some of the helpful guidelines, get a little experience and you will soon fall in love with delighting your child through unit studies.

What usually happens is that moms begin using a unit study curriculum as their guide. Once they gain some confidence they switch to using prepared guides for some topics and even creating their own from scratch for other topics. At first moms NEVER believe this will happen with them and they are just sure they do not have what it takes to even carry out a unit study successfully. One where her children will be excited and delighted - let alone create or plan her own from scratch. But, it truly does happen and I have had many, many mothers come back and tell me how great they are doing!

CAUTION - IT'S EITHER/OR... NOT BOTH!

One mother I talked to at a curriculum fair was excited and convinced that she should do a unit study. I sort of winced because I knew she was going to add a unit study to her already very full schooling schedule. Even though you certainly CAN do this, I don't recommend it. Instead, I suggest you take time off from your main course of study and incorporate as many of your academic skills and subjects into your unit study as possible. You could continue with reading and math daily, spelling and grammar once a week for an hour or so, and set the textbooks or other curriculum aside while you are doing the unit study.

As you learn this "Steward Method" and follow the simple guidelines I teach, you will learn which subjects to include. Their completed work in different subject areas will allow you to see that your children are indeed learning and you will feel justified and confident that you are still doing valuable and worthwhile "things." You can tell this by their responses.

Too many parents try to use both textbooks and the unit approach

to teaching, practically wiping out both themselves and their children

because they were afraid to let the textbooks go... just in case.

(Ibid., 129)

No matter which avenue you decide to try, you will soon find your own niche!

How Much Should a Unit Study Cost to Conduct?

Of course, the cost of a unit study will vary depending upon which avenue you choose. As you seen, with The Steward Method - I give some specific suggestions for how to schedule your unit study time. One important part of that is reading aloud and another part is Information Time. During Information Time, often you will want to do some sort of connecting or related activity (in some subject area). You will get the idea for this activity either from your teachers guide or you may come up with it yourself - more later! So, undertanding this, now we know what we need 1) a book to read aloud, 2) some nonficiton books which contain the "information" you'll be teaching, 3) a teacher's guide for ideas and reproducibles and also perhaps 4) an educational colorbook. That's four items. With our homeschooling supply company, Steward Ship, we print a catalog and though we'd like to carry ten different resources for each unit study topic, we cannot possibly do this - so we strive to carry at least these FOUR basic items. You would probably want to gather a few more books and resources for any topic, **but you COULD do a unit study with these four basic items**. We could calculate the cost of: **a read aloud, a nonfiction book, a topical teacher's guide and an educational colorbook** at around $20 to $30 - that's not too bad!

I had a distressed mother ask, "How much do you spend for curriculum each year?" She was upset because she had just placed a textbook order for her two elementary grade daughters for the upcoming year. The company's recommendation for materials she needed exceeded her budget of $1,000 so she wasn't able to get everything they suggested. I answered but was a little embarrassed, "Well, about $200 - $300 - for my whole family."

If you spent a GENEROUS amount, say around $50 on each unit study (which would allow you to buy some educational coloring books, perhaps a model, and several books), and then you planned to conduct nine studies in a school year (which is more than I ever get done!), you would be spending about $450 - for your whole family AND that's for all kinds of neat books, models and other goodies. That's pretty good, plus you get to keep them and add them to your home library or resell them when you no longer need them.

Conducting unit studies doesn't have to cost you a great deal. The amount of money you spend will also depend on how many extras - such as videos, field trips, games and models you use. We use the public library and our own home library quite a bit. Also, if you know what you are going to study in advance you can keep yours eyes open when you go to thrift stores or yard sales! Another good thing is to pick up a packet of stickers here or a coloring book there and even though it adds up, you won't notice it as much spread over time!

SUMMARIZE THE THREE AVENUES

These three categories offer you some options, and at any time you can use any or all of them together combining the best of each to suit your needs. We all have different preferences and one avenue is not really better than another - its a matter of choice according to each family's needs. One family might choose an option because it works best for them, but it may not work for the next person. There is always room for variety and sometimes the changing needs of your family will lead you to take another avenue or to use a mixture from the three categories.

I personally prefer a combination of using topical guides and creating my own studies from scratch. At times I have benefited from ideas used in a unit study curriculum. If I have a topical guide for my study, I will always get a few ideas or reproducibles from it. I used a complete curriculum for my daughter when she began high school called *Far Above Rubies*. I chose this option for high school so I didn't have to do all the work myself.

A COMPLETE UNIT STUDY CURRICULUM

Remember, a unit study curriculum is an investment you will use for years. The initial cost might range from at least $100-$200 for the curriculum itself. You will still need to acquire books and resources but, here again, you can space out your expenses. Before purchasing one, ask other homeschoolers which ones they prefer and why. Ask them what they liked about it and what they didn't like about it. It would even be great if you could check one out of your homeschool support group library or borrow one from a friend so you can spend some time evaluating it to see if you want to own it.

A TOPICAL GUIDE

Most topical guides cost $10 or less. Some might cost a bit more… some might be less. The benefit here is that you can spend less at the outset and have what you need for the present time. Keep watch for these at used curriculum fairs! You can also pick these up at teacher stores. They are more commonly known as thematic guides.

CREATING YOUR OWN UNIT STUDY

Because you will still purchase some resources, the cost for creating your own study will be about the same as using a topical guide just minus the cost of a topical teacher's guide.

WHAT DOES A UNIT STUDY MEAN TO YOU?

When you start shopping for topical guides or various unit study curricula, you will find much diversity in style among authors and publishers. Some authors lead you in one direction, some in another; others include lots of this and not much of that. Sometimes I feel confused by some of these guides because the authors approach to a unit study is different than mine. The differences in people and our diverse thinking is what makes "the world go round." I have learned to use what works for me and leave the remaining material alone. It is important to make this point to spare you any confusion when choosing or comparing unit studies. Sometimes a particular style or author really leaves an impression upon you. Other times the assignments or projects don't appear to apply. There are also times when I think of something to include in the unit study that the guide doesn't offer. Remember, the choice is yours!

Because unit study is such a flexible methodology, every advocate seems to approach it from a slightly different perspective. – Loyalty to the method, though, is nearly universally based on thematic, integrated study. – The appeal for Unit Study advocates is that it is natural, child centered and informal.

(Clay and Sally Clarkson, *Educating the Whole Hearted Child*,
[Walnut Springs: Whole Heart Ministries, 1996], 60)

WHICH RESOURCES SHOULD YOU CONSIDER USING?

There is so much available - I can't even begin to list but here are a few ideas:

Topical Guide series available:

- Teacher Created Materials - Secular - suggests a piece of literature so assignments and reproducibles would coincide. Drawback? If you don't choose that piece of literature - the guide will be almost useless.
- *The Study of... Unit Study Guides* by The Steward Family (that's us!)
- *Unit Study Adventures* by Amanda Bennett
- *Five in A Row* (literature based - great for young chidlren)
- *Good Apple Guides*
- Castle Heights Press

Listed below are some complete unit study curriculums to consider using:

- *The Prairie Primer* (based on Laura Ingalls Wilder books)
- Diana Waring (for history)
- *Prairie Primer*

Listed below are some complete unit study curriculums to consider using:

- *Far Above Rubies* (Jr. High/High School girls)

- *Blessed is the Man* (for boys)

- *Lessons From History* (3 volumes)

- *Heart of Wisdom* (Ancient History - extensive)

- *The Quick Look Unit Study Series* (Hands-On units from STEWARD SHIP States, World, Explorers, Inventors, Composers)

- The Weaver Curriculum

- Konos

- Alta Vista

- TRISMS

WHAT SHOULD WE STUDY?

Once you decide which avenue best suits your needs, make a list of topics you would like to study. If you're going with a complete curriculum, the topics may be laid out for you - now you have to decide if you are going to follow it as per the recommendations or if you are going to use it as a guideline skipping topics, leaving some out, inserting others or switching the order.

Whatever interests your children—the sky is the limit! Unit topics tend to fall into the categories of history or science but others might include: literature, character or miscellaneous/other.

HISTORY—Ancient History (Egypt, Greece, Rome, etc.), Art History, Exploration, Famous People, Historical Costume, Inventions, People Groups, Time Periods (Medieval, Renaissance, etc.) U.S. History, Wars, World History, 1800's, American History (Pilgrims, Colonial Times, Transcontinental Railroad, Pony Express, etc.)

SCIENCE—Ants, Creation Science, Dinosaurs, Human Body, Insects, Nutrition, Ocean Life, Plants, Reptiles, Rocks & Minerals, Space/Planet, Volcanoes, Weather, Lighthouses, Trees, Weather and so on.

LITERATURE—Dickens - *A Christmas Carol*, *Charlotte's Web* (great Farm Life or Spiders unit study Read Aloud!), The *Little House on the Prairie* series (great for Westward Movement/Pioneers), *The Red Badge of Courage* (Civil War), *The Secret Garden* (read during a study on Plants), Mark Twain (read his works), Robert Louis Stevenson (a Scottish immigrant). Use simply as great pieces of literature since literature studies can stand alone or you can use them as read alouds during any study and expand the literature aspect of it by jumping off and studying things that pop up during the story (more explained later).

MISCELLANEOUS—Agriculture, Canning, The Decade of the 1920's, Factories, Occupations (Firemen, Pilots, Veterinarians), Textiles, Trains, Woodworking, etc.

GEOGRAPHY—*Around the World in Eighty Days*, Amos Fortune Freeman (Africa), Mark Twain (traveled the U.S. and abroad in his life - a great geography study), Pirates (*Treasure Island*), Lighthouses (also a great Geography study!) U.S. or World Geography unit studies are the most fun!

How Do I Know What to Study?

- Consider what has already been studied and teach what's next in chronological order.

- Ask your children what interests them.

- Make a list of all topics you think you "should" study.

- Use a course of study as a reference guideline (such as Kay Milow's *Homeschool Guide*).

PLAN FOR THE "LONG TERM"

I prefer to make an annual unit study plan. When you make your annual school plans, try to determine how long each unit study will take. My plan lists nine units which begin in September and extend over a period of 12 months. Please bear in mind that this is an ideal plan and we don't often (or ever!) fulfill our original hopes and plans. We would be extremely happy if we actually got nine units done in a year but realistically we usually get around six or seven done. That would be in the course of the regular school year and then we might try to do something more fun (and definitely lighter) during the summer.

Use the planning sheet called "The Big Picture Plan" (in the Appendix) to help make a tentative long term schedule. This sheet is your tool so scribble on it and use it to help you. If you don't like your plans start over and use it to help you get a roadmap for your upcoming year.

If you can, plan for two or even three years to give you an idea of the direction your studies might take. **Remember, knowing what you plan to study in the next year or two allows you to collect books and other resources ahead of time**.

PLAN TO DO A CO-OP

Since you are going to be planning your whole year, you can look over your chosen topics and decide whether you would want to conduct any of them in a co-op, either with a large group or maybe just one or two families. If you decide to, you'll need to decide which topics, which month, and which family. There is more information about co-ops later.

STUDY SOMEWHAT CHRONOLOGICALLY

People ask frequently about the idea of studying history topics in chronological order. This means to study things in the order that they happened as dates in history. When we first started doing unit studies, I just picked any topic and jumped in. We would study Civil War, then something like Volcanoes, then Colonial Times and so on. Before long I realized that the Colonial Times period came before Civil War in American

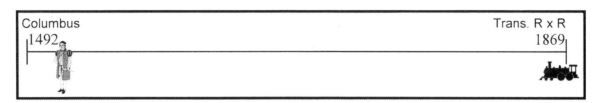

History so I started trying to put my topics in more of a chronological order. Chronology really only matters where time periods are concerned. In other words, you can study science topics in most any order. The same with geography and so on. If you are doing literature studies, you might look at the time period of the book but this can also become too much work and confusing.

I tend to think chronologically - this just makes sense to me, but chronological order is something that parents and teachers are "hung up" on and the not the kids - they don't really get it. In fact, it has taken many years of studying different topics for my kids to really build a mental timeline and I find it takes lots of review and reminding them where the topic fits in history before they really understand time periods and how they fit together.

My advice, then, is to study "somewhat" chronologically. Let me explain. If you were going to study topics chronologically and started at the dawn of man with Creation Science, moving into ancient Egypt, Greece, Rome and so on, you wouldn't get to the Space Age until high school! Since there are many important topics to cover throughout the elementary school years which you wouldn't want to miss, I feel it works better to study somewhat chronologically. If you studied one or two American History topics each year and one or two Ancient History topics each year - plus mix in other science topics and some in the "other" category, you would have a nice mix of topics to study - thus holding your child's interest. Studying some-what chronologically means that you might study Egypt one year and the next time you pick up an ancient history topic (whenever that would be), it would be Greece - enabling you to keep them in order. The same for American history - study Columbus in October and Pilgrims in November then go on to a science topic.

Another thing to consider is how much history and/or science you want to tackle in one year. I personally don't usually study history topics one right after another where some parents, (especially those who are using the Classical Approach), study the ancients in a row. The reason I don't generally do this is that history topics can be very similar in nature - looking at people, religion, homes, food, wars, architecture, and art, so all your studies end up taking on the same "look" or "flavor" and follow a similar pattern, thus the students can become bored!

I have had an emergency change of plans when I realized that I had covered American history topics like Pilgrims, Colonial Times, American Revolution, etc. with my older children, but my younger children were so young, that they only got a bare bones, juvenile study of those topics. I had to make plans to "get it all in" so we studied many American history topics over the course of about two years. In this case, we still mixed in some science topics and some "other" topics, which helped keep things interesting, but we were able to cover the American history topics we needed to.

A WORD TO THE WISE

There are times when a child really wants to study a topic, like Medieval Times, and the parent might be tempted to hold off because they have not studied other ancient history topics like ancient Egypt, yet. My suggestion is... don't wait. If your child shows interest and you make them wait for a year so you can keep those topics in chronological order, they will most likely lose interest. If this is the case, tell them where your topic fits in history, and explain that you are going to jump ahead but will go back and study those other topics… in order! Viewing a list of topics we studied in one year might help you get an idea of how you can study "somewhat" chronologically.

What We Studied in One Year:

Finishing California History - (2 to 3 weeks to finish last segment from previous year)

Trains (4 weeks - October)

Columbus and Pilgrims (6 weeks - November to early December)

The rest of December - "Christmas activites," visiting people, baking, reading, etc.

Colonies (4 weeks - January)

History of Clothing (a 3 week mini unit on sewing/textiles - February)

Shakespeare (4 weeks - February into March)

American Revolution (at least 6 weeks - April and May)

Please note: *It is good to take at least a few days between studies for Mom to plan and regroup. During that time, the kids can do some reading and math plus finish loose ends. There may be assignment sheets which need to be finished and organized into the notebook, vocabulary words that need to be looked up in the dictionary, and photos of field trips pasted in. (This explanation will help account for some of the time which might seem to be "missing" from my schedule as you read along through what we've studied for a few years.)*

Also note that I have been doing unit studies for about sixteen of the twenty-one years we've been homeschooling. So, you might get confused when you see me repeat a topic in a list of topics studied. You're not losing your mind! Since I have several children, in the past few years, I have started repeating topics for the second "round" of students - so it may be difficult to really follow my examples as I have offered so many from so many years of teaching… please bear with me as I try to tell you EVERYTHING!

The Next Year:

Art History (4 weeks - September - finishing from summer)

Lewis and Clark (6 weeks - October/November)

Lighthouses (4 weeks - November through early December)

December (no unit study in December - time spent as described above)

Rocks and Minerals (4 weeks - January)

Mark Twain (4 weeks February)

Astronomy/Solar System (4 weeks March)

The rest of the year we worked on a study of the United States (which is a continuing study which we pick up from time to time) and finished up loose ends.

One More Year:

Incas Aztecs, Maya (4 weeks - September)

Westward Movement (6 weeks October/November- Conducted a co-op with a large group)

Trees (4 weeks November/December)

December (finished Trees… then no unit study in December… as in other years)

Ancient Egypt (6 weeks January/February - co-op with another family)

Insects (4 weeks - March)

Farm Life (4 weeks - April)

The Alamo (2 weeks - May)

Many moms (especially those who are new to homeschooling), ask "How do I know where things fall in history?" Well, believe me, before I started teaching interactively with my children, I didn't have a clue either (this was basically before I started getting an education!). Below you'll find a chronological list of the main historical events for elementary grades. From such a list, you can plan several years of history unit studies.

Chronological List of Main History Topics

- Bible History

- Creation, Ancient Civilizations, Jewish People

- Ancient Egypt

- Ancient Greece

- Ancient Rome (The time of the Roman Empire and of Jesus Christ)

- Medieval Times

- Renaissance

- Reformation

- The Age of Discovery/World Explorers

- Columbus

- Pilgrims

- Colonies

- Founding Fathers

- Revolutionary War/Early Republic

- French and Indian Wars

- Frontiersmen (Daniel Boone)

- Lewis and Clark

- The Age on Inventions (1800's)
- Westward Movement/Pioneers
- Pony Express/Transcontinental Telegraph
- Transcontinental Railroad/Trains
- Pioneers
- Mark Twain/Mississippi River boats
- Cowboys
- Abraham Lincoln
- The Civil War
- Industrial Revolution
- Immigration
- World War I
- The Great Depression
- World War II
- The Space Age World

Try to formulate a general plan and group topics somewhat chronologically instead of jumping around time periods like a ping pong ball.

EXAMPLE:

One year we studied Creation Science first, ancient Egypt next and then ancient Greece. We grew tired of ancient history and moved on to something else, but I knew the next time we studied an ancient history topic, it would be ancient Rome. In another year we studied Colonial Times, Birds, Abraham Lincoln (as a character study), Immigration, World Geography, Musical Instruments, and Westward Movement. Now I make an annual plan which helps me to order my units. Since I taught Colonial Times last, I planned to teach Revolutionary War as my next American history topic. Likewise, after studying Westward Movement, Cowboys would be a good choice to follow with in the near future. This way, topics which can be tied together are still fresh in our memories so we can take advantage of what has been learned without becoming burned out on any one area.

You could literally study anything under the sun! Below is a partial list of ideas...

IDEAS FOR UNIT STUDY TOPICS

People

Founding Fathers	Inventors	Explorers	Indians
Christian Heroes	Church Fathers	Patriarchs	Composers
Women in History	Scientists	Presidents	First Ladies
Astronauts	Authors	People of the World	
	World Leaders	Athletes	

People

Founding Fathers	Inventors	Explorers	Indians
Christian Heroes	Church Fathers	Patriarchs	Composers
Women in History	Scientists	Presidents	First Ladies
Astronauts	Authors	People of the World	
	World Leaders	Athletes	

Science

Rocks and Minerals	Volcanoes	Creation Science	Soil
Environment	Weather	Disasters	Oceans
Water	Zoology	Plants/Botany	Insects
Ants	Bees	Gardening	Canning
Food	Cooking	Solar System	Planets
Human Body	Nutrition	Electricity	Textiles
Light	Sound	Trees	Penguins

Animals

Cats	Dogs	Horses	Farm Animals
Dinosaurs	Birds	Fish	Reptiles
Pets			

History

Transportation	Historical	Costume	Medieval Times
Castles	Reformation	Renaissance	Ships
World Wars	Historical Figures	Kings and Queens	Immigration
Vikings			

Ancient History

Archaeology	Ancient Egypt	Ancient Greece	Ancient Rome
Life of Christ	Civilizations	Architecture	Incas, Aztecs, Maya
Ancient China			

Crafts

Woodworking	Cake Decorating	Furniture Refinishing	Upholstery
Ceramics			

Vocations

Pharmacist (medical field)	Doctors	Nurses	Engineers
Pilot	Veterinarian	Law Enforcement	Fireman
Farmers	Carpenters	Computer Tech	Lawyers
Forestry			

American History

Slavery	Pony Express	Gold Rushes	Canals
Industrial Revolution	Inventions	Trains	Wars
Civil War	French and Indian War	Revolutionary War	Your State History
Westward Movement	Pioneers	Frontiersmen	Cowboys
Transcontinental Railroad			

Geography

U.S. Geography	Islands	Jungles	World Geography
			(to include customs, dress, homes, food, religion)
Oceans	Seas	Mountains	Deserts

Literature

A Christmas Carol   *Charlotte's Web*   *The Secret Garden*   *Treasure Island*

Little Lord Fauntleroy   *Carry On, Mr. Bowditch*   *Works of Shakespeare*

Little House on the Prairie series   *The Red Badge of Courage*

Miscellaneous

Agriculture   The Decade of the 1920's   Factories

The Arts

Art History	Ballet	Music	Musical Instruments
Composers	Art (sculpting, painting, etc.)	Art Appreciation	Types of Dance
Architecture			

Character Traits (Examine the character of godly people, i.e. Abraham Lincoln)

Honesty	Integrity	Truthfulness	Perseverence
Patience	Dependable	Hospitable	

Topics for Young Children

Animals	Farm Life	Fall	Pumpkins
Butterflies	Trains	Ocean Life	

HOW LONG SHOULD YOU STUDY ONE TOPIC?

Unit studies come in all shapes and sizes and take on many different forms. How long each of your studies takes to complete is up to you. There are some determining factors and guidelines which can help. With "The Steward Method," **we recommend doing one unit study topic and studying for about one month**. This is not a rule - just a guideline and seems to be about the right amount of time to cover your topic and get through your books, without losing the interest of your students. Some people say, "I don't know how you do it. I could never finish a unit study in a month."

Consider the following:

- Your goal is not to teach everthing there is to know about your chosen topic, but rather to become familiar with it.

- The content of your chosen topic (more material requires more time) For example: A vast topic like Animals or a long period of time in history like Medieval Times will take more time.

- The number of books/literature you wish to get through or cover.

- The interest-level of your children.

- What kind of study it is: World Geography will take a long time (try every Friday for two years!). Your state history will probably take a year.

- If you are using unit studies for your core of teaching, then most of your subjects will be integrated into your unit. This saves time you would otherwise be spending on many subjects… thus taking more time to complete a unit study.

- How you are using the unit study? Is it a sideline to another study, a context study, or a mini-study? Is it a whole unit study?

- How long it will take to meet your educational goals for the topic.

MORE ABOUT THE BIG SECRET

Now, here's the Big Secret I've been waiting to tell you but you must promise not to tell your children! As the teacher, you are using your chosen topic to work at necessary academic subjects you wish to accomplish. You will be doing maps but your children never have to know it's Geography! You can have your kids copy a poem and they will never know that one of your motives was for handwriting practice. You can have them look up something on the internet and read about it and they don't realize they are doing research. But the minute you tell them to do some research, they begin to complain and get the jitters. By the end of the study your child's notebook will be filled with papers and assignments which are all the result of valuable learning and skills - an outpouring of many subjects - and it becomes a report without them even knowing it… AND they love it AND they learn. Just don't ever tell them our little secret!

Another thing which may help you determine how long a unit study topic will take is to select a couple of nonfiction source books to use for information. Sometimes your unit study guide will help you divide your study into workable or senseable sections. If the guide doesn't offer help in this area, turn to your books for help. Usually each two page spread in a nonfiction book is about one aspect of your study. The book I used when planning a human body study, was divided so each spread was a different body system which helped me decide how to organize the study. The same thing was true for our study on "Pilgrims." I found I could teach one week on "life in England and Holland," the second week we investigated "life on the Mayflower voyage," and the third week we studied what it was like as "the pilgrims made their home in the New World." We tied everything together the fourth week and prepared a feast. A unit on "Weather" could be divided by seasons or types of weather: hurricanes, tornadoes, rain, snow, etc.

During a study on Medieval Times we found these sections: knights, castles, war/weapons, the Church/Monks, social ladder (Nobility to Peasants), feasting, sport (hawking, tournaments, chess, etc.) When you begin to see what the study will consist of, it will help you figure out how long it might take. You might be able to cover a certain number of pages to cover each day. Let your books help you plan your units. I am amazed at how many ideas I get just from looking over my books.

On the other hand, continuing a unit study beyond the children's interest span is usually a waste of time. You've seen that look before - it's a blank stare - and when you see it you better take note because it means "nothing more is going in!" During our study on Medieval Times, I discovered that four weeks would not be long enough to cover the 1,000 years of culture, people, places and events but my children were tiring of knights, castles, chivalry, peasants and the "darkness" of the Black Death! I knew I needed about two more weeks so I just told them, "Hey you guys, just hang with me and we'll finish in two weeks." Because I had given them a time frame (and hope!) they hung in there. This also happened with our study on Animals. We were studying by habitat and we had gone for about six weeks and made it through all the habitats except Oceans and Arctic. When I realized this, I decided to quit because we had recently done a complete unit study on both of those topics. Here's what we homeschoolers do to ourselves though. We realize that if "they" ever looked into our child's Animal notebook, they would discover that those two important habitats were missing.Believe me, I thought about this… for exactly one minute. Then I realized I don't know who "they" are and next I realized that I am the teacher and it's OK!

I recommend a break in between units so everyone will be refreshed and excited about starting a new one. We try to take at least a week off between units and will continue working on some some loose ends and other skills during that time.

If you're not using unit studies as your full time teaching method, you might wish to add a mini-unit as a sideline to your regular studies to liven things up. In this case, a unit might only take a week or two. Even if you use unit studies full time, it is fun to conduct mini-units from time to time. I know one time I had come back from Indiana where we were doing a workshop. We had visited an Amish village and I brought home a few books about the Amish. We took a few days to do a mini unit on the Amish.

The other extreme is to have more than one unit study going at the same time! We did a World Geography study for one whole school year one day a week while doing other units at the same time. Our children enjoyed breaking away on the fifth day to study something different.

Still some can't swallow our suggested guideline of doing History OR Science… not both at the same time within a unit study topic. I still prefer not to try to force science fit a history topic or visa versa, so my suggestion is to do a history topic for a couple days a week and a science topic the other days.

While individual, prepared curriculums outline a schedule, much of the planning is still left up to the parents. You tailor the schedule according to the number of children you have and their differing ages and can adjust to the plans and the schedule to suit your needs. Some unit studies are designed to be studied continuously over a specific period of time and outline the entire school year or even two. I know of some families who have used *The Prairie Primer* with the Little House series over the course of a whole school year.

GRADE-LEVEL LEARNING GOALS

One consideration while we're trying to plan and also a frequently asked question is "How do you know what a child is supposed to learn and when?" There are several publications which include information regarding what children typically learn at different ages. Use this information as a reference to show you what you COULD study - don't allow it to intimidate you. You do not have to study the whole list and you do not have to do it in the order listed AND you don't even have make sure your child knows all that by a certain time!

Parents new to homeschooling are constantly asking us, "What is my child supposed to learn in the _____ grade?" This question always ruffles my feathers a bit because those who ask are trying to adhere to teaching standards established by the public school system. In your "private school," you set the requirements for your own children. Imagine saying, "Uh oh, my child didn't learn about the U.S. Presidents in the fifth grade, so now he can't learn about them." It just doesn't make sense. It is perfectly acceptable to use these standards as your general guideline, but I would like to officially give you permission to decide for yourself what is next in line to teach your child. Here's the big "IF." If you are planning or think there is a good chance that your child might be going back into public school, you should know what is required and follow it. If you took your child out of school in the 3rd grade and didn't teach them your state history (which is typically covered in the 4th grade - in the U.S.), then you put your child back into public school in the 5th grade, they would have missed their state history.

Here are a few resources:

- *The Home School Manual* by Ted Wade
- *What Your Child Needs to Know When* by Robin Scarlata
- *A Typical Course of Study* (booklet) from World Books
- *How Do You Know They Know What They Know?* by Teresa Moon

I'm not too worried about what others say we should be teaching our children or when they say we should be teaching these things. Remember, you are teaching the children, not the book.

(Valerie Bendt, *How to Create Your Own Unit Study* [Hawthorne: Common Sense Press, 1990], 22)

WHY ARE WE SO AFRAID?

Now, how are we going to take one more step in planning if we can't get past this issue? The issue we've been talking about is what I refer to as a fear based approach to teaching. I talk to many parents who wrinkle their brow in worry and say "But I'm afraid of this or that." Usually they are afraid they will miss something important. They worry that their children won't be able to pass SAT tests. They worry over whether their children will be able to go to college. Some of these fears are in relationship to using the Unit Study method but often they are just homeschooling fears in general. Often those who express these fears (over college especially) are homeschooling their first child who is still only preschool age! We must go back to the reason we are homeschooling and ask ourselves whether this is something we thought would be fun and neat or if this is a serious decision brought about by the prompting of the Lord. We must evaluate our philosophy about education and remind ourselves often of what we think about the value of education. Is education all about academics or is it about raising godly children who fear the Lord? It is possible to have academically superior children who love the Lord but we parents must always keep priorities straight and keep these things in perspective.

If we are home educating our children because we have a religous conviction, we must go back to the source - our Faithful Lord who knows our needs before we can say them. We never need to say "I'm afraid."

Our society worships education and knowledge… but that issue will have to wait for another book! The Word of God warns "…we know that we all possess knowledge. Knowledge puffs up, but love builds up. The man who thinks he knows something does not yet know as he ought to know. But the man who loves God is known by God." I Corinthians 8:1-3

We need to be responsible to educate our children well, but we also need to make sure we are seeking the God who called us into home education and not be fearful. Also, there is a whole army of those who have gone before you in your efforts paving the way for the future. Scores of children have met with success after graduation in all areas of life. They are turning out as excellent people who have leadership qualities, are interested in learning and know HOW to learn. They are able to communicate and get along well socially despite the fact that they have been so called "sheltered" and have lacked in socialization!

Folks - we have nothing to fear because God is with us! I am going to challnge you to write that in BIG words and post it on your refrigerator so you can remember this, simple but profound truth,daily!

One more thing… and that is the fear over missing something important. The question over missing something important needs to be settled here. YOU WILL miss something important! It's just a fact.

And while we are on the subject of God - WE are NOT God so WE WILL miss something important! I'm going to be bold here...invariably, those who use the textbook method, are even more likely to miss something… IMPORTANT! I went to public school for twelve years and used textbooks and I missed something important - I missed getting an education. As I said earlier, I got A's and B's and still did NOT get an education. How? All you have to do is your work. Complete your work and turn it in and you can get a good grade but in my case, I didn't learn much because it wasn't interesting to me.

I've seen it over and over. Parents use textbooks because of the security they seem to offer - everything there in one place. BUT because they are usually dry and boring, kids go through them, but they don't absorb or remember the material because it's not interesting to them...they are just "doing school."

Let me give you an example. At different times I have done co-ops with other families. Since the unit study approach is interactive and I am usually the mom who knows more about unit studies, I do most of the teaching. During a co-op on Insects, I decided to include some literature so I read some of **Aesop's Fables** like "The Ant and the Grasshopper." I also read a story from Rudyard Kip-lings **Just So Stories** titled "The Butterfly Who Stamped." (I knew about these books from a study we had done a few years prior, on Animals.) After I read the selections,we did a connecting acitivty by reading a bit about both authors from a short bit of information I had searched for on the internet. Next, we copied black line maps of Europe to find Greece, the home of Aesop, and England, the birthplace of Kipling. We outlined the land brown and the water in blue. (We do this sort of thing constantly and that's how my children have learned so much about world geography - we're always "on the map!")

One thirteen-year-old student had never heard of either author… and none of the children knew where Europe was let alone Greece or England. My children were waving their hands wildly (which is embarassing - I knew they were not trying to be "know-it-alls", they just wanted to answer). I am always a little startled when I see this in other children because I am used to the way my children respond. **The truth is, kids really DO learn through interaction and they really DON'T RETAIN that much when they are sitting alone working through a stack of textbooks/subjects**.

Over the years, in group settings when I ask children questions, many times their faces are blank. They don't know the answers to simple and important information because they haven't really learned it. The thing is, students who are in the 5th or 6th grade and are using textbooks should know this kind of information - I KNOW that information is in those books.

I should qualify the previous observation by saying that kids who are well read, not just stuck in their textbooks, meeting the status quo… doing school… checkiing off required boxes - they ARE able to answer. Once again solidifying my belief that a person can get their whole education from reading!

THAT'S A CAPITAL IDEA!

CAPITALIZING

Capitalizing means looking for opportunities you can use to enhance your child's education. Unit studies allow you more freedom to capitalize on the teachable moments or local events. We must remember that we want our children to learn and be enthused about it so we should never be afraid to step out of our comfort zone (which includes leaving our "fear" behind) in order to feel guilt free over stepping away from the books in order to capitalize on the opportunities which are at hand. Sometimes we feel so obligated to stick by the book (usually textbooks) and so afraid to get "off track" that we won't tap into the neat extras that would add so much to our studies. I just want to remind you that this is part of the beauty of home educating our children. We certainly have more time and opportunities coming our way so we should take advantage of them! Of course, we must maintain balance or we could find ourselves running around doing alot of educationally enhancing activities and neglect the needed basics we need to accomplish.

CAPITALIZING ON A CHILD'S INTERESTS

One afternoon a friend wanted to "pick my brain." She had a question concerning one of her children. I would describe her son as a boy who loves to learn. He gets totally involved in his interests, and if he gets your attention, he'll talk constantly about his latest interest! He expressed to his mom that he felt frustrated because he had to "do school" and couldn't pursue the projects he was really interested in. He had everything he needed to start building a model ship. Her question was, "Should I make him "do school" when he wants to work on this ship? He says he's willing to do writing and spelling and other things related to his project."

What do you think my answer was? "If that boy is so interested in his project and says he'll wrap his studies around it, jump on this opportunity! Take his core interest and build your study around it." I then proceeded to give her ideas for things he could do to study along with his ship building project.

- Read a novel such as *Carry On, Mr. Bowditch*.
- Write a fictional story about the man who owns the ship.
- Make a map showing a route of exploration he made with his ship.
- Create a poster showing different kinds of ships.
- Create a list of spelling and vocabulary words connected to the project.
- Draw a diagram showing the different parts of the ship.
- Look up Scriptures that talk about sailing.

She went home and told her son he could go ahead with his project and showed him some of the things he could do during his "unit study" on ships. He was delighted and told his mother, "I like it when you go to the Steward's house!"

CAPITALIZING ON EXTRA-CURRICULAR ACTIVITIES AND EVENTS

Check the community calendar in the local newspaper for events scheduled in the area and capitalize on the unique opportunities that come to town such as an museum exhibit, theater performance, IMAX film related to your study topic and the like. Remember, your annual plan and school schedule is designed to compliment your family's lifestyle so tap into any available extracurricular activities. Our car insurance company publishes a bi-monthly magazine listing events occurring throughout our state. If something corresponds with a study and is logistically possible, we include it. We were in the middle of a unit study on California History when our family took a trip to the beach which was a about an hour's drive to Monterey - the first capital of our state. We capitalized on some "living history" and took a "super" field trip. While there, we visited the original Customs House, watched a video in the museum about early California and then stopped to visit a mission on our way home. The field trips really brought the study to life for the children.

One year, we studied Lighthouses in October then Lewis and Clark in November. We found out that an IMAX theater was showing a Lewis and Clark film so we took a "field trip" and visited two lighthouses on our way to the IMAX. (An IMAX theater is where a film is shown in a special circular theater with the film surrounding you and the effect of the film is spectacular!)

Videos, both films and documentaries, can have literary, cultural, and educational value. For instance we watched *Fiddler on the Roof* when Cacey was studying Jewish culture, Disney's *Pete's Dragon* when we studied Lighthouses, *Cleopeatra* when we studied Egypt (watch the rating and the film selection on this one!), *Journey to the Center of the Earth* when we studied Volcanoes, *A Bug's Life* when we studied Insects and so on.

When we studied Shakespeare, we watched videos of many plays, renting videos from video stores or checking them out from the library. This really helped the children understand the stories and appreciate the time period.

Videos are a good resource to add to your home or support group library. We purchased an educational video about California history that was featured in the museum gift shop at Monterey. One mother told me she bought discounted videos which each featured a health topic like: ulcers, the heart, etc. to use in her study on The Human Body and all for a discount price. The videos were two dollars each!

During our study on The Civil War, we went to a Civil War re-enactment. They had suttler vendor tents where people were selling books, uniforms and other Civil War memorabilia. We found some great historical cookbooks from the Civil War and other time periods. This series of cookbooks (published by Foodways Publications), are filled with historical information as well as period recipes.

EXTRAS HELP YOU CAPITALIZE

Children love trinkets and "doo-dads" - little "extras" that add so much to your study. Build models, use historical paper dolls to show what the period clothing looked like, or make your own thematic writing paper (children can do their final drafts for writing assignments on paper with decorative borders or pictures that match the topic and can be colored in - or use stickers or clip art). Most boys aren't too fond of coloring. I allow my son to either place the picture in the notebook without coloring it. If he is really adverse, I tell him to pick one picture from an educational coloring book in our topic, (he usually picks a battle scene!) and tell him he must color THIS picture throughout the entire study, a little each day, while I read aloud. Sometimes we laminate something special a child has prepared or cover it with contact paper so they can save it in their notebooks. Use stencils or stickers for the younger children. Dover Books carry stickers and stencil books in a variety of topics for only one dollar. These "extras" require little or no work at all on your part and make such a difference to the children.

CAPITALIZE ON THE CONTEXT/CONTEXT STUDIES

Context studies help you take a topic from your reading material and explore it further so you would take time out to explore! For instance, if you were reading *The Golden Goblet* while studying ancient Egypt, your children might become interested in learning more about gold and the art of goldsmithing. Take a couple of days and do a context study - take a trip to a jewelry store, research the different gold rushes in history, see what God's Word says about gold, find out the current value of gold, and look up the symbol for gold in the periodic table. You might or might not want to make a little notebook or folder for your study. Also, you could make a section in your Ancient Egypt notebook and label It Gold.

The hidden message of a context study is that there is always more to learn.

(Clay and Sally Clarkson, *Educating the WholeHearted Child*
[Walnut Springs: Whole Heart Ministries, 1996], 114).

STEP-BY-STEP PLANNING

Now you are ready to start planning... step-by-step. There is a rumor going around saying that unit studies require too much planning, but they really can be quite easy! Once you have chosen the avenue you wish to use (which we discussed in "Options to Consider") you can start planning your unit study. This can be done quickly, easily, and stress free using what I call my "Quick, Easy Stress-Free Planning Method" (QESFPM)! Though you may be an old pro at unit studies, if you've been struggling in the area of planning, the following method will help you understand how to simplify the process. Try doing a "mock" planning session as you read step-by step.

Warning!

Planning is always an issue. Universally, moms are concerned over this and feel that planning a unit study is stressful and difficult, but once I discovered the problem areas with unit studies, it has helped me so much in the area of planning! Stay tuned for help!

Newsflash!

Here's the news of the day regarding planning. Ready? If you study your topics as history OR science, then this solves a lot of the work where planning is involved. I mentioned this earlier, but if you are trying to fit a subject (just for the sake of "getting it in" or because you think your supposed to), but it ends up either not really fitting in or creating a lot of extra work for the one planning it... my advice is, then don't. Just leave it out and let the topic stand alone as history or science.

Where to start:

- Choose your topic.
- List sub-topics (bubble diagram).
- Determine the length of your study. (Can it be divided by weeks?)
- Combine your list of areas to study to corresponding activities. (Write up assignment sheets.)
- Find out what's available in unit study materials, publishers, etc.
- Select and gather materials. (Your books will help you plan the rest.)
- Make your rough plan. (Length, schedule, activities, etc.)

ALLOT YOUR PLANNING TIME

Planning is the key to stress free, worry-free units because when you have it all laid out before you, it is easy to see how the whole unit will proceed. Time spent on planning prepares you to present a successful unit study with confidence. Most of the time, I spend only a couple of hours on the actual planning; and there have been times when I did the main core of my planning the night before - but please bear in mind that I can do this because of years of experience! The more you do it, the easier it gets and you'll find that even after three or four unit studies you will become a pro!

PICK YOUR TOPIC

For your first unit study, choose a topic you know something about and keep the study fairly short in duration. Otherwise, refer to your annual plan and pick the next topic you would like to study. Remember, if you choose uncommon topics, you may have a difficult time finding books and resources.

Your next step is to decide whether this study is going to be in-depth - one where you would need to spend more than four weeks. Refer to our sample Planning Grid for the topic "Pilgrims" which lasted four weeks.

LIST SUB-TOPICS

If you are designing your own study, the next step in our QESFPM is to organize your study into sections or sub-topics. Some topics cannot be divided up in such a way to make sense and work smoothly,but if it is possible to divide it up, it really helps with planning. Again, your books often help organize your study. Listing sub-topics uses the planning tool we call brainstorming.

Our study of ancient Greece divided easily into time periods. To further break it down, we zeroed in on one specific period and divided it into: Greek society (food, clothing, etc.), Theater, (drama/comedy), Olympics, Philosophy, Famous people, Architecture, and Religious beliefs (gods and goddesses). I divided the study of Birds into (1) Types: ground and game birds, sea birds, birds of prey, etc. (2) Characteristics: feathers, beaks, feet, wings, and (3) Habitats: woodlands, marshes, and seaside.

BRAINSTORMING

The purpose of the brainstorming session is to allow you to think of **everything** that relates to your topic. You may be surprised at how extensive this list can get. Because it is easy to "get carried away," set parameters for all your grand ideas! Once you have "brainstormed," you can begin to narrow down the list to what you wish to teach. Obviously, if you included everything that pertains to the study, it could become too involved and take too much time both in planning and conducting the study.

Try to have someone else brainstorm with you. Ask your husband, friend, or children to brainstorm with you. For me, it is the driving force that makes my brain gears start moving and that person doesn't even have to contribute a thing, but it "makes" me get busy.. Their presence tells my brain it must begin to work.

USING A BUBBLE DIAGRAM

You will find a sample of a Bubble Diagram from a brainstorming session on Pilgrims in the Appendix. This is just a tool to help put your thoughts and findings down on paper so you can see it in all in one place. Once you see how much you could study, it makes it easier for you to decide what part you'd like to include. Your bubble diagram can be huge so please don't let this information overwhelm you - it is meant to decrease the stress of planning... not add to it.

To make a bubble diagram, just use a blank sheet of paper and write your topic in the center. As you think of things you could study which relate to the topic, place them n the field around your unit study topic and draw bubbles around them. As you look at the sample, notice our sub-topics categorize things which played an important part in the lives of the Pilgrims and their journey to the New World.

This list of sub-topics includes:

| Religion | Sea Travel | Cultures |
| Geography | Food | |

If you know something about the topic you've chosen to study, it will help you with brainstorming If not, gather your materials and books and begin to look over them so you can get a feel for the information that can be taught. There is no right way to make a bubble diagram. It belongs to you and is only a planning tool. You can start one, scratch it out, throw it away, and start over again. Your bubble diagram demonstrates the thorough job of teaching that can be accomplished by unit studies and helps you see how you can explore many of the different aspects of your topic.

For Pilgrims we used the book *Stories of the Pilgrims* published by Christian Liberty Press as a read-aloud title, *If You Sailed on the Mayflower* by Ann McGovern and *Daily Life in a Pilgrim Plantation* by Paul Erickson as our nonfiction source used during information time. These included needed information for all areas listed on our bubble diagram. You can usually find the information from your stack of books used during planning to make your bubble diagram together with any topical guide or curriculum you are using.

WHAT WORKS FOR YOU?

We have found the bubble diagram a helpful tool in planning, but be comfortable and use whatever works for you. Many times I just scratch my thoughts on a blank paper and then transfer them to a "planning sheet" where my plans begin to take shape. My planning scratch sheet for a Westward Movement study looked something like this:

Areas to study - Events involved with and leading up to Westward Movement:

Louisiana Purchase - Lewis & Clark Expedition - Exploring the West (mountain men and trappers) - Geography (mountain ranges, prairie, rivers, etc.) - trails, Pioneer Life - Indians/Buffalo -The Homestead Act - Types of homes built (soddy, log cabin, etc.) - Wagons (types of, provisions, etc.) - People (pioneers, frontiersmen, cowboys, The Donner Party, Laura Ingalls Wilder, Mark Twain, etc.) - The Pony Express - The Gold Rush - The Railroad.

Further notes might include: ideas for writing activities, group acitivities, assignments to place on assignment sheet, field trips, arts and crafts, cooking, etc. I discovered these "areas to study" by purusing through the stack of books (both collected over time and added to our home library and borrowed from the public library).

CHOOSE AND GATHER MATERIALS

Once, you have decided what to study, you can begin to gather your materials. If you're using a prepared guide or curriculum, refer to their resource lists for suggestions on books to use. People often ask me how I know which books to use. Here are some guidelines:

- The recommendations of other teachers or homeschooling moms.
- Look through homeschooling catalogs (they arrange books by topic and usually carry Christian resources you can count on).
- Experience - the more you are "around" books, the more familiar you will be with authors, publishers, and series.

Chapter Four is devoted to books and includes many suggestions for gathering quality materials and unit study treasures. I've also listed some favorite publishers there.

When I refer to the term "materials", I am mostly refering to all kinds of books but since we approach our studies from many different angles, we use stickers, stencils, (especially for younger students), models, video and audio tapes, hands-on trinkets, brochures, magazines as well as lots of books!

Try to select one or more books (nonfiction, in most cases) to serve as a main source of information. As mentioned, this book will present ideas for ways to divide the information into sections or areas to teach. As I pour over my materials I begin to see a sensible way to organize the material. I am always amazed at how many ideas I get just from looking over my books. As your plans come together for a specific unit study, you may find different activities which can be put into slots to do on a certain day which happens to correspond to the information you are covering.

The book I used when planning a Human Body study, divided the information into sections about body systems. This helped me determine how many systems to present each week. When I planned a unit on Pilgrims I found I could teach "'life in Engalnd" one week, "life in Holland" the next, "life on the Mayflower and life in the New World" the third week and ended by planning a "feast" for the last week. For Musical Instruments I broke the study into groups: Woodwinds/Brass, Percussion, Strings, and Keyboard. Often it is possible to organize your material by studying from the smallest to the largest (i.e. animals, plants, etc.) or chronologically (i.e. Westward Movement events: The Louisiana Purchase, Lewis and Clark Expedition, Explorers of th West - Mountain men and Trappers, Trails West, Pioneers Life, Gold Rush, Pony Express, Transcontintal Railroad). I enjoy teaching unit studies so much, I seem to turn everything into a unit study and can't go anywhere without thinking, "This would make a great study!" A couple came to our church to put on an evangelistic program and the story line was centered around the Erie Canal. I leaned over and told a friend, "I can see a study on the Erie Canal coming up!" Another time we took a trip to San Francisco to talk with my relatives from Italy about our family history - having just studied Immigration. We know we were going to be returning to the city again soon and could make a little "fiield trip" out of it. I took that opportunity to conduct a mini unit study on the history of San Francisco using a few books I found in a museum gift shop.

Some of the books were:

- A children's book about the San Francisco earthquake and fire.

- A copy of an authentic newspaper from the earthquake.

- A booklet with actual photos of the earthquake.

- A pictorial history of San Francisco then and now.

- An educational coloring book.

- A kids' activity book chock full of information and activities connected with the city.

- Postcards, maps, and brochures to use in notebooks.

I always say **"It is really the books that make the study!"** Truly, my stack of books and materials are what inspire me when planning a unit study. I know what you're thinking, "'YOU can come up with ideas because you are the creative type. But I know I would just sit there and stare at the pages!" This is not true - once given a few helpful hints and guidelines, I see moms blossoming and gaining confidence to create their own studies all the time! One of the things I have moms do when I teach our one day Unit Study Workshop, is to pass around stacks of books to groups of moms to brainstorm ideas by looking over the books. You'd be surprised at the wonderful ideas they come up with - things I didn't even think of!

Soon you will begin to think "UNIT STUDY" and you'll start to see "things" of value which you could use to enhance a study to help bring it to life. Whenever I "spotlight" a unit study at our monthly unit study meeting, I bring lots of the resources we used during our study to show. The moms sit in eager anticipation as I share about each book, model, magazine article, coloring book, map, etc. Being mostly visual, tactile creatures, our children also look forward with eager anticipation when I introduce a new study and bring out all the "goodies" we will be using. It's really the books!

I admit, I have a problem with books - you might call me a "book-a-holic!" But then, you're probably one too, aren't you? See, I can't decide which book looks best because one has something great but then the other one has something else that is really great - so I must have them both! In fact, during our Medieval

Times study, the librarian said frowining at me over her glasses, "I think you have taken out ALL the books we have on this subject!" I used them to help me plan and after a few days, then I returned the ones I didn't need. I noticed that our library implemented a policy allowing a person to only check out three books under one Dewey Decimal System number!

To choose a read aloud title (and other books):

- Pray and ask God to show you good books. The Lord might lead you to the recommendation of others, homeschool supplies catalogs, a book fair, a literature guide, or the library computer system seraching your topic. (Search the topic and the age. Example: Medieval fiction/juvenile.)

- Use the Internet as a resource.

- Try to devise an annual plan so you know future topics you're going to study so you will know what to look for.

If you have an annual plan, you will know, ahead of time, about future units you intend to teach, so you will be able to gather materials along the way for these units.

MAKE A LIST OF CORRESPONDING ACTIVITIES

Once you have organized your study into subtopics, add ideas for activities in each area of study. There should be a balance of writing assignments (compositions, creative writing, poetry, etc.), research, hands-on visual aids to add to the student's notebook, a field trip, a video, experiements, reading (dictation, spelling/vocabulary, etc.).

Use Literature Guides like:

- *Books Children Love* by Elizabeth Wilson
- *Honey for a Child's Heart* by Gladys Hunt
- *Teaching Children* by Diane Lopez
- *Hand That Rocks the Cradle* by Nathaniel Bluedorn
- *Great Books of the Christian Tradition* by Terry Glaspey (upper level)

Dividing the study of Creation Science into sections/four weeks:

Creation	Evolution	The Flood	Dinosaurs/Fossils

Additional activities:

Experiments - Boil a whole chicken until the bones fall apart. When cool, have the children try to assemble the chicken bones. This activity helps children understand how scientists reassemble dinosaur bones.

Hands-on visual aid - Make a map of the world with a key showing where dinosaur bones have been found.

A writing assignment - Write an argument defending creation or disproving evolution.

Handwriting - Copy scripture pertaining to creation - God's handiwork.

Projects - Build a box model complete with dirt, plants, and dinosaurs and reenact the flood.

Activity - Do a biographical sketch on Charles Darwin.

Reading Aloud - Read chapters from Adam and His Kin.

Silent Reading - Read a chapter in It Just Couldn't Happen.

Videos - Watch a video from Creation Scientist Kent Hovind (www.drdino.com). Older students take notes.

Research - Research the names of all known dinosaurs. List important facts about each kind. Alphabetize the list.

Activities listed should be carried out in conjunction with the correct section listed above. When planning, I list the corresponding activities into three categories: (1) those we will study in our "information time;" (2) those which work well on the assignment sheet for students to do on their own; and (3) those we can do in a unit study co-op.

PLAN TO INCLUDE YOUR PRESCHOOLERS

This next section will be devoted to discussing how you can teach your young children using unit studies. Many parents of young children ask "How old do my children need to be in order to start teaching them? What is a preschooler?" Any child who is not in school yet. Preschoolers are full of energy and curiosity adn this is a prime time to begin teaching, but we need to be ready for eager early learners and patient with late bloomers. Parents need to be discerning about the uniqeness of each child and their readiness to learn. When you are doing a regular unit study with older children, include preschoolers by planning activities in which they can also participate. They like "doing school," too.

Some of the basic early skills can be incorporated into a "preschool unit study" including:

- Introducing letters.
- Learning upper and lowercase letters.
- Numbers and counting.
- Colors and shapes.
- Clock/time.
- Calendar and seasons.
- Sorting or classifying.
- Order (first, next, last).
- Size (big/small).
- Learning to obey and follow directions.
- Learning to recognize their name (write it?).
- Alphabet and beginning phonics.

EXPLORATION AND DISCOVERY

Teaching children in the early years should be fun. Their wide-eyed faces are ready to explore and learn, but notice I did NOT say they are ready to sit still! Most everything children learn at this age is through exploring, so place your emphasis on taking nature walks and remember to tune in to your surroundings (wherever you are), pointing out and explaining things to them.

A unit study for preschoolers will look different than for elementary grade students. People often ask us what we have available in unit study guides for preschoolers. We might say "There isn't much available - because you don't really need much!" If you are looking for a unit study curriculum especially geared for young children, check out "Five in a Row" - a literature based unit study. We always suggest studying nature topics like: ants, penguins, whales, bees, farm life, gardening and topices like these which allow you opportunities for lots of hands-on activities and things to "do." History topics like Pilgrims, Trains, Children around the World, George Washington, etc., are great for young children and you will find plenty of books at their level.

Since young ones generally do not read or write at this age, the world of exploration will be theirs. For example, bring your preschoolers into the kitchen and let them help you cook or bake. Or you can buy them some seeds and help them plant them outdoors. Get them an ant farm and read some books about ants. Give them some chores like feeding the pets and learn about cats, dogs, aquarium fish, and tropical birds. Take them to the zoo and read books about animals.

It is easy to leave your little ones out of your study because they might seem too young and disinterested in the topic, but you can simplify most unit study topics for young children and present basic teaching they can digest and can participate at their own level - right along with the rest of the family.

At the present time, I am schooling my youngest child, Laurel (or as she calls hereself - Lo Lo), at the kindergarten level. So far this year we have studied topics like Aztecs, Trees, and Ancient Egypt and though she has been learning many of the basi skills (listed above), I found that I was "leaving her out" of our study. For this reason, we decided to study two topics at the end of the year, just suited for her: Butterflies/Insects and then Farm Life.

Get a few books, incorporate exploration and discussion; add in some read-aloud times, some art, music and a few hands-on projects, and you have a preschool unit study! There are so many ways to include the little ones!

READING

If you want your children to love books and reading and to discover how fun it is to learn, this is the time to start. Begin reading to your little one to introduce and develop a love for books, reading and literature. Read picture story books, the juvenile section of the library is full of them. I call these PICTURE STORY BOOKS because there are more pictures than words. You will find these in the JE section of the library. Choose books, both fiction and nonfiction, which are geared to younger children.

NOTEBOOKS

You've read the section in Chapter 2 on notebooks and there is just too MUCH to say on the subject of notebooks so we've directed you to our Notebook Package for more help. Let me just say DO NOT exclude your preschoolers from the notebook project! Once they see brother or sister working with a notebook, they REALLY want to have their own binder and they want to have lots of papers in it! I personally don't do sections for subjects, but what does work great is to divide the notebook into different mini-unit studies. Since the younger children aren't writing much, you can do their writing as they dictate to you what they want to say on broken line, preschool paper and accompanied by their very own pictures. If their motor skills are developed, allow them to copy some words you have written down for them. They also love to color pictures from educational color books or juvenile color books that follow your topic.

A wonderful tool we have recently discovered is that you can go on the Internet. Type in www.google.com and if you were studying birds, you would type in "Birds Coloring Picture," and many options will come up for you to print off. This is a really great resource when you are looking for simple pictures because some educational color book pictures are too detailed for young learners.

Another fun tip for young children is to put pictures of them in their notebooks. They like to see their faces "in print," so think of creative ways and places to use them. For our Solar System study we placed a picture of Anna's face in the bubble helmet of an astronaut suit. When we studied Cowboys we had the kids choose a nickname (because all cowboys have a nickname like Slim or Cookie), and we copied a picture of a cowboy from a book and then placed a photo of their heads onto the picture - so cute!

HANDS-ON ACTIVITIES

Prepare hands-on activities so the children can experience what they are learning. Young children cannot use scissors very well, so plan on helping them cut things out. They ARE good at pasting though, so include lots of stickers and magazine collages for art. They love to paint, draw, color and put things together. Your preschoolers will be happy if you plan just a few activities here and there. Keep watch because little ones tire easily and get bored, so don't go out of your way to include them and force them to "do school" when they are not interested. Send them o their way to play, which they can also learn to do quietly nearby.

BOOKS AND MATERIALS

Remember to collect some items for your preschool age children when you are collecting books and "thematic" treasures for your studies. Getting their hands involved making and doing will help cement what they are learning. Remember...

> # Tell me, I forget.
> # Show me - I understand.
> # Let me DO and I remember!

PLAN TO ADD FIELD TRIPS

Field trips MAKE the study come alive and they are a great way to end or culminate your study. There are usually a number of options for places to visit for most topics that would correlate with your study. We don't always fit a field trip in, but we try whenever we can!

Plan the trip:

- Make a list of possible places to visit that would enhance your Unit Study topic.

- Call to ask if they offer tours and, if so, the cost, number of students and adults required, etc.

- Try to keep your group small if possible. When you have too many people, it can detract from the trip's purpose and any learning you hope the children will gain (i.e. too much noise, children can't see, distract each other).

- Arrive on time.

Preparing your children for a field trip:

- To get the most out of the field trip, try to read books and look at pictures realting to the field trip. Explain what they might see and hear.

- Tell them you expect them to learn something. They need to take notes, ask questions, etc.

- Remind them about their behavior and that they are representing the Lord, homeschooling, and their family. This is a good time to teach them proper conduct and manners.

- Talk to the person in charge of scheduling tours. Make sure you get their name to avoid a mix up when you arrive (like saying they never heard of you!). Let them know you are a homeschooling family or group.

- Arrange a date and time.

- Poor weather or other factors might affect your plans, so on the day prior to your trip, or the morning of the tour, call to confirm your trip (and, again, to make sure they don't say they've never heard of you! It has happened to me!). Weather or other factors might affect your plans.

- After the field trip, plan to talk about the different things you saw and learned. You could even make up a sheet which students can fill out and save.

- Have the children write "thank you" notes to let the tour guide or organization know how much they enjoyed the trip and learned from the experience.

PLAN TO TAKE PICTURES

Take pictures of your students while on field trips and then place them into their study notebooks. Use the reproducible template in our resource guide, **Everything You Need to Know to Build a Unit Study Notebook**. Make copies on colored cardstock and then paste your photos onto the sheet and place in your notebook. Lines are provided to write a description of the picture. This is such a great addition to the child's notebook and helps make it truly an educational keepsake. Those little ones grow up so fast, in a few short years you'll love having those pictures to look back on.

This picture is of _____
Our trip to Yellowstone _____

This picture is of _____
Some buffalo we saw _____

PLAN TO AVOID CONFLICTS
AS THE FIELD TRIP COORDINATOR

If you are the field trip coordinator for your homeschool group and plan a field trip, you MUST be emphatic with your instructions regarding the field trip, fees, deadlines, required numbers, age limitations, sign-ups, etc., especially if you are dealing with large numbers. It can be a difficult job for the one coordinating as you may seem like "the bad guy" because you have to be so firm about the guidelines for the field trip.

As you may already know from experience, you will find those who can't make a commitment, drag their feet, don't return phone calls, and complain about everything! In order to have a positive experience for everyone - including the one who is doing the work coordinating - you must set your guidelines making known what is required (offered in a firm, but loving spirit of kindness!) and the stick to your guns!

Field Trip Resource:

The A-Z Guide to Home School Field Trips by April Purcell, Elizabeth and John Gaunt and Ross Tunnell. Edited by Gregg Harris. Ideas for field trips are offered alphabetically in this book. It also includes "Tips from Barnabas" or a biblical application for each place you visit.

PLAN FOR UNSUPERVISED LEARNING TIMES

Plan to have some other things in your "back pocket" that your children can do that have value… things they can do while you are occupied elsewhere in the house. We don't want to create what I would call busy work - time fillers or fluff! But rather what we can call unsupervised learning times. These might include looking through nonfiction books on the study topic, watching an educational video, playing a computer game or using a computer resource and so on.

PLAN ON USING AN ASSIGNMENT SHEET

I used to be frustrated with unit studies because I had so many other things to get organized in regard to my home and family before I could feel ready to start school for the day. Remember in chapter one I gave you an example of what our daily school schedule might look like starting each day with our Bible time, followed by the read aloud time, then going right into the information time, reading from nonfiction books on our topic. Many times I have either planned something to do in a subject area that "connects" to what we just learned (which is an idea I got from a planning guide/curriculum) OR I may have thought of something while I was just reading to them.

Information Time usually takes us up to lunch time, but if we still have some time and I don't have something planned, the children can do an assignment listed on their Assignment Sheet. Also, some mornings I am not quite ready to start the study, so I tell my children to get their "basics" out, which they can work on by themselves. These basics consist of their Math and Phonics workbooks and their silent or independent reading time - plus a few other things they work at on a less consistent basis.

Using Assignment Sheets is another pillar in our concrete framework. Before we made this discovery, I found that I would lose the continuity of my study time if my children had to wait for me to come up with the next thing they needed to do. In no time, they would wander away to play or start wrestling with each other on the floor! Chaos quickly ensues without a plan and the Assignment Sheet solves the problem.

Now I can't take credit for the idea of assignment sheets, but they have really revolutionized unit studies for me. Now, instead of having to stand over my children, they can continue because they have some directions. So what exactly is an Assignment Sheet? This is a sheet you make up during your planning time… listing assignments - arranged by subjects - for your students who are able to follow directions and work independently (usually 3rd-4th grade). There are many parts of a study children can do on their own and the Assignment Sheet allows for this. Not only is it a great help for me to keep my kids moving and on track, but they like it, too. Often they really desire to have a check off sheet so they can work in a more self-directed way. As you create your planning guides, you will be able to determine which assignments and activities your students could do on their own.

The assignments I list on the sheet are things my children can do apart from our read aloud and information times. This Assignment Sheet doesn't include ALL unit study activities because there will be other things you do together.

I try to make my Assignment Sheet at the very beginning of our study. If I do, the study goes more smoothly. I start by listing assignments for the oldest child I am teaching and then simplify or eliminate assignments for the younger ones. The work your older students do will be more advanced and they will have more assignments than the younger ones. You CAN make an Assignment Sheet for younger children, but since they can't read or understand the directions, it will really be something which will help keep you on track as you refer to it for ideas for assignments you will have to initiate with them.

Some mothers like to provide an Assignment Sheet for their students on a weekly basis. I prefer to do the work once for the whole month (because I'm lazy!). Though some subjects will differ from unit to unit, you can list assignments by school subject: Bible, Writing, Art, Activities, Geography, Handwriting, etc. A helpful tip for moms when writing up assignments is to list the subjects that students have made in their notebook section divider tabs. This helps the students to know which section their work should go into when it is completed. You'll have to decide what you require of your child in regard to finishing assignments, but I allow my children to complete the assignments in any order they wish - as long as they are doing them and not saving them until the last week!

I suggest you leave some blank spots on the Assignment Sheet because as the study progresses, you will always get some new idea or some great things to add, but if you give your kids too much, they will protest! If you already do unit studies, you kow they can sort of "evolve," taking on a different shape, with new ideas popping up as you read through your books. Some kids like to have a lot to do. Go with each child's ability and interest and either add them to the Assignment Sheet and let them do all of them, or just pick the ones they are most interested in. If they complain too loudly, eliminate some.

Remember... THERE ARE NO RULES!

Benefits to using Assignment Sheets:

- When added to the notebook, Assignment Sheets serve as a record of accomplishments.

- Students enjoy being able to follow through as they complete each assignment and check it off.

- Children won't be able to use the excuse, "I don't know what to do."

- The study is well organized, which relieves stress and helps Mom feel that her time is well spent as she sees her children accomplishing necessary academics and learning skills.

Where do you get the ideas to put on the Assignment Sheet?

You will either get your ideas from a teacher's thematic planning guide, your unit study curriculum, or if you are creating your study from scratch - you will come up with the ideas during your brainstorming sessions, often getting ideas as you look over your books. You can also get ideas from the Internet by looking for unit study ideas on your topic. For example: type in Lewis and Clark Unit Study and you'll be amazed what you find.

A question which often arises concerning unit studies/Assignment Sheets is, "How do you know if you are doing enough or doing too much?" Experience will help you determine the answer to this question for each child. While we want to always challenge our child's ability and skill level so they can advance at a reasonable pace. We certainly don't want to overwhelm them or push too hard, especially if it is for the sake of what "looks good" or because we're worried about where we think they should be. Remember it is up to us to foster delight and not create stress brought on by OUR fears. We start worrying how our children compare to others academically. Remind yourself often that one of the benefits of home education is to allow each child to progress at their own pace without pressure. Undue pressure kills delight for learning. So often it is the fearful parents who temporarily forget their goals and start to "drive those little doggies!" Soon the doggies get bored and begin to complain and, after a time, we are zapped back into reality, let go of our fears, trust the Lord once more and go back to what we KNOW works.

Since THERE ARE NO RULES, follow these Guidelines:

- Consider age and ability level and the length of the study.

- Observe your child - give them plenty to do as you can always eliminate items from the list.

- We must examine our children's responses - are they delighting in the study or complaining? If they are complaining, we must determine if they are complaining about their work because they can't do it or because they are lazy.

If they follow you around the house telling you things they learned - you haven't a worry. Follow your heart and enjoy the JOY. Don't worry about what you might not be doing… enjoy the fruit of what you ARE doing!

In Summary - A Recap About Planning

Planning Your Year:

1. Evaluate what's been learned - if using unit studies, consider what you've already covered. If you are taking your child out of another program, evaluation is necessary.

2. Plan ahead and decide - if you'll study history chronologically, how many history/science/ literature or other topics you want to do in a school year.

3. Choose a schedule that works for your family.

4. Decide if any of you will conduct any of your studies in a co-op.

    Try to figure:

    - Number of weeks on and off.

    - Number of days to do unit studies in each week (3 to 4, etc.).

    - A general plan on how your school day will go - Bible first, read aloud next, information together time, break, look up vocabulary words, children do silent reading while Mom works on phonics with younger child. Children work on an assignment from Assignment Sheet, etc.

    - How many units you hope to do this year - length of units.

5. Make an annual plan for units by choosing a balance of: history, science, literature or other topics. Start out using scratch paper, bubble diagrams, planning sheets, big picture plan, etc. Once you have your annual plan, transfer all of your plans onto one sheet and put into your plan book.

Books

4

If you want to get a job done right, you need to have the right tools. Since good books are an important tool for unit studies, knowing how and where to obtain them is crucial. Books will become like your right hand when you're trying to delight your students with unit studies, so use these tools to their fullest potential.

What you need to know:

- How to use the library.

- How to build your own home library.

- How to recognize a book that has value.

- Where to obtain good books.

- Why look for older books.

- What distinguishes a "Living Book?"

It's Really the Books That Make the Study:

It really IS the books that make the unit study. I can't say enough about books and hhow a growing stack of books about one topic can get everyone excited about starting that study! Our family has a pretty impressive home library, but I have a friend whose home library is five times (at least) the size of mine. You can imagine that for me, going to her home is like going to a candy store! I love going to the library, but what's so great about my friend's library is that she is a Christian homeschooling mom, so I can trust that her choices and recommendations are dependable! (You can, too, since she has a bookstore! Check out - www.buriedtreasurebooks.com!)

Using the Library

The library is an important asset for unit study lovers since one cannot possibly afford to purchase all the books you might like to use for a unit study. Allowing children to spend time at the library will help them foster a love for learning. When I was a child, the library seemed dull and boring because I had not yet developed a love for reading and learning. Since then, I have been introduced to the exciting world just waiting to be explored behind all of those book covers. In fact, almost anything I would want to know can be found by searching through books.

Children love to have their own library card… It's like having their own driver's license. A library card helps teach children that with responsibility comes certain privileges. I remember the smiles of anticipation on our children's faces as they reached the age to have their own card.

Watch out for past due books. (Right now, we're hunting for "Benjamin Franklin," he's overdue again.) Some libraries charge as much as $.25 per day. By all means, however, don't let this deter you from using the library. My husband jokes, "Have we given enough money yet to add the west wing to the library?"

You can avoid overdue fees by following a few guidelines:

- Set a limit for the number of books each child can check out.
- Count the number of books you check out.
- Choose a spot on a table where children can replace books when done.
- Mark the number of library books and their due date on your personal calendar.

Children love to have their own library card because it's sort of like having their own driver's license. It will help teach children that with responsibility comes certain privileges. I remember the smiles of anticipation on our children's faces as they reached the age to have their own card. I can also remember the shocked look when they could not find a book and had to help pay the overdue fine! Keeping library books in a designated spot helps us keep track of the books. It also helps save time looking for books when we are ready to use them for our study.

Sometimes it is hard to find books you are looking for and even the biggest and best libraries will not have some books. If you are looking for specific books your library doesn't own, you can request the library to get titles for you. If your library participates in an interlibrary loan program, you may be able to request books from other libraries nationwide. If you will primarily be using library books to plan your unit studies, try to make a special trip without the children. Your ability to concentrate will help make the whole planning experience much more positive. You can do much of this from home using the internet.

Library Resources:

How to Create Your Own Unit Study by Valerie Bendt. Includes a 16-page section called "A General Guide to the Reference Section of the Children's Department of the Public Library."

The Ultimate Guide to Homeschooling by Debra Bell. This book includes a categorized list of the Top 150 Titles Available at Your Local Library which you can utilize as a helpful unit study resource.

BUILDING YOUR OWN HOME LIBRARY

It is really hard to get out to the library with any regularity. You have to set time aside and usually the children want to go - which is a good thing, but it can be stressful when you are trying to concentrate and get the books you want. Because of this, I suggest you begin collecting your own books, building and filling up your own home library. As one of the most valuable tools a family can have, a home library will not only provide you with treasures at your fingertips, but will also provide a lasting heritage for the next generation of home-educated people in your life - your grandchildren! **<u>Building up your own library with good books is one of the most valuable tools a family can have</u>**.

The dynamics of our family life, combined with the way we study, makes having a home library a necessity. Even a quick trip to the library means grabbing the shoes and coats, getting everyone out of the house and into the car, and driving to town. We don't have "naptime" anymore but when we did, I had to juggle this with our small town library hours. A trip to the library interrupts our school day and even if we have good intentions of returning to our studies when we come home, we seldom do.

We've been adding books to our shelves for years and have quite a variety so we can just walk across the room and have needed information at our fingertips. I know what certain books contain so we are constantly pulling them from the shelves to use in our studies. One book might picture has a great picture of this, a needed diagram of that. I obtained a booklet on Lewis and Clark and as I leafed through it I noticed an original copy of the letter President Jefferson wrote when he sent them on the famous expedition. Later, when we studied Westward Movement, I remembered the document so we grabbed the book and made a copy of the letter for their notebooks! When Cacey was looking for information about the digestive system she found all she needed right at her fingertips, in a book entitled *The Incredible Machine* - a book purchased for one dollar at a thrift store!

Once the word gets out that there's a library in your home, others will want to borrow your books. I prefer not to loan books simply because we DO use our books frequently - especially reference type books. If you decide to loan your books, set some rules about how long they are on loan, what condition you'd like them to be returned in and so on. When I do loan a book I make sure our name is written inside the cover and I also tape down any tattered bindings before they go out. It is common courtesy to take good care of books and return them in the same condition, so express that you would like your books cared for.

When you begin to build your own home library, you will wonder which books you should acquire. You really will develop a real "trained eye" for choosing the right kind of books in no time. You also get to know different series and publishers you like and as you become more and more familiar with them, you will be able to spot them easily.

One good rule of thumb to help you classify "kinds of books" is to think of your silent reading titles and read aloud titles as "stories" and the nonfiction books which I call source books, are the books which contain and provide the bulk of "information" you will use in your study.

Read aloud = Story   Source books = Information

RECOGNIZING A GOOD BOOK

People ask me how I can tell if a book is a good one - it comes with the job... being around alot of books all the time!

A quick and easy way to make sure you are getting a "book of value" is to:

- Ask others for their recommendations.

- Get to know series.

- Recognize that "classics" can usually be counted among valued favorites.

- Read the back cover and a few random pages throughout.

- Don't judge a book by its author. Since not all works by the same author can be depended upon to be "good" literature, each book needs to be evaluated individually.

The best way to find a good book is through the recommendation of others. I have been led to many great books this way. You can also be spared from the "not so good books" when friends let you know about books that weren't worthwhile. Over time you will be able to discern propaganda and bias in books. There might be a subtle bias that undermines the Christian family value, has a secular world view, or is evolutionary. I personally have a difficult time detecting an author's bias, but my husband can identify it almost immediately. We are quite selective in choosing books and only have room for GOOD books.

Books Resource

Great Books of the Christian Tradition by Terry Glaspey. A literature guide which recommends
    higher level learning and church history.
Books Children Love by Elizabeth Wilsom
Honey for a Child's Heart by Gladys Hunt
Invitation to the Classics published by Baker Book House

OBTAINING GOOD BOOKS

Book hunting is a fun family hobby. There are many places you can find good books:

- The library.

- Your grandmother's bookshelf.

- Nationwide book search by used bookstores (www.adall.com).

- Companies who sell homeschool or educational materials.

You can also find books that are worth owning (sometimes whole sets) at flea markets, estate sales, second-hand thrift stores, used bookstores, garage sales, library book sales, and used curriculum fairs. We've even found several books at antique stores even though they are not antiques. Our local used bookstore sells books in good condition for half the new price. Keep a wish list of books you are looking for in your wallet or organizer for quick reference. Also, keep an updated list of books you already own to avoid duplication. The bigger the library... the bigger the list!

Good literature can also be found in Christian homeschooling catalogs or seminars. Many catalogs categorize books into easy-to-find sections: American history, ancient history, biographies - even sometimes displaying pictures of the books they carry. Try to attend homeschool seminars or curriculum fairs. It's nice to see what is available and be able to examine the materials instead of trying to figure out what they are like from catalogs. You can add books to your personal library one at a time without spending a lot of money. I try to exercise some self-control and only come home with one or two books. (An amazing feat for a book lover!)

Many publishing companies provide educational books and series for different age groups. Most of these are secular publications, but instead of "throwing the baby out with the bath water," we just avoid the incorrect information or discuss what is in error.

Companies include:

Usborne	Eyewitness	Living History
Dorling Kindersly	Dover Publications	Christian Liberty Press
Bellerophon Books	The Nature Company Discoveries Library	

Series include:

Historic Communities	Once Upon America	In Their Own Word s
Landmark	The "I Can Read" Books	Cornerstones of Freedom
Scholastic Biographies	New True Books by Children's Press	
	The "*If You...*" series mostly by Ann McGovern	

Most children love books with pictures - me too! It's true… a picture IS worth a thousand words! Many of the books I've listed are in a larger format and the pages are covered with pictures with accompanying text blocks.

WARNING! Proceed "book looking" with your friends cautiously. If you and your homeschooling friends (who are also book-a-holics) all go "book looking" together, you could end up brawling over the same book! Homeschoolers are vicious when it comes to books and I know because I'm one of them!

LOOKING FOR OLDER BOOKS

The date a book is published should be a determining factor in many of your book choices. You can usually count on books published prior to 1930 to be morally sound and have more of a Christian worldview.

If you look for older books, you will avoid much of the present day propaganda and abide with stories that uphold virtuous values. Perhaps you have noticed in some of the more recent books that history is being rewritten and that America is quickly losing her Godly heritage. Our Godly heritage has been documented and preserved in older literature and I believe that's why schools and libraries are discarding them - for this reason, library book sales are a good place to pick up books. Recently my library discarded a book I often checked out on the American Revolution. They told me I might be able to buy it at the next library book sale so I made the effort to go but could not find it. The lady told me they did not take discards anymore because they don't sell very well. I found out that they put them in the dumpster to be recycled for paper! I was horrified and almost asked if I could go "dumpster diving!"

Older books also support and solidify our resolve to follow Christ because they are laced with a strong moral fabric woven throughout the text, encouraging the reader to acknowledge the Providence of God. It's just the way things used to be. Laying hold of older books is not only an asset to your home library, but in a small way, you are doing your part to preserve truth. Did you know that recent textbooks are saying the pilgrims came to the new world because they liked to sail?

Over the past several years, many family-based Christian ministries have begun to reprint and republish old treasures. Because of their efforts, we are able to obtain some quality books.

Publishers Reprinting Old Treasures

Mantle Ministries   Back Home Industries   Lamplighter Publishers   Beautiful Feet Books

LIVING BOOKS - WHAT SETS THEM APART?

Most references to Living Books are traced to Charlotte Mason, an educator who lived during the first part of this century. She believed Living Books were those that had literary power. To determine whether a book is a Living Book or not is to judge whether it is "lively," or just enduring.

A Living Book stirs emotion, pricks the heart, challenges the mind, and impacts your life. A Living Book is timeless. Such a book would be added to our list of classics. Read the first few pages of the book to your children and see how they react. Remember, Living Books = real life experiences. All novels are not Living Books.

All of the great literary "classics" are whole, living books. They contain stories that feed your child's imagination, touch the heart, and challenge the intellect. They are classics not simply because someone decided they should be, but because they are enduring stories with a life of their own.

(Clay and Sally Clarkshon, Educating the WholeHearted Child
[Walnut Springs: Whole Heart Ministries, 1996] 80)

The chart below outlines the difference between Living Books and textbooks.
(Excerpted from *Educating the WholeHearted Child* by Clay and Sally Clarkson, page 80)

LIVING BOOK	TEXTBOOK
Written by a single author, a real and knowable person.	Written by various authors or contributors, usually unknown.
Literary expression of the author's own ideas and love of the subject	Nonliterary expression of collected facts and information
Personal in tone and feel. Touches the heart, emotions, and the intellect.	Impersonal in tone and feel. Touches only the intellect.
Author addresses the reader as an intelligent and capable thinker.	Looks down on the reader as one needing to be instructed.
Ideas are presented creatively in a way that stimulates the imagination.	Facts are presented without creativity in a way that deadens the imagination.

IT'S NOT JUST A LIBRARY - IT'S A HERITAGE

Reading and collecting good literature means much more than having a home library. If you have used textbooks over the years, by the time your child graduates from high school, you will have acquired quite a collection. These can be sold at a used curriculum fair for one third to one half their original value. However, if you have used Living Books whole books, you will have built a library of lasting value which can be enjoyed by your family and others for generations to come. Perhaps there is another generation of homeschoolers in your future who will need to borrow those books from grandma! Before we know it, our little grandaughter, Elaina, will be over to have Grandma read to her - and I can't wait!

Here's an analogy comparing textbooks to living books:

> You're the boss and you need to hire someone for a job opening so you conduct an interview. The first person comes in and introduces herself. Your first impression, based on her appearance, is that she is cold, stern and not very open. In a monotone voice she beginsto tell you her name, address and some other facts about her qualifications. You can tell she is uncomfortable and wants to get the interview over with quickly. She's just there to do what is necessary, tell you what you need to know so you can decide whether or not she is qualified for the job. It ends up being a brief conversation because you've made up your mind already. When she leaves you think, "She might be qualified to do the work, but she has no personality."
>
> The next person you interview walks through the door bubbling over with enthusiasm. She confidently shakes your hand and takes a seat. She can't wait to start the interview and is relaxed and seems to have all the time in the world. At your first question, she smiles and begins to tell you about herself, her family, and her work background. Everything she says is interesting. You think, "Now, this girl would be an asset to my business. She will help the customers enjoy shopping here and they'll want to come back."

J. Steward

- Now, that's the difference between textbooks and living books. Textbooks are filled with facts students are expected to digest in one sitting. I wonder how students might use allthose facts - even if they could remember them.

- *Heidi* by Johanna Spyri, is a Living Book. We read Heidi as one of our first read aloud books and it DID stir emotion and prick the heart. Morality, integrity, and virtuous living were all qualities portrayed in the characters. This is the standard way of life in most older books. Notice how prayer was an important part of Heidi's day:

"When Heidi was lying that night on her high bed of hay she thought of the grandmother on her low pillow and of all she had said about the light and comfort that awoke in her when she heard the hymns. She thought: "If I could read to her every day, then I should go on making her better." But she knew that it would be a week, if not two, before she would be able to go up the mountain again. This was a thought of great trouble to Heidi, and she tried hard to think of some way which would enable the grandmother to hear the words she loved every day. Suddenly an idea struck her, and she was so delighted with it that she could hardly bear to wait for morning, so eager was she to begin carrying out her plan. All at once she sat upright in her bed, for she had been so busy with her thoughts that she had forgotten to say her prayers, and she never now finished her day without saying them. When she had prayed with all her heart for herself, her grandfather, and the grandmother, she lay back again on the warm, soft hay and slept soundly and peacefully till the morning broke."

(Johanna Spyri, *Heidi* [Chicago: John C. Winston Co., 1924], 211, 212)

Living Books, often historical fiction or biographies, are based on real people and events. They are captivating and the kind of books you don't want to put down.

Steward List of Facts About Living Books

Living Books have helped my children develop a passion for books.

- My children have a passion for living books and never want me to stop reading.
- My children have learned so much (information) from real books.
- Living books have been a key to my children's hearts.
- I'm not nearly as interested in what I see in their heads (information and facts) as what I see in their hearts.

"For a bird, flying is its life and the mother bird must teach that skill.

We can say, "Flying is more important than hearing about flying."

In the same way, we can apply this logic to our own children's learning and recognize that using knowledge is more important than having knowledge."

(Barbara Wagner, *Learning Life's Lessons*
[Washougal: Hewitt Research Foundation,1991], Introduction)

Reading good literature allows you to be carried off into the pages of history as you visit villages, big cities and palaces walking among the wealthy and the poor. There are many ways to bring good literature into you home. You could soak your kids in good literature by letting them fall asleep at night listening to books on tape. One friend gives grandparents a Christmas wish list of books and resources. This way grandparents can shop wisely for family gifts everyone can really use and enjoy. Another way to "soak" them is to let them see how much you love books and reading and make sure lots of books are available to them.

See for yourself and pick up a living book and read it. See if you discover the charm they possess. If you still prefer textbooks, that's okay, just don't use textbooks because you think you must and at least incorporate a read aloud time along with your textbooks! I have heard mothers say they taught from kindergarten through grade twelve using textbooks. They did it ALL. They will argue that students must know all thosedates and events in order to pass college entry tests. Remember your goals. Do you want information in - information out, or do you want children who are fascinated with the world and love to learn?

WHAT BOOKS SHOULD I CHOOSE?

Many of the books you choose will depend on the ages of your children. If you have one child and you start teaching at age nine, you won't need books for early childhood. If you have more than one child and intend to teach them all in the future, try to get books on the same topic for different age levels. Look for books with pictures. Get novels for older kids and easy readers for younger ones.

Dover Publications, Spizziri Publishers and Bellerophon all publish educational coloring books. These aren't juvenile "Boo Boo Bear" coloring books but are black and white line drawings done by talented artists. Each picture is accompanied by an information caption which you can use for teaching. Even if your children aren't fond of coloring, you can use these for reference only as teaching resources.

The great thing about these coloring books is:

- They are inexpensive (just $3-$5 each).

- Numerous topics are available in educational themes.

- They are a great resource for unit studies providing your children with something to do and something visual.

Some publishers give permission to photocopy, which allows the children to use them for reports or include them as pictures in their notebooks. These coloring books also provide a great activity for the younger children to do while you are reading aloud to them. Coloring pictures which show a picture relating to your topic can be a great accompaniment for writing assignments. So, you can put your picture on the left side with the paper you wrote facing it - in your notebook.

Organizing Your Home Library

What in the world are you going to do with all those books? Husbands please build shelves! We started with one large bookcase and soon had a bookshelf in every room of the house! It was such a blessing when we added on a family room and built one whole wall with built-in, floor to ceiling bookshelves.

Organize your home library so that you and your children can access books easily. Start by making a list of books you own. If you carry an organizer, make sure the list is in it to help you avoid duplicating titles you already have. I admit this is too big of a job for me so I just keep a mental record. Very seldom have I bought a book I already have, but when I do I can place it in my "Used Book" section on our website.

I do stress that the children to take good care of our books so we can use them for years to come but I also DO want them to enjoy spending time at the bookshelf looking at books. I have one shelf with books for the little ones which I usually read to them at bedtime. The rest of the shelves contain all other books. The shelves are not labeled, but the children know how the books are grouped.

The different sections are:

- Dictionaries, thesaurus, language arts and grammar handbooks, phonics, writing.

- Bible/church history, character, devotional books, Bible atlas/map books.

- Classics

- "All about books" - Antarctica, Bees, Pond Life, Shells, Submarine.s

- Patriotic books, Government, Presidents, General American history.

- Art, Music, Crafts

- By topic - Ancient Egypt, Ancient Greece, Ancient Rome, Animals, Colonial life, Columbus, Immigration, Pioneers, Rocks & Minerals.

- Geography - atlases, world resources, U.S. and world maps.

- Encyclopedias

- Reference books, textbooks, curriculum, teacher's helps, books about homeschooling.

- Miscellaneous - books that don't fit anywhere else or that I don't have others like it to make it a group or topic.

- Textbooks,"school books and resources," homeschool how-tos, teachers manuals.

Our other "family" books are catagorzied as much as possible: cookbooks, how-to books, landscaping, health and first aid, Chrisitian books etc. The books are placed, basically, where they fit! When I have acquired too many books in one topic, I move them to another shelf where they fit better. All the books and resources in one topic are placed on the bookshelf together. So, we group together silent reading for many ages, read alouds, coloring books, sticker books, thematic guides, nonfiction books, how to draw books on that specific topic, and picture story books.

We have arranged our history and related books on the shelves, chronologically which not only helps with how to organize them but it helps the children find books they need. Over time, if your children use your books often and are accustomed to getting books from the shelves, they will build a mental timeline just from seeing the books in order on the shelves. (Use the chronological list of history topics in Chapter Three to help you arrange your books.)

Smaller books and booklets can get lost so try using plastic magazine organizers for these. Some of my friends use plastic magazine shelf organizers to place smaller items into. A thrifty alternative is to cover sturdy cereal boxes with wrapping paper and use them the same way. It is difficult to keep book bindings dusted and arranged evenly on the shelves so I go through the shelves now and then to tidy things up.

When you no longer need to use a tool, lay it down. For teaching, books are your tools and you can do the same with them. If you have used all the information you need you don't have to finish the book. When you need it again, you pick it back up.

KEEPING YOUR BOOKS ORGANIZED DURING A UNIT STUDY

When the time comes to plan and conduct a unit study, I gather all my books on that topic from our home library shelves. When added to the books borrowed from the public library and other resources, I usually end up with quite a stack. To keep the study organized, I store all of these books in one place. We've found the best place is a large basket I keep by MY chair in the living room. The children know they are supposed to return them to the basket when they are finished using a book. The important thing is to keep them togetherin one place so you don't have to search for them when you are ready to use them.

HOW MANY BOOKS DO I NEED?

I always say, **"A unit study is a stack of ten books."** My unit study lover friends think I'm crazy and say it's impossible to limit a topic or study to ten books. This is just a guideline and I usually have far more than this in my stack! Since you'll probably be studying with varying ages, these materials might include novels or silent reading titles for all age groups, educational coloring books, nonfiction books, "how-to draw" books, books of poetry, a biography and such. I will caution that you can have too many books. At times I've had so many books on a topic that it gets confusing. You thought you saw a map that would be perfect, then you can't find it again!

TAP INTO YOUR BOOKS

One speaking session I present at conventions I call "There's a Teacher Inside You… Let Her Out!" The main point is to help moms gain confidence and see themselves as their childs teacher. Part of this is owning your role of teacher and tapping into the awesome resources contained in books. I can't tell you how many times I've opened a book and found a wonderful map right inside the front cover. The publisher probably put it there just to decorate the inside but you now have a usuable resource at your disposal. Books contain, poems, quotes, maps, diagrams, pictures and so many NEAT things to use in teaching. One children's book we used during our Westward Movement study, had a full color labeled, diagram of a stagecoach. Since we had just seen a real stagecoach on a field trip and learned all about the different parts of it, we copied this picture, used "white out" to erase the labels, then used the diagram to test our knowledge and placed the finished paper in our notebooks under the Geography - Maps - Diagrams section.

USING BOOKS WHEN CREATING YOUR OWN UNIT STUDIES

If you choose this option and are the kind of person who feels comfortable and excited about creating your own unit studies from scratch, it will be your stack of books that helps you plan how you will execute the study and give you ideas for what kinds of skills you can work on and develop and what kind of activities you will include for specific subject areas.

COLLECTING UNIT STUDY TREASURES

Your library can provide other educational treasures. As you become a unit study enthusiast, you will begin to look at life as one big unit study. If you have a long term study plan, you will have an idea for the topics you will be studying in the future. Even without your list, there are some topics you will surely be teaching in the future, such as World Geography, Indians, Plant Life, Space and other common topics. It's the "stuff" that kids can use to make and do that will make learning more interesting and fun so make sure you include these treasures - especially for your younger kids.

Way back when Brooke was turning eight we celebrated her birthday at a Mexican restaurant and she was given a sombrero. Well, of course, I tucked it away for our future World Geography unit. The chopsticks we took home from a Chinese restaurant came in handy too! Maracas for $3 while visiting Old Town San Diego? Yes! I had to get them!

Why am I telling you to clutter up your home with a collection of educational trinkets? Because, if you collect items as you find them, you won't have to search for them when it's time to start a study. When the price is right, pick up those trinkets and treasures, books, and extras.

But really, collecting unit study treasures need not cause a clutter problem. The best way to deal with all your "finds" is to purchase a few put-together cardboard file boxes with lids and label them "Unit tudy Treasures." Compile your treasures by topics in ziploc bags and file folders. Store these boxes in a closet or in the garage where you can get to them easily.

As you can see, books are certainly one of the most important aspect to conducting successful unit studies so now you know EVERYTHING YOU NEED TO KNOW ABOUT BOOKS!

Unit Studies
(5)
and High School

PREPARING YOUR HIGH SCHOOLER FOR THE FUTURE

When the time comes to educate your high school students, please return to your philosophy of education and reevaluate your goals and ideas to see if you still feel the same way about your philosophy now that your children are in high school. You should consider:

- What goals do you have for each child?

- What goals do your students have for themselves?

- What do they want to do after high school?

The answers to these questions will play a big part in how you proceed with planning for high school. Many Chrisitan parents start to panic (or they were panicked from the beginning and it is just time to deal with it), when their children start nearing the junior high years. We are very concerned about this because we believe it is out of fear or pressure (either brought on by ourselves, family, our peers, or society in general) that they begin to struggle with the issue of whether it is still wise and responsible to home school their children throughout high school. So it seems they either never really knew why they were homeschooling, they forgot, or they changed their mind. My challenge to parents who find themselves in this category is to remember the Big Picture of God's purpose for your child and how that might be better accomplished if kept within the context of their family. We must remember that this is more important than all the acadmic accolades or accomplishments they might achieve by going to a conventional school.

The good news is it IS possible for your high school student to use unit studies and still get the best education. You can adapt any subject area to fit your needs. If they have always enjoyed learning through unit study exploration, why should things change because they enter high school? Please don't be intimidated by high school. Before we get there, we tend to think of it as a new, different and scary thing. But once we arrive at the ninth grade and start our whatever program we've decided to use, we find it is really the same thing as what we've always done. It's different in that there is more work, the material is more in depth, the papers are longer and so on, but it is not really not a different thing.

COMPARING HIGH SCHOOL TO ELEMENTARY UNIT STUDIES

High school unit studies do differ from elementary studies. First of all, they do not center around the read aloud time. (you'll find you miss your older kids so make sure you have a "family reading time" in the evening so you can stil enjoy this time together.) The biggest difference falls with the topics they study and the level of work they do - compositional writing, grammar, research, reporting, and so on. Part of this upper level work will come as a result of the books they will use. Cacey groaned when she found one of the units she would be doing was "The Human Body" because we had just done that unit a couple years before. When she looked at the books she was going to be using, she knew it would be a totally different study.

My sister, also a home educator, has taught high school classes for homeschoolers. She has been surprised by the students inability to research and find the answers needed to complete assignments. Many of them have never been taught how to research a topic. This is often the result of those who have been learning (or using) textbooks. Because unit studies are interactive, students are familiar with research, writing, reporting and such. One of my children were so interested in the study of Ancient Egypt they followed me all around telling me about the pharoahs and dynasties. It was helpful to be able to use her notebook a couple years later when we studied it with the younger children. We were able to benefit from her research.

Though our kids still do unit studies in high school, one area of difference is that they are not studying with the rest of the group anymore nor are they (in most cases) doing the same unit study topic. Another thing which is different is that my high schoolers read alot choosing selections from a high school literature list, so often they are not reading a novel which ties into the unit study topic.

There are other "things" or subjects my high school students do as well, but we always keep a unit study going too and remains the "core" even though there are some other areas they are studying and working on. The reason we have a unit study going on (in the background) is that it offers the place where they can accomplish skills/subjects like: geography/maps, writing, research, organizing information learned in various papers, fact sheets, art, history and science.

Some of the other things our kids do besides the unit study they are working on are: foreign language, world geography, government, vocabulary, taking part in a monthly book discussion group (so they read an assigned piece of literature), debate club, math, driver's education and a few other miscellaneous areas. They do not do the things I listed at once.

NOTEBOOKS AND HIGH SCHOOL

It was actually when my first daughter was in high school using Far Above Rubies (for girls), that we were introduced to the use of notebooks. If you enjoy using notebooks and seeing your elementary grade children delight over them, imagine how great they are for high school!

Notebooks can serve an important purpose in high school:

- Notebooks provide a place for students to make contact with their work.

- Notebooks give students a place to document what they learn and do.

- Notebooks allow students to exercise their creative flare.

- Active participation helps students retain the material covered.

- Notebooks can serve as a portfolio if needed for college entrance.

- Notebooks provide a living record for what the student has studied and can be used to help you make up transcripts.

STILL THINK TEXTBOOKS ARE NECESSARY?

If your high school student plans to attend a four year university and major in something MAJOR, the security of a standard textbook may help provide a proficiency in some subject. If you choose to use textbooks for your course of study, I would encourage you to still approach studies from a standpoint of "delight." For example, skim over a chapter in a biology, history or any other textbook with your student to see what is to be learned, then fashion it into a sort of unit study. Students could compile a notebook including section dividers for different chapters of the book. Each section could have pages labeled "Terms to Learn," and include pictures or diagrams of the material discussed. Many of the questions provided at the end of a chapter ask students to do an assignment. Include these assignments in the notebook so the students are allowed to DO something rather than merely read chapters and answer questions.

Remember that all books, including textbooks, are your tools. In fact, textbooks can be very good "source" books.Not only do they offer information on "what to study next" but contain the upper level information needed when doing research. When Cacey was studying genealogy during her Immigration unit, she referred to her biology textbook for information about genes. When she was studying birds, again, she used the textbook to find information about bird family groups, types of feet, beaks and so on. (Most of the textbooks I own were purchased at used curriculum fairs for a very reasonable price.) Use your textbooks to obtain important information, but don't use them as your core of teaching and only source - you'll be back into the mold of going through the motions trying to memorize dry facts.

A friend told me that her tenth grade son (homeschooled all his life) pleaded with her that instead of doing unit studies and ntoebooks, to just lay a stack of textbooks before him so he could get his school work done. She had seen the difference in real learning accomplished through unit studies so she held to her position. To prove her point she had him read a couple of chapters from a textbook. He was astonished by what he found and in his own words described them as "dull and boring!" Not only that but he was also amazed at how little the book had to offer on any one topic.

IN OUR EXPERIENCE...

At the time of this printing, three of our children have graduated from home school high school and our fourth child is in the tenth grade. We have seen many changes in the homeschooling movement and one of them is the vast amount of materials available for all ages including high school. This has not really affected us too much because by the time our kids are in high school, they pretty much "write" or design their own unit studies. I will say the girls did more than my son did but I believe if you've found success in developing a love for learning… this is the result. They don't need a curriculum, they just need books to study topics which you have helped them lay out as a plan for high school. You (the teacher) can look at what they've covered, and what you think still needs to be studied. Some topics they covered, may need to be studied again depending on how long it has been.

Cacey was our first to enter "high school" so we used a unit study curriculum because I didn't want to have to come up with high school level assignments and a scope and sequence for what to study. This program wasn't perfect and we did have to tailor it to our needs but it was helpful to have something to go by. We used a unit study program for boys when Tyson was in high school called *Listen, My Son*. It was laid out in a more simple format than Cacey's but it was also helpful to at least have something to use.

If you are tired of struggling with conventional methods and just now (around the high school years) jumping into unit studies, having high schoolers proceed on their own probably won't apply to you so much since you will need to be more involved with your beginning unit study student.

READY TO FLY?

Our high schoolers are excited to be able to work more independently in the ninth grade, but it has been our experience that they are not quite ready to soar on their own. I have found them sort of floundering out there on their own. So, be advised that they still need you to stay in touch with them (pretty much daily) to keep them on track. They can easily develop a sense of failure - so help them out. My girls were better able to work independently than my son, Ty, who would do whatever I told him but was not able to just go on to the next thing without clear direction each time.

I MISS YOU!

When they enter high school students go off to another part of the house and study by themselves. You'd think they were going off to school but they are just in the next room. Still it's so hard to let them go! It is such a joy to study together that I really do miss them when they are no longer in "my" class! You can imagine how hard is when they get married and leave home! Life is full of seasons of new changes, challenges and blessings. My newest season is having my five year old (and probably my last little one) start school. We are constantly facing new seasons of life and they are all a blessing.

MEET OUR GRADUATES

I thought you might like to meet our three high school graduates. From left to right…

I'd like to tell you a little about what we did in high school for our three older kids. Of course, Cacey was first so she was sort of our guinea pig! I mentioned that we used Far Above Rubies for her and liked it pretty well. The curriculum is set up so you can complete it in three to five years and Cacey wanted to graduate in three so we allowed her to. Unless there was a good reason to do this, I would not do it again because she really had to press herself to do it and it put alot of stress on the rest of the family. When she graduated, she didn't have any real plans and wasn't going to college to seek a career because she knew the Lord had called her to be a wife and mother. Cacey decided to take some enrichment classes at the junior college and did very well. She spent the next few years managing our homeschooling business and was a great asset to me. I remember how much she disliked having to make phone calls but I encouraged her to do it anyway. Guess what she does today? She assists her husband a couple days a week in their very successful software business and she often spends most of the day on the phone! Cacey was a good student and very well read. I would consider her an academic student who excelled in most subjects… maybe not math!

Tyson had the unique opportunity to work with his dad in the construction business so whenever he was needed or had time, he went to work with Jim. Though Ty liked to read, he was not as well read as his sister and I would consider his high school skills to be more "remedial" and not so academic. He was bright and picked up on things quickly but was not a very motivated self starter. Sometimes when we have a kid like this we wonder how they'll do when they have to make it on their own. Well, Tyson is married to Amy and they have a little girl. They own their own home, and though he still works in the construction field with his dad, he runs a side business building bookshelves and custom furniture. Now twenty-two, he has been a deacon at our church since he was eighteen, is loved and respected by other men, is industrious and responsible. I'll tell you more in "Tyson's Story."

Whitney is probably my most academic kid so far. She loves a challenge, loves to write and do research. She is the quote lady around here and is always coming up with some deep thougt or profound quote. She spent a year of high school doing debate and did so well she and her debate partner qualified and participated in the national debate tournament in Tenessee in their first year! She has read more books than I can count and even though she has graduated, I can't keep her out of the library! She still takes part in the monthly book discussion and reads a literature selection for that each month. Whitney is still praying for direction and she would love to go to college just because she'd like a teacher to give her challenging assignments. We (and she) are still not so sure that is the direction the Lord would have for her. She keeps very busy helping Mom with the family, running errands, helps teach Laurel (the five year old), works in a couple ministries at church, works part time locally, and helps out with the debate club.

Please don't think that I am boasting - I give all the glory to the Father but really all of my children love books and learning. How rewarding for me as a mom to hear my kids say "Mom, I don't see how people don't like school!" I don't believe it is because of ME - I believe it is because years ago when I was about ready to give up - the Lord allowed us to find an alternative.

One year on Mother's Day my husband, Jim, had the kids all say something they liked about me. This was a little embarassing for me but as I listened most of them said they liked the fun we have as a family and mom's sense of humor. But what was such a blessing was when each one said something like "I like the way Mom teaches us." They didn't really mean that I had special gifts or abilities - they meant that I work with them interactively and teach through living books. They enjoy the unity of being together and truly learning. The tree of investing in our children's education is yielding good fruit!

Tyson's Story

I would like to tell you a story that has a happy ending which, I think, will inspire you. It is really a "shame on me" story but I hope you may learn by my mistake! I mentioned that when Tyson was in high school he worked with his dad quite a bit. This truly was a great opportunity for him to not only learn all the skills needed for working in the carpentry/construction trade, but he also benefitted so imagine, trying to fit in "school." Many days Jim would say he needed Ty to work with him and I would say, "He needs to stay home and do school!" Other moms would tell me to let him go because math could wait. My problem was if Ty missed what I was doing, I'd have to do again with him when he got home but I didn't have the time or energy to do that in the evening. Ty was in the middle between his dad and me. Soon my relationship with him was suffering because of the stress.

I finally told him he could go ahead and graduate that June but that he "owed" me another year and would have to work all the next year on the side at fulfilling MY requirements for what I thought he needed in order to have a good high school education. That never worked out, he didn't "pay" his dues and with resentment, I released him. I did have a chip on my shoulder - a sort of subconcious attitude of "go ahead and be stupid!" It was horrible.

We've seen that there is an important growing up period between the age of eighteen and twenty one so we don't buy into the idea that a young person is an adult when they turn eighteen. Tyson accepted Christ as his Savior when he was a little boy but during those years he wrestled with his relationship with the Lord and the Lord really drew him unto Himself and Ty came to a full understanding of The Cross. Tyson always had a heart for young people wanting to impress the importance of living purposefully for Christ during the young years not wasting their time. He felt the Lord calling him to put on a conference for teens so he prayed about it, asked his friend (who was also serious about the Lord) if he would do some speaking too. The two of them prepared for three months and I witnessed something amazing!

Tyson bloomed into this studious person as he began to study and apply himself to learning. He spent hours on the computer preparing three talks he'd be presenting. He was making outlines, writing, cross referencing scriptures and looking up words in the dictionary. When the Lord gave him a task, he put all these "skills" to work in one place. I didn't help him at all besides making a few suggestions.

When he was finished he asked me to come down to the church to listen to him practice. I sat there with my mouth open (not really), but he was amazing. When it came time for the conference about eighty kids came and it was so neat, both the guys did very well. I still can't explain it but I would have never guessed that Tyson would be what he is today. Tyson is outgoing - not at all shy. He is a talented hard worker and he has always had great character, but I would never have classified him as a public speaker. He is a very relaxed, natural leader and has done some preaching for our church and is a great leader.

The whole point of my story is that "I" never sought the Lord for how he wanted me to direct Tyson's education. I had decided what he needed to do and learn and had never consulted the Lord about it. The suggestion I have for parents is not that we should abandon our studies and find a way to have our sons go to work with their dad, but that we seek the Lord for direction and see if we can determine our child's bent. Tyson is very bright and his experiences have helped him to be a well rounded man who knows about life, he understands what is important and he is very responsible.

I don't know if you picked up all the "me's" and the "I's" and all the things I wanted for Ty's education! Can you see that this was really a pride issue for me? We need to examine whether the educational goals we have for our children have anything to do with making us look good!

THEN THERE'S BROOKE

I almost forgot to mention Brooke. She is our fourth child and is, at this time, in the tenth grade. Brooke is a very bubbly and delightful girl and like the others, she loves to read, is self- motivated and continues to do unit studies in high school. The older girls all work in our business so if you should call, you might have the pleasure of talking with one of them. They truly understand how this teaching method works and can explain it to you! Brooke loves history and without even suggesting this assignment, she chose to write out the WHOLE Declaration of Independence during a study on the American Revolution. She also wrote out *Paul Revere's Ride* by Longfellow! Brooke enjoys her studies and it shows when she talks with others about life. It might comfort you to know that none of my children have been really strong in math and that is mostly due to the fact that it is not my strongest subject. Dad is the "math man" so I have him help all the children when they have a problem or a question and are stuck!

Teaching Teens

By the time a student reaches ninth grade, he should have mastered the basic skills of reading, writing, and arithmetic. He should also know how to use research materials and think things through to a logical conclusion (or be getting better at it). If he has not mastered these basic skills, spend time at beginning of high school to review, strengthen, and master them.

Assuming your younger teenager can read well, can express himself verbally in writing, and has mastered general arithmetic, your job as a high school teacher at home is relatively easy. At this point, your student is ready to become an independent, self-motivated learner.

You do not need to know everything that your student is learning. Do not be intimidated by well-meaning people who ask you how you can possibly teach high school without a degree. What your home schooled high school student needs most is an encourager, a resource person, someone to bounce new ideas off, and someone to keep him in line as he works to meet his goals. These jobs are challenging, but certainly do not require a degree or state credential.

(Mary Scholfield, *The High School Handbook*
[Norwalk: Christian Home Educators, 1992], ix)

MEETING STATE REQUIREMENTS

I have heard many conflicting stories from several reliable home school parents and leaders who talk about what is required for high school and what is necessary for applying to colleges. Some say you must have two years of this and one year of that. Others say, "Oh no, you don't have to do that, you have to do this!"

Though requirements differ from state to state, the law concerning private schools in my state does not say we must meet public requirements. We CAN follow them as a guidelines if we choose to for helping us set up our own requirements.

I sat in on a session about homeschooling high schoolers and the speaker said that as long as those requirements, which were initially written by godly people decades ago, do not go against biblical standards, we are safe to follow them. But you, the parent, CAN determine what you wish to require your student. Since we are all very concerned about giving our children a quality education it is obvious that we are going to be as responsible as possible. Part of this means finding out about state requirements, determining, if possible, what our child's interest is for the future, and then requiring what we think will help them achieve their goals or encourage their talents.

As your children approach high school you can begin to think about whether they need or desire higher education. If you know what area they are interested in pursuing, you can research the schools and programs to see what will be necessary for them to "have under their belt" and then make sure they accomplish that in high school.

Most parents who have kids in high school are concerned with points, hours, credits and transcripts. I really can't take the time or space to address this in detail, but today there are many resources available. There are not only a miriad of books written by homeschoolers who have gone before us, but there are also many resource people who have figured this all out for us!

Unit studies are more elusive when it comes to keeping records but we do have some forms in the appendix which may help you to feel more comfortable for keeping track.

We are very pleased with our children's education and there is no contest between my public school education and the joy filled education my children have attained at home. When we look over our philosophy of education, we can say that we are reaching the academic and spiritual goals which we set out to attain. Our children are all doing well as adults and most importantly, they love the Lord with all their hearts.

High School Resources

Senior High Designed Form + U + la by Barbara Shelton

The High School Handbook by Mary Schofield

The Christian Home Educators' Curriculum Manual for Junior and Senior High written by Cathy Duffy

Home School, High School, and Beyond by Beverly Adams, Gordon

How Do You Know they Know What they Know by Teresa Moon

High School Unit Studies at Home, Volumes 1, 2, 3 and 4 by Steward Ship

There's
6
Still More!

Now you know all kinds of things about unit studies… but there's still some more! In this last chapter, we will talk about:

- Unit study co-ops
- Unit study support meetings
- How to bring a child home to school
- How to wrap up or conclude a study
- Testimonials

- Unit studies and learning disabilities
- Drama
- Oral presentations
- Record Keeping
- Flapbooks

UNIT STUDY CO-OPS

Many families enjoy doing unit studies by conducting a "co-op."which is short for cooperative. Technically this means that you get together as a group with other homeschoolers and everyone shares in the work and the planning. There are times when I've conducted a class, doing most of the planning and teaching, but have still referred to it as a co-op. Co-ops are nice because families can get together and pool materials, ideas, and efforts and conduct a unit study together. We have conducted many studies with other families and it can be alot of fun. One main reason I do co-ops is it MAKES me do the fun things that make studies more fun and memorable.

Co-ops have both benefits and drawbacks:

Pros

- When starting out it is helpful to group with others who know the ropes so you can learn.

- They are cost-effective because resources are shared.

- Provide such things as activities and field trips.

- Group situations challenge students through healthy competition.

- Co-ops help moms share the workload.

Cons

- Group problems with behavior do arise.

- Children get distracted and don't pay attention so learning is limited.

- One or more of the coop mothers might become uncooperative.

- Co-ops require more organization and energy.

I've done both large group co ops and smaller ones with one or two familes. I generally prefer smaller groups. It's nice when you can find another family who you are compatible with and have children with like personalities and are close in age.

Unit study co-ops motivate me to provide more of the fun activities my children love and remember. Isn't it a shame how we homeschooling parents can plan and prepare crafts, nature hunts, collages, art projects and field trips when we know other people's children are counting on us, but can't seem to get it together often enough for our own children?.But it's so true - I know these people will be arriving at my door by a certain time which means I must get the copies made, the books out and figure out how our time will go.

Co-ops give homeschooled children the opportunity to be around other children, which can be either a positive or negative experience. One advantage of getting outside the family environment is that it gives the children a chance to have a little healthy competition. Sometimes this factor motivates them, and they often feel more challenged to not only get their work done but also to do their best. It can also help them view where they stand academically. As the scriptures say, "Iron sharpens iron!"

When I'm planning a large co-op, I meet with the other mothers ahead of time to make plans. We usually keep our units to about four to six weeks in length and meet in our church fellowship hall. We've had groups as large as 40-50 kids! Once I know which families are participating and how many children we have, I can split them up into groups so mothers can be in charge of a group. I will give her the instructions for the activity and the materials. For large groups like this, I will set a fee for each family to pay to cover the materials. We usually go from about 9:00 a.m. - 2:00 p.m. and have each family bring a sack lunch.

When we're doing a family co-op, depending on the family, I usually do most of the planning (being the Unit Study Queen that I am!) and ask for help for the project or activities. We then take turns having the co-op at each others homes on Fridays. When we meet in homes, we usually split the cost of materials and decide who will bring the items needed each week. Some moms like to do a full study and just do activities on our co-op day, while others don't really want to do anything else during the week connected with the study but only take advantage of what will be offered in the co-op class time.

To help the co-op run smoothly:

- Keep home groups small.

- Hold a mothers' meeting and explain guidelines.

- If there is a materials fee, be sure to charge enough money.

- Delegate - give each participating parent a specific area to oversee.

- Make guidelines known and enforce them so everyone has a pleasant experience and the intended learning takes place. .

- No dropping off kids! Each of the homeschooling parents are required to stay and supervise his/her own children.

- Organize, plan, and be prepared.

HOLDING ON TO A GOOD ONE

Once you find a family you are compatible with, try to keep a good thing going. There are a couple of families we really work well with so we have done quite a few co-ops together. One of the things that has worked well, is one mom takes the older (high school kids) and goes in the other room and does grammar with them. They are in there having a good time, while I am working with the elementary grade kids and we are having our own good time! The two little ones go off and play together during our time. We usually do co-ops with other families once or twice a year.

LARGE GROUP CO-OPS

Large group co-ops can be a lot of fun but require alot more work and if your not careful they can turn into a big, loud, "free-for-all." Co-op day can be a socail day for Mom and this can also be difficult if mothers end up standing around visiting with each other. You have to make your guidelines and expectations clear in order for things to turn out successfully.

It is nice to have planning sessions together because you can brainstorm up some great ideas. One thing that I've found though is that if you get too many parents in on the planning process, it gets confusing.

Unit studies came to my rescue when I was discouraged with the homeschool program I was using initially. For that reason I do a co-op on occasion to encourage other mothers with this method and they can learn the method as they watch and take part. If you are just starting out, joining a co-op will help you understand how unit studies are done. A co-op experience will also give you the confidence to conduct unit studies with your own children.

ONE DAY CO-OPS

One day co-ops can offer the best of both worlds. You have all the benefits of cooping with friends, but the short commitment eliminates the long-term planning and required energy! During an election year, we held a one day unit teaching the election process. I thought it would be exciting to run a mock campaign, have a headquarters, hold primary caucuses, and even go through an election. The only problem was that I needed people. Therefore, I "put the word out" to determine if anyone else was interested and it turned out that most of the other homeschooling moms thought it was a great idea.

That day we decorated the hall with red, white and blue streamers, balloons and flags, and gathered materials to make campaign buttons. The students who sat on one side of the room were Democrats for the day; those on the other side were Republicans. One mother wore an "Uncle Sam" hat and walked around the room she asking students questions about the political process, passing out candy for correct answers! Along with teaching sessions about all aspects of an election, the children did many hands-on activities, had contests to see which group could find answers the fastest, and held a primary to see who our Presidential candidates would be. The two candidates each wrote a short campaign speech and held a political platform.

In the end they elected one of the students to be our next president. The group was also able to visit a mock poll conducted by our local homeschool support group. They decorated and ate patriotic cupcakes and went home that evening to watch the results of the real presidential election. The events of that one-day study were rich and memorable and they learned so much. One day co-ops still require planning and parent participation like longer unit study coops, but the nice part is that it is all over in a single day.

CO-OPS AS A BUSINESS OPPORTUNITY

Many parents would pay dearly to have a unit study class available to their children. Somebody else does all the planning and gathering of materials and then you just have to show up! A couple of my daughters have done this with great success and it has helped them earn a little money while doing something quite rewarding and fun! Depending on the size of class you take, you might need to ask the moms to stay and help too. Remember, you aren't providing a babysitting service.

This is a great service to many homeschooling families because it gives them an outlet for enrichment studies and activities for their children. If God has given you the ability, time, space, and the heart, you might consider conducting a co-op in your area. You don't need years of experience either.

The amount you decide to charge would depend upon the economy in your area, the materials you provide, and the length of the study. Considering haviing a day of lively instruction and fun enrichment activities, parents consider it a bargain, comparable to fees for music lessons or other workshops. If you wish to place your child in an enrichment unit study co-op, be sure to consider the information in the next paragraph.

HOMESCHOOL CO-OPS VS. CLASSES

The growth in the homeschooling movement continues everyday along with an ever increasing number of parents interested in finding enrichment classes for their children. There is a difference between co-ops and **unit study co-ops**. You should already understand the various types of unit study co-ops from my previous comments. A **co-op**, on the other hand incorporates classes in which homeschooling (and sometimes non-homeschooling) parents share their area of expertise or talents. Though this concept sounds good, use wisdom in choosing your children's outside activities.

Pray and evaluate:

- How the experience might affect your children and your family - whether your children deem it as a "chance to see my friends" or if they are serious about learning.

- Whether the experience will add or detract from your goals - both academic and spiritual.

- Who the teacher is and how well you know them; how many will be in the class; the value system that will be relayed; and what they will be taught.

- How it will help your child academically.

- How it will affect your schedule.

Unit Studies and Learning Disabilities

One reason you should consider doing a unit study with a child who has learning disabilities is because it removes all stress. Your children don't have to fit into a curriculum mold. You have the freedom to explore whatever you or your children find interesting, and at your own pace. Many children with learning disabilities learn best by getting their hands involved. They are often very slow to learn phonics, therefore they can't read, but they can bloom when you read to them - just be sensitive to their attention span. As I said before, the read aloud time gives so many wonderful opportunities for discussion. Take the time to discuss and explain things to your child.

Many parents are trying to work with their children who struggle with Attention Deficit Disorder (ADD). These children have a difficult time focusing on one thing or staying with it. Unit studies work well with an ADD child because you can diversify as often as needed for the child and yet tie together whatever you are trying to teach.

The Unit Study Support Meeting

I have been hosting a monthly unit study meeting in my area for the past seven years. Whenever I mention this to moms at my workshops, they perk up and say, "We could do that!" Not only is it a "moms night out" and a great homeschooling meeting, but it is a great way to learn and share about unit studies. Over the years we've used different formats for the meeting always trying to determine what would be most helpful. They are always pleased to have new information and ideas they can use when teaching their children.

Often when you hear speakers at seminars, you only see the side they want you to see and it is hard to imagine that their children would ever do anything naughty or that they have difficult days like the rest of us. This meeting has met a real need because moms can ask questions and share areas they struggle and ways they've found success. If you know of a mother who uses and understands unit studies, and would be willing and able to lead a meeting, consider holding one in your area.

Our monthly meetings, which we publicize in a couple of local homeschooling newsletters, run for two hours. The way we manage the meeting is one person (usually me!) leads it. We make announcements of upcoming field trips or events and then have introductions. We schedule in advance a full year of unit study topics to spotlight. Whatever the topic, we tell moms to bring their books on that topic and then we have a brainstorming session. We break up into groups and get ideas for assignments you could do by looking at the books.

We also do a bubble diagram on the board which helps get ideas out of your head and down on "paper" so you can see them all in one place. These excercises help moms learn what a unit study is and how to plan one. The one or two moms who do the "spotlight" will bring a child's notebook and show us what they did during their study on that topic.

Unit Study Spotlights

I will share a two examples of some of the spotlights, ideas and resources, and testimonials from the mothers who have attended one of our Unit Study Meetings.

ART HISTORY UNIT ~ by Jennifer Steward
Read Aloud title: *I, Juan de Pareja*

Other Resources:
Start Exploring Masterpieces, Introduction to Art (Usborne)

Taking the Mystery Out of Studying Art History Unit Study Guide

- Do a chronological study of art history and art appreciation.

- Read a chapter a day from I Juan de Pareja.

- Read about a time period in The Story of Painting. Younger children look at art print.

- Read about an artist from Start Exploring Masterpieces coloring book. Color his painting and place it in the notebook.

- Design section dividers for an art history notebook.

- Paste pictures on a timeline.

- Experiment with different modes of art that coincide with an artist, time period, or method. Paint on a large rock when you study "Cave Painting," use watercolors during a study of impressionists, lay on your back and paint on a paper taped to the underside of a table when you study Michaelangelo, do sculpting for early Greek art, etc.

- List famous art galleries around the world.

- Visit an art museum.

FRONTIERSMAN - TRAPPER UNIT ~ by Debbie Fuller
Read Aloud Title: *Daniel Boone* - Childhood of Famous Americans series

This unit is one of our favorites! Our boys were 3, 6, and 8 when we studied this unit. Here are some of the activities that we learned from and thoroughly enjoyed:

- Take a wilderness hike.

- Track raccoon, deer and other animals.

- Identify animals as either predators or prey.

- Hunt, catch, and cook food. This can be accomplished by going to the grocery store!

- Read about Lewis & Clark and trace their trail on a U.S. map.

- Journal findings after going on a nature walk, like Lewis & Clark did using an ink pad and quill.

- Examine a real covered wagon on a field trip or by looking at pictures in a book.

- Study bears common to North America.

- Make a coonskin cap.

- Make butter from real cream.

- Make a "possible bag" (mountain men carried only their necessities).

- Practice using a compass.

- Read about Pooh Bear's "expotition" (expedition).

- Visit a mountain man, dressed in authentic clothing, at a living history event if possible.

- Learn what a musket is and write about the difference between a musket and other guns.

This study was taken from Konos Curriculum.

IDEAS AND RESOURCES

This section is filled with ideas and resources which have been offered at our unit study meetings. Many suggestions are good all around teaching tips, while others are specific helps to the unit study method.

Ideas:

- Homemade timelines go well with history unit studies. Use timelines to show the chronology of any event. Use a six-foot length of butcher paper taped to the wall. Make copies of pictures or draw your own to paste on. Label with dates and information. When you are done, laminate and save the timeline for future reference.

- Keeping toddlers quiet when you're "doing school" is challenging. Give your preschooler his own time early in the day to fill his emotional tank. Spend 30 minutes with your preschooler and call it his "school time." Then he will be more willing to let you have your "school time."

- Often children dawdle at mealtime. Rather than waiting for them to finish so you can get on with school, do your read aloud time while they eat. Then let them go play for 20-30 minutes so you can eat.

- If you don't have the space or don't want all your unit studies stored in notebook binders, remove them and place them into gold craft 10x13 envelopes, label and store. If you put a snap ring in the corner, it will help keep all the papers together. You can store many of them in file boxes and have easy access to them.

- Clip articles from homeschool magazines to start a file for unit study ideas. File ideas from past unit studies you've completed and make copies of any bubble diagrams. Many home-schooling publications feature unit studies every month and list activities and resources. You can build your own curriculum by using the ideas they offer.

- Purchase a prepared unit study curriculum with another family and share the cost. Some curriculums like *Konos* or *Weaver* come in volumes so you can work from one volume while the other family uses another volume.

- Start little informal studies with your preschoolers to get them excited about learning - for instance, sprout seeds, set up a bird feeder, collect rocks, shells, coins, or stamps.

- Allow older students to organize and teach a unit study to younger children. You always learn as you teach.

- Encourage students to keep adding things to their unit study notebooks as they discover new information even after they've completed the topic.

Resources:

- If you are a "book-looker" and go to used curriculum fairs you can find great books on all topics for great prices while everyone else is snatching up those buys oncurriculum. Train your eye to look for books for all age groups for different topics you will study in the future.

- *Kids Discover* magazine publishes magazines on dozens of topics. The phone number is (212-677-4457)

- Scholastic Books has great prices, sells to homeschoolers and there's no shipping or tax. Scholastic Book Clubs, Inc., Jefferson City, MO 64102-7503. 1-800-246-2986. www.scholastic.com

- Get a double-sided write-on, wipe-off laminated map with the U.S. on one side, the World on the other. To save space, fasten a wooden yardstick to the wall and put velcro on the stick and on the map so you can lift it off and turn it when you need to use the other side. (map carried by Steward Ship)

BRINGING A CHILD HOME TO SCHOOL - WHAT'S NEXT?

What if you are bringing your child out of a classroom situation. What's next? Should you try to do unit studies? Absolutely! But one of your biggest obstacles is going to be… yourself. Let me explain. Folks will bring a child into home education for a number of reasons.

Perhaps your child:

- Was not thriving in the classroom - academically or emotionally.

- Was getting in trouble in the classroom.

- Was becoming peer dependent.

- Doesn't fit into the classroom mold.

- Has an insatiable desire to learn.

- Desires to be homeschooled.

Parents have the tendency to feel they must put on a "show" for others to prove they are doing a good job when they bring a child home to school. They want to get started immediately on the academics and make sure that what they are doing looks good and acceptable to others. What they usually don't realize is how important it is to gain and reclaim some ground with the child. The child needs time to adapt to this change and YOU do, too. If your child has had a hard time and a negative experience in school, you MUST foster a stress free atmophere. The last thing they need is for you to say they are "behind" and you need to get going. The way to foster delight is to sit together and read - ALOT!

Some children are not happy about being brought home and might have a rebellious nature. If a child has been suffering emotionally or academically, he definitely needs time to gain self confidence and discover the joy that comes from spending time together and learning. Because you can go slowly as you enjoy studying something - anything, unit studies are so appropriate in this time of adjustment. Begin to build your child up during this process.

It's Never Too Late to Teach with Unit Studies

No matter what age or grade level your child is, it is never too late to use unit studies. I have parents constantly tell me that they wish they had known about unit studies sooner and now that their children are older, it's too late. If you understand that the unit study method as a vehicle which will enable you to lead your child to the wonderful world of real and meaningful learning - you'll realize it's not too late. It's never too late for that! The reason WE think it is too late, is because we get caught up in the high school "gotta do a bunch of hard stuff now" syndrome!

Sometimes people think it would be too difficult to figure how to go about using unit studies when a student has been so used to textbooks. I think parents owe it to their children to do some research and try out alternative teaching methods instead of coming to negative conclusions. If you determine that you have a will (reason) to do it, then there's a way. The fact remains, if someone doesn't fit the mold of the classroom, why bring the classroom home? Remember, home education offers the freedom to explore learning the way it should be because it does not have the limitations of a classroom.

Oral Presentations

The unit study approach provides opportunities for a wide range of experiences which contribute to a well-rounded student. Having your children plan oral presentation at least once a year can really add to a study and also help conclude it. Oral presentations help kids have the ability to communicate thoughts as well as encouraging them to become involved in leadership by addressing issues through speech and give elementary grade students opportunities for public speaking. By the time your students reach high school they should be able to write and present a speech. Help them to see public speaking as a necessary skill rather than just a requirement to complete their formal education. When your family is involved in a unit study co-op more children are involved and many age groups are present so the experience can move outside the family and be a positive challenge to your students.

CAUTION: *Presentations should not be looked upon as a competition.*

Giving an oral presentation:

- Introduces students to public speaking skills, and helps in overcoming shyness.
- Teaches important communication skills.
- Enables students to focus on a topic or an aspect of their study.
- Helps students plan and organize information they have learned.
- Helps students develop creativity as they design poster board.
- Enables students to incorporate props and diagrams into their talk.

Guidelines for giving an oral presentation:

- Make the presentation about five minutes in length.
- Know your information well but don't memorize word for word.
- Use two or three pieces of poster board.
- Use props and visual aids to enhance the topic.
- Once you have offered the body of information, recap what you've discussed (use a pointer on the poster board).
- Be confident and smiile.
- Make poster board bright and attractive, original and creative.
- Conclude by asking "Are there any questions?" then "I'd like to thank you for listening to my presentation."

Your posters should be bright, attractive, original and creative. The FIRST poster should contain a catchy title and gain the interest of listeners without giving away the topic of presentation. The SECOND poster contains the body of information and the THIRD contains the conclusion. Some catchy titles, for example: when my daughter gave a presentation on the care of rabbits she titled it "Who Cares." Another child titled a presentation on birds "Awesome Aves" and another child chose the title "The FAX Are In," referring to interesting facts about birds. She drew a picture of a fax machine and had the title flowing out of it with the title written on - very cute!

When choosing a topic to use in preparing an oral presentation, I find it helpful to go back over the areas we have studied and also our source books to help provide ideas. I usually list topics my children can choose from. Although they are not limited to this list, it helps get them started, especially the younger ones.

Public Speaking Resource:

From Playpen to Podium by Jeff Myers

PLANNING MY PRESENTATION

Topic _____

Plan an outline to organize all information

1st Poster board _____

2nd Poster board _____

3rd Poster board _____

Ideas for props I can use _____

Length of presentation (timed in practice) _____

Date and place I will give precontation _____

QUICK AFTER DINNER PRESENTATIONS

A good way to introduce children to giving oral presentations is to start by (but continue doing even when you get to be an old pro) giving mini presentations after a meal, while the family is still gathered at the dinner table.We've had our children each prepare something, to tell about briefly. For example, when we studied World Geography, we often made a craft from somewhere "around the world." The children would show their craft and then share a few interesting facts about that country. This is an excellent way to include everyone - from the youngest to the oldest, by incorporating some aspect of a study which provides another "connection" andopportunity to expound on something learned.

INCLUDING DRAMA IN UNIT STUDIES

Do you have some hams in your crowd? You might never know until you give them a chance to perfrom! Drama experiences are another way to encourage creativity and develop kills. I tend not to go the extra mile it takes to do too many extra curricular activites, but one year I found out about a drama club my friend was offering. She happened to be doing a Shakespeare play and since we had done a unit study on Shakespeare the year before, I wanted my kids to have this experience. I really didn't know that either of my daughters had acting abilities, but I found out how very talented they both are through this experience.

You can include a play as a culmination to a unit study which has been conducted over a whole school year. Since unit studies are topical, they provide a perfect opportunity to plan a play that fits your topic. For example for a study on cowboys - The Buffalo Bill Show; for weather - The Day it Rained Cats and Dogs; for Ancient Greece plan a comedy or tragedy. For a study on Farm Animals try a presentation of *Charlotte's Web*.

Drama activities might be a source of stress for Mom so add it in if you want to but don't feel like you must! You might have success by allowing the students to orchestrate the whole activity with you just setting some guidelines (i.e. how much time you will allow for writing, practices, etc.; whether they will have sets, props and so on.)

You could use the experience to encourage writing skills and plan to have your children write their own play! Keep the play within your family and have the playwright include parts for all family members. Put the play on for close friends, grandparents, etc. If your prefer, rather than putting on your own production become involved in one at your church or homeschool group.

Writing and putting on plays:

- Can be simple or complex, short or long. Can involve practices and set making or be done without props - asking the audience to use their imaginations.

- Helps students present ideas through words and gestures - acting!

- Allows students to interact with each other and their audience.

- Allows the writer to express a point of view. A story worth telling can involve writing, acting, music.

Drama Resource:

Putting on a Play - the young playwright's guide to scripting, directing, and performing
by Nancy Bentley and Donna Guthrie

How to Wrap Up or Conclude a Unit Study

Whatever length of time you have chosen for a particular unit study, the time will come when the study needs to come to an end. In fact, during the planning process (which, remember, should only take you a couple of hours once you have gathered your materials and started brainstorming), consider how you will conclude your study. As mentioned before, most unit studies can be completed in about four weeks.

By the end of the third week you should be evaluating:

- Whether you've covered all the information you planned. If you have not, how much more time do you need?

- If your students are still interested in the subject.

- How the notebook project is progressing. The notebook project is like a REPORT and actually helps you conclude your unit study because your students will be finishing and organizing assignments that go into the notebook. When it is completed, it will be filed on the shelf with other unit study notebooks and makes for an official end to your study.

It is also a good idea to review what has been learned by going back through some of the source books used during the study.

Other ways to conclude a study:

- **Spelling words** - If students have been studying a list of spelling words, give them both oral and written tests. If you have been giving weekly tests, you might want to give them one at the end of your study.

- **Vocabulary words** - Before they put everything away in their study notebook, make sure they understand the vocabulary words they learned during the study and have used the dictionary to look up all their words.

- **Book Reports** - If your children have been reading a Living Book for their topic for silent reading, have them do a book report. They can also write a book report for your Read Aloud Title.

- **Tests and Quizzes** - I often find it helpful for my children to take a quiz at the end of a unit study.

- **Record and Assignment Sheets** - Each child's notebook should have a record sheet and an assignment sheet placed in the front. At the end of a study, the record sheet (sample included in Appendix) should be filled out by the student (or the parent for younger students) including the topic, the date, books and resources used, field trips taken, projects, etc. The assignment sheet should have all the boxes checked off telling which assignments have been completed.

- **Flapbooks** - We usually make a flapbook once or twice a year. These are a great project to use as a sort of report. A student can decide what aspect of a study to "report" on then make a flapbook. Flapbooks fit nicely in the back of the notebook!

TEACHING TIPS YOU MUST KNOW!

I have a couple of really great tips which make doing unit studies and notebooks so much fun. The first one is to scan the covers of all your favorite books you used during your unit study. You can place them on a page and place lines by them for your students to look up the author and title. Kids love to remember what books they used so this is fun for them and they don't even realize it is a writing assignment!

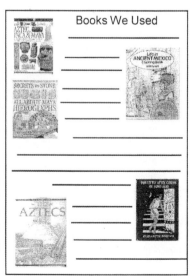

The next awesome tip requires using the internet and is probably a good idea for something that Mom or Dad to do. If you go to Google (and other search engines too) and click on **images**, then type in the picture you want (like ladybug) you will get a whole page of images. If you are looking for a black and white coloring picture, you need to type in ladybug coloring picture. (See next page.)

Google

Web   Images   Groups   News   Froogle   Local

What is so cool about this is that each image is actually taking you to a website with an article. I have found some really great information (connected with each image) which might have otherwise taken me hours of searching. You will get a few "strange" and possibly inappropriate pictures so that's why I caution to have Mom or Dad use this resource. You can right click your mouse and copy the imgae to a program where you can place it and size it, then print the image. You can find crosswords (type that in under your topic: ladybug crosswords) and even worksheets. If the image is copyrighted, I don't believe you will be able to print it.

Once I discovered this "treasure," I use it all the time for making connecting assignments for our studies You will be able to make your own custom worksheets tailored to what you are studying just right for your child's age. I made this sheet using pictures I copied from two places and pasted them in. I had a younger student write a fun fact about a ladybug and we used the bottom picture to make a little diagram.

The Fun Has Just Begun

Probably one of the most exciting aspects of learning through unit studies is that even though the study is officially over, the notebooks are completed, and all the books have been placed back on their home on the bookshelf, the fun has really just begun. Once you have explored a new area of study, a whole new "world" is opened up to you and your students. You have become an expert in a particular field and now that you know so much more about a topic, you can enjoy it. When we finished our birds study, we began to really enjoy the world of birds. Usually we acquire books and resources "before" a study but when we studied birds, we began to really enjoy the world of birds. We found some bird feeders for our yard and added a couple of beautiful bird books to our library - AFTER the study was over. We found out about a Egyptian museum exhibit months after we had studied ancient Egypt but because we've "added" this interest to our lives, we were interested in going to the museum.

Our daughter was watching a cartoon video about Hercules. She was excited because she could identify most of the Greek gods and could understand what was happening due to our extensive study on ancient Greece. This excitement is common in our home and is further proof that learning can be exciting and interesting… and it should be.

Keeping Records Using Unit Studies

Keeping unit study records is not a problem once you develop a system that works for you. Each person must decide how, and to what extent, they will keep records. Part of the record keeping depends upon any requirements made by your state or your independent study program. If you are signed up under an independent study program (ISP), keep your records according to their specifications. Many ISPs are flexible and allow you to modify your records to suit your family situation once you explain what you are doing and how you are going about teaching subjects.

Do not rely on hearsay, but seek accurate information regarding record requirements. Your ISP might have something they obtained in writing from the state level or local school district. Contact Home School Legal Defense Association (P.O. Box 3000 · Purcellville, VA 20134-9000 · Phone: (540) 338-5600 · Fax: (540) 338-2733 · E-mail: info@hslda.org) to find out what they recommend for your state. The important thing to remember is that if you were called to account for your child's education, the court would want visible proof showing that your child displays reasonable progress in his education.

Keeping daily school records has always been a struggle for me because I find I either keep records or teach. It has always been a huge stress for me and is almost impossible for me to do both well - so I prefer to TEACH! Over the years I have tried many different methods until I found the balance that works for me. I have developed a system of using my children's notebooks along with monthly record sheets. Thus, these notebooks can serve two purposes:

- Educational keepsakes to be treasured and enjoyed.

- Records of work accomplished and learned.

At the beginning of each school year I pray about "goals" for each of my children and try to figure out where they need to be challenged or helped. There is a monthly record sheet in the Appendix which will help you keep records when doing unit studies. The notebook stands as a living record and even includes a students (not teachers) record sheet listing: books used, read aloud title, unit study topic, child's name, date of study, field trips, projects etc. Together, using these two records, I have a clear conscience and feel like I could easily show (if I ever had to) what my children are learning and what I've been teaching them.

You can also choose to design your own unit study record sheets with any type of boxes and places to record what you are doing daily or weekly for each child. To save time, take your unit study planning sheets and adapt them to be used as records.

If you are required to keep detailed records, you can create codes for different subjects like:

DI for dictation   RA for read aloud   ACT for activity

If you are the organized type you could make copies of your child's work choosing samples from different subjects and place them in a records binder making sure that you have collected them from September, January, and June. This way you have everything in one place. This is too much work for me especially since I have a number of children to consider, so I am content to know each child has a notebook I could pull off the shelf.

Many people get overly "caught up" in records, requirements, transcripts, and credits. We can lose some of the most valuable opportunities we have in home teaching if we allow meeting the academic requirements to hinder delight. Many life skills occur simply by coming along side them in your natural environment. How would my daughter homemaking skills, hospitality and servanthood if her nose is stuck in a book all the time? How will my son learn to fix a fence or visit the sick if he has to spend all his time meeting requirements?

TESTIMONIALS

The following testimonials are written by mothers who have seen unit studies make a difference in their homeschooling experience.

- *Unit studies have brought the joy back into not just our homeschool, but into our lives. In the five years we have homeschooled, we have tried many methods available: textbooks, packaged curriculum, etc. The Lord has always led us back to unit studies and we are here to stay! Our children are excited about learning which excites us in our teaching efforts. Units can involve the whole family (even toddlers) in the learning process. We count it a blessing that the Lord has shown us a painless, joyful, enriching way to teach our children at home.*

  L. Vidal - Mother of 5 (2 Girls - 10 & 4 and 3 Boys - 9 & 3, infant)

- *Our children love to learn. This love for learning is fostered by the unit study method which allows them to contribute to their studies. They discover truths. When they make a discovery, not only do they remember what they have learned but they have an incessant desire to share with anyone who will listen. So we listen! Unit studies glue "subjects," as well as a family together!*

  D. Fuller - Mother of 4 boys (those still at home are 12, 10, 7)

- *After fifteen years of homeschooling I've tried about every method out there! What experience has shown me is that the material my children have retained the best is what they learned through the unit study approach. My guess is their retention increases as their subjects are integrated, which happens during a unit study. These are also my fondest memories of teaching. It is so easy - vocabulary words from your read aloud time - you almost feel guilty, it's so painless!*

  B. Klein - Mother of 5 (2 Girls - 17 & 10 and 3 Boys - 20, 12, 8)

- *I really appreciate unit studies now that I have three school-age children. Some of the things that stand out with unit studies is that it unifies our family. Because we all study the same thing I know what all the kids are learning and I feel more in touch with them. Before, I was over whelmed when I tried to cover all the subjects for all my students. Being able to incorporate writing and other subjects around one topic really helps and makes more sense. Unit studies enable my children to study, explore and enjoy things they are interested in. When they are enthused they seem to remember what they learn.*

  S. Schwegler - Mother of 6 (2 Girls - 8 & 3 and 4 Boys - 13, 11, 6. infant)

- *When I started teaching my children, like most people, I didn't have a clue as to what to do or how to go about it. I went to a couple of workshops that taught about different educational "methods" at some conferences my first couple of years and always seemed drawn to unit studies. Once I started and saw what fun it was for me and how excited my children got in being able to participate in the choices of what we studied, I was HOOKED! I didn't know at the time I would have 4 (or more) children, but even if I only had one or two, it would still be the same! My children love delving in to a subject, they STILL love to be read to (and, I discovered I still do, too!) and I know WE have learned more, enjoyed our time together learning and will remember, retain and keep on learning throughout our lives. I look forward to many more years of teaching (and I have a LOT!) "the unit study way". I believe it really is the best way to develop a love for learning in ALL of us!*

  D. Eldridge Mother of four - (three girls and one boy ages 14,10. 6, and 4)

SUMMARIZING WHAT WE'VE COVERED

- Decide where your children will acquire their education.

- If you have chosen home education, evaluate your Philosophy of Education.

- Consider the different teaching methods - benefits and drawbacks.

- Pray for direction.

If you have chosen the unit study approach:

- Evaluate where your child is academically.

- Choose the avenue that suits your needs (complete curriculum, topical guide, or create your own study).

- Evaluate what topics have been learned.

- Choose a topic.

- Make a rough annual plan for topics you'd like to study.

- Choose materials - read aloud, main source of information, etc.

- Use the QESFPM (Quick Easy Stress-Free Planning Method) - Brainstorm ideas; construct a bubble diagram; or use books to help divide study and think up activities.

- Jump in and get started!

For Successful Unit Studies:

- Let your materials be YOUR tools - don't be intimidated by them.

- Choose good literature - older books, living books.

- Use the library and build a home library.

- Go with your child's interests whenever possible.

- Capitalize on teachable moments and extras to enhance studies.

- Write up assignment sheets starting from oldest child to youngest.

- Use suitable subjects; do not expend the energy to force them in if they don't fit.

- Choose a Bible, math, and phonics program to incorporate separately.

- Use your read aloud time to its fullest potential.

- Prepare a unit study notebook for each study as a main project.

- Simplify; teaching should be a delight for you and learning should be a delight for your child.

- Try to make most of your units no longer than six weeks in length.

- Consider doing a unit study co-op from time to time.

A NOTE FROM THE AUTHOR

Well, thanks for spending this time with me! You know by now that I am excited about learning and teaching! Often I talk to parents and see the distressed looks on their faces and sometimes even tears, wondering how they are going to teach. I know I could help them if I had the time to answer their questions. So, it brings me great joy to put something into your hands that will help you explain how practical and easy unit studies can be. It is my earnest prayer that now you can say, "I CAN do unit studies!" and better yet…

"I WANT to do unit studies!"

I have tried to tell you "Everything" I know about unit studies and have organized and outlined the details into a method you can easily adopt and adapt into your family. Use any or all parts of the method to bring delightful learning to your homeschool and once again…

Remember all the little light bulbs you saw throughout the book?

These are what I consider the most important guidelines and truths

about the unit study method.

I will leave you with these words of encouragement - Winston Churchill once said, "**Never, never, never, never, never, never, never, never give in**." When we started our homeschooling business we felt we HAD to take advantage of our last name and call our business Steward Ship. This word is often associated in Christianity as meaning to be responsible in regard to finances. We want to use it in the context of being responsible with parenting. The choice to home educate our children is part of our responsibility toward God to bring them up for Kingdom purposes. We feel the best way to help our children become people prepared for Kingdom work is to give them a real education which is not necessarily the same thing as the kind of education we're "supposed to" give them. Our business logo a ship - a mascot of sorts - with a banner inscription saying: "Don't Give Up the Ship." We think of the ship as homeschooling - we don't want you to get frustrated, discouraged or desparate and QUIT. We want you to experience the same joy we have in learning.

It's natural to feel a little anxious and unsure when you are trying something new, but once you start using unit studies and see your children responding, you WILL understand more and more, and it will become easier and more natural. Whether you "throw in" a unit study now and then or embrace them for full-time teaching, you'll quickly discover what works best for your family. Just try it, I know you and your children will love it! And, when they like something, they will stop complaining about schoolwork, thus removing the burden we feel when our children constantly grumble about schoolwork.

Jennifer Steward

Appendix/Toolbox

INCLUDES:

Glossary of Unit Study Terms

Resource Section

Samples and Examples Section

4 Sample Units (*World Geography, Birth of Christ, Revolutionary War, Colonial Times*)

Variety of Planning Sheets (*to photocopy*)

Samples of Planning Sheets (*filled out*)

Sample Assignment Sheets (*for varying age groups*)

Record Keeping sheets (*monthly and also for notebooks*)

Sample High School Record Sheets

Book Report Form

Reading List Form

Ideas for Things to Include in Reports/Notebooks

USING THE PLANNING SHEETS

The following pages include samples of several different planning sheets. Some are already filled out so you can see how you might use them. Other forms are blank and ready to copy and use in your own planning. There are examples of planning and assignment sheets from two studies: Pilgrims and Pony Express. Hopefully, the different examples will help you get a well-rounded idea to help you in planning.

You can photocopy, adapt, or expand the planning sheets according to your own style or particular needs for planning. Use them for ideas on how to create your own forms for your unique situation (i.e. the size of your family, the ages of your children, the unit study curriculum you are using, etc.).

A brief description of each one follows:

- **The Bubble Diagram** - gives you an example of what your plans might look like after a brainstorming session.

- **Brainstorming My Plans Sheet** - can accompany your bubble diagram as a place to sort out and transfer the information after you have finished your brainstorming session. After you have made an extensive list of areas you COULD study, you will then choose only those things you WISH to study.

- **The Big Picture Plan** - offers a place to write out your unit study plans for a whole school year. It will help you keep a balance to your plans.

- **Annual Calendar** - lists all the months of the year so you can see your unit study plans for the whole year at a glance.

- **Daily Calendar** - a daily unit study calendar is yet another option for writing in the different activities you plan to include.

- **Weekly Planning Sheets** - The Four-Week Column Sheet enables you to plan the activities you will cover each week for a month. The Four-Week Daily Sheets will help you to further detail, day by day the unit study activities. Listed are the interactive, group activities, not the individual ones for the Assignment Sheets.

- **The Planning Grid** - provides a form for: Topic, Sub-topics, divisions or areas to study, Books/Resources, and Activities. A sample of the Planning Grid is filled out for your consideration.

- **The Planning Boxes Sheets** - a two-page set of planning sheets that provide boxes to fill in if you are the type of person who likes to keep things neat and organized. "A place for everything, and everything in it's place." Even unit study information!

- **The Personal Notes Sheet** - shows you how you can scribble out your own plans on a plain piece of paper.

- **Assignment Sheets** - samples to help you see what you could include.

- **Student's Notebook Record Sheet** - a copy of this sheet should be placed in each unit study notebook. This form provides a permanent record for each study listing the books and resources used, the date of the study, topic, projects and field trips accomplished during the study.

- **Monthly Record Keeping Sheet** - has been designed especially for filling in information pertinent to the study.

- **Book Report Form**

- **Reading List**

- **High School Forms** - a sampling of two pages for keeping daily records of work accomplished in high school. We keep track of hours which we translate into points which translate into credits. This is what we have for our children, but standards vary from state to state, so you will have to adapt the form accordingly.

- **Daily Record Keeping Forms**

- **High School Subjects List**

- **High School Subject Record Sheet** - list the many areas our students study and how they fit into academic categories counted for credits. Use to transfer data from daily record sheets.

- **Things to Include in a report**

GLOSSARY OF UNIT STUDY TERMS

ACTIVITIES - anything educational you DO - not just arts and crafts.

ASSIGNMENT SHEETS - a list of activities for a specific unit study that students can accomplish on their own.

AUTOBIOGRAPHY - the story of a person's life written by himself.

BIBLIOGRAPHY - a list of books on a specific subject.

BIOGRAPHY - literature devoted to the writing of the life stories of individuals.

CLASSIC - of model excellence in literature; 1) some define a classic as any book which ought to be read by or to children because THEY read it as a child 2) a book written by an author who has been dead for more than fifty years 3) a story or book you love and hold dear.

COPYING - the first step taken before dictation; student copies a selection to build skills.

CO-OP - teaching children in a group situation; the lessons are shared by the teachers and focus primarily on hands-on activities.

CURRICULUM - a specified course of study [at a school].

DELIGHT DIRECTED STUDY - an enduring interest and joy toward learning. One might be directed to study something out of interest and will thus delight in it.

DICTATION - to read aloud a passage for another to write down in order to master writing skills.

EDUCATIONAL KEEPSAKES - any work that the child is proud of and wishes to preserve (Especially items collected and placed in students' notebooks).

FICTION - literature dealing with imaginary characters and situations.

GRAMMAR - a system of general principles for speaking and writing according to the forms and usage of a language.

INTEGRATED STUDY - combining subjects and students of varying ages into one topic.

INTERACTIVE - time spent working on studies and activities together.

LITERATURE - the body of writing of a language, period, subject.

LIVING BOOKS - NOT textbooks! These are books that allow the reader to interact with real and interesting people in real life experiences. They stir the emotion and prick the heart.

NARRATION - to relate, to tell (a story) in detail; to describe.

NON-FICTION - factual books/source books = information.

NOTEBOOK - an important part/project for unit studies. May be a three-ring binder with dividers to serve as a place to keep paper work or comb bound and kept as an educational keepsake, a record or report compiled during a unit study.

PHILOSOPHY OF EDUCATION - your own set of values that exemplify what you feel are the necessary components to give a child a good education. Your goals and ideas develop over time through your experiences and observations in educating your children.

PROJECTS - engaging in a planned activity usually requiring some research, making or building of something, putting together a model, etc.

READ ALOUD - a piece of valuable and enjoyable literature chosen for family read aloud time to use during a unit study.

REFERENCE MATERIALS - extra-curricular resources you would refer to for study such as encyclopedias, National Geographic Magazines, books, tapes, maps, etc.

ROTE LEARNING - mechanical repetition.

SUBJECTS - academic school subjects i.e., history, math, science, geography, writing, etc.

TEXTBOOK - a manual of instruction.

THEME - subject or topic of study.

THEMATIC - about a specific theme (sea life, Civil War, rocks and minerals, the life of Abraham Lincoln, costumes of the Renaissance Era, etc.).

TOPIC - area of interest to be studied.

TOPICAL TREASURES - items to collect for conducting unit studies by theme.

UNIT STUDY - a teaching method where subjects are combined to center around one theme or topic.

WIPE CLEAN BOARD - a dry erase or wet erase board. Do not use permanent markers!

RESOURCES

This section is devoted to helping you find some of the great resources
mentioned in this book - sort of like a bag full of goodies!

A BEKA BOOKS
Pensacola, FL 32523
1-800-874-3597
For elementary math

BELLEROPHON BOOKS
36 Anacapa St., Santa Barbara, CA 93101
(805) 965-7034
Educational coloring books

CHRISTIAN LIBERTY PRESS (CLP)
502 West Euclid Ave., Arlington Heights, IL 60004
(708) 259-4444

DOVER PUBLICATIONS, INC.
31 East 2nd St., Mineola, NY 11501
(516) 294-7000
Call to request Juvenile and Booklist catalogs

MANTLE MINISTRIES
228 Still Ridge, Bulverde, TX 78163
(210) 438-3777
Richard "Little Bear" Wheeler - speaker and publisher of
historical audio and video tapes/also republishes old books

SPIZZIRRI PUBLISHING, INC.
P.O. Box 9397, Rapid City, SD 57709
(605) 348-2749
Educational coloring books

STEWARD SHIP
P.O. Box 164, Garden Valley, CA 95633
1-530-333-0803

USBORNE BOOKS (Educational Development Corporation)
EDC, P.O. Box 470663, Tulsa, OK 74147-0663
1-800-475-4522
Check your area for local distributors first

Miscellaneous BOOKS and RESOURCES Mentioned:

Adam and His Kin by Ruth Beechick

Advent Foretold by Gary and Wanda Sanseri
Back Home Industries

The American Revolution by Bruce Bliven
ISBN # 0-394-84696-6

Bible Truths for School Subjects by Ruth Haycock

Carry On, Mr. Bowditch by Jean Lee Latham
ISBN # 0-395-13713-6

Celebrate With Joy by Sondra Burnett
Available through Steward Ship

A Cricket in Times Square by George Selden

The Far Frontier by William O'Steele

For the Children's Sake by Susan Shaeffer Macaulay
ISBN # 0-89107-290-X

Girl of the Limberlost by Jean Stratton Porter

He Went With Marco Polo by Louise Andrews Kent

I, Juan de Pareja by Elizabeth Borton De Trevino

It Just Couldn't Happen by Lawrence O. Richards

Johnny Tremain by Esther Forbes

Journey to the Center of the Earth by Jules Verne
(Children's Illustrated Classics)

Kids Discover Magazine • 212-677-4457

Kids Multicultural Art Book by Alexandra M. Terzian

Mary Emma and Company (Little Britches series) by Ralph Moody
ISBN # 0-8032-8211-7

My Brother Sam is Dead by James Lincoln Collier and Christopher Collier

The Price of Liberty by Wayne Whipple

The Read Aloud Handbook by Jim Trelease
ISBN # 0 14 046 534 0

George Washington's Rules of Decent Behavior

Sam the Minuteman and George the Drummer Boy by Nathaniel Benchley

Scholastic Book Clubs, Inc. • 1-800-246-2986
Jefferson City, MO 65102-7503

Stories of the Pilgrims (Christian Liberty Press)

The Story of the American Revolution coloring book (Dover Publications)

The Tale of Three Trees by Angela Elwell Hunt
ISBN # 0-7459-1743-7

Uniforms of the American Revolution

Unlocking the Mysteries of Creation by Dennis Peterson

Will You Sign Here, John Hancock? By Jean Fritz

FIELD TRIPS

The A-Z Guide to Home School Field Trips by April Purtell, Elizabeth Gaunt, John Gaunt,
Gregg Harris (Editor)

LITERATURE GUIDES

Books Children Love by Elizabeth Wilson
ISBN # 0-89107-441-4

Great Books of the Christian Tradition by Terry Glaspey
ISBN# 1-56507-356-8

The Hand That Rocks the Cradle by Nathaniel Bluedorn
Trivium Pursuit, PMB 168
429 Lake Park Blvd., Muscatine, IA 52761

Honey For a Child's Heart by Gladys Hunt

Teaching Children by Diane Lopez

COURSE OF STUDY

The Home School Manual by Ted Wade

A Typical Course of Study • World Books

What Your Child Needs to Know When by Robin Sampson
ISBN # 0-9701816-1-2

LANGUAGE ARTS

For the Love of Reading by Valerie Bendt
Bendt Family Ministries
333 W. Rio Vista Court, Tampa, FL 33604-6940
813-758-6793

The Great Editing Adventure
Common Sense Press

Simply Grammar
P.O. Box 172, Stanton, NJ 08885
ISBN # 1-89920-901-5

Wordsmart Computer Program
Smartek Software
1-800-858-WORD
For vocabulary

Writer's Express, The Write Source 2000, and Writer's Inc.
Great Source Education Group
P.O. Box 7050, Wilmington, MA 01887

The Writing Road to Reading (WRTR) - Teaching Reading at Home by Wanda Sanseri
Back Home Industries
P.O. Box 22495, Milwaukie, OR 97222

UNIT STUDIES

Alta Vista
12324 Rd. 37, Madera, CA 93638
1-800-544-1397

Developing Godly Character in Children
Hands to Help Publications
P. O. Box 3464, Orange, CA 92665-1203

Diana Waring - History Alive
621 SR 9 NE, PMB B-14, Lake Stevens, WA 98258
(425) 397-0631

Five in a Row by Jane Claire Lambert
P.O. Box 707, Grandview, MO 64030-0707
(816) 246-9252 • Fax: (816) 246-9253

Food for the Hungry (missions)
7729 E. Greenway Rd., Scottsdale, AZ 85260
1-800-2-HUNGER

KONOS
Box 250, Anna, TX 75409
(972) 924-2712

Learning Life's Lessons by Barbara Wagner
Hewitt Research Foundation
P.O. Box 9, Washougal, WA 98671
(206) 835-8708

Lessons from History
Hillside Academy
1804 Melody Ln., Burnsville, MN 55337

Weaver Curriculum
2752 Scarborough, Riverside, CA 92503
(909) 688-3126

HOMESCHOOLING

The Basics Steps to Successful Homeschooling by Vicky A. Brady
ISBN # 1-56384-113-4

The Christian Home School by Gregg Harris
ISBN # 1-56857-025-2

How to Home School by Gayle Graham, Common Sense Press
ISBN # 1-880892-40-5

The Ultimate Guide to Homeschooling by Debra Bell
ISBN # 0-89-499-3988-7

Educating the Wholehearted Child by Clay and Sally Clarkson
ISBN # 1-888692-00-6

MATH

Math-U-See
1378 River Rd., Drumore, PA 17518-9760

Saxon Math
1320 West Lindsey, Norman, OK 73069
1-800-284-7019

ART

Draw Write Now
Barker Creek Publishing, Inc.
P.O. Box 2610, Poulsbo, WA 98370
1-800-692-5833

Taking the Mystery Out of Studying Art History guide
1-888-4 R-UNITS

How Great Thou Art
http://www.howgreatthouart.com

SCIENCE

Lyrical Life Science book and tapes
Lyrical Learning
8008 Cardwell Hill Rd., Corvallis, OR 97330
1-800-761-0906

HIGH SCHOOL

Christian Home Educator's Curriculum Manual for Junior and Senior High by Cathy Duffy
Home Run Enterprises

The High School Handbook by Mary Schofield
CHEA of California
P.O. Box 2009, Norwalk, CA 90651-2009
1-800-564-CHEA

Home School, High School, and Beyond by Beverly Adams Gordon
15436 42nd St. Ave. South, Seattle, WA 98188
(206) 439-0248

A Senior High Form+U+la by Barbara Shelton
ISBN # 1-887-639-03-9

PUBLIC SPEAKING

From Playpen to Podium by Jeff Myers
ISBN# 1-56857-068-6

DRAMA

Putting on a Play-the young playwright's guide to scripting, directing, and performing by Nancy Bentley and Donna Guthrie
ISBN # 0-7613-0011-2

MUSIC

Basic Library of the World's Greatest Music by Lee Lambert
P.O. Box 25212, Ft. Lauderdale, FL 33320
ISBN # 0-962163-007

Music Education in the Christian Home by Dr. Mary Ann Froehlich
ISBN # 1-56857-031-7

SAMPLES AND EXAMPLES SECTION

This section is devoted to providing samples of different unit studies and examples of how to use some of the planning sheets and how you might schedule your unit study day. In chapter one, I demonstrated a typical schedule for us during a unit study on birds. To show you how studies and schedules vary according to the topic and the age of the children consider the following examples.

SAMPLE UNIT STUDIES

COLONIAL TIMES UNIT STUDY

At the time of this study my children were:
Students - Cacey 18, Ty 16, Whitney 13, Brooke 10, Kally 7

Length of study - 4 weeks (4 days a week) = 20 days. Normally, we would work on a unit study for five days but this particular year, we did a colorful, fun filled World Geography study with the younger three children. The older ones used that day to work on foreign language and other areas. **This is a great idea - to study on one topic four days then step away to do a completely different type study one day a week - perhaps a more "fun" study - it can be more of an activities type day. The kids really look forward to this.**

Time required - During this unit study we finished all skills and activities before lunch (taking two to three hours). Anything not accomplished like studying a list of spelling words, silent reading, looking up any new vocabulary words, working on writing assignments, or doing math could be done after lunch.

Subjects incorporated - Reading, Writing/Grammar, Spelling and Vocabulary, Reading Aloud, Arts, Crafts and Hands-On Activities, History, and Geography.

Resources Used:

Colonies Colorbook by Spizzirri Publishers

13 Colonies Colorbook by Bellerophon (contains beautiful pictures of seals - have child choose their favorite to color different details each day!)

If You Lived In Colonial Times by Ann McGovern

The Witch of Blackbird Pond by Elizabeth George Speare (The Read Aloud Title - don't be scared off by the title as this is a very good book)

Tools and Gadgets (Historic Communities series)

The Courage of Sarah Noble by Alice Dalgliesh (silent reading for Brooke)

Young Abigail Adams by Francene Sabinea Troll Associates book (Mom read to Kally)

Benjamin Franklin - a biography (independent reading title for Ty and Cacey)

Little Maid of Massachusetts Colony by Alice Turner Curtis (silent reading for Whitney)

Early Trades coloring book by Dover Publications

Cut and Assemble Colonial Houses by Dover Publications

The Story of Jamestown (Cornerstones of Freedom series)

I started each day by reading a chapter from *The Witch of Blackbird Pond* sometimes offering vocabulary words from the text. Each day, for 13 days, I read about a different colony (from educational color books listed). As I read, the children cut out colonial houses, colored pictures of the colonies to place in their notebooks, or took notes.

The first day we started making a group wall timeline and marked dates from 1607 to 1776. As the children learned about each colony they placed a cut out (traced from a map) of each colony by it's founding date and wrote some information about it. They each had a U.S. map to color for their notebook, and made a key to go with it. Each day we started (information time) by reviewing the colonies we had studied and marked the colonies on a large wipe-off U.S. wall map.

Next, I would read a page or two from *Tools and Gadgets* or *If You Lived In Colonial Times*. These books gave us ideas for some colonial activities. Fortunately, we have a few antique gadgets in our home so we were able to do some of the following simple activities using them - usually just one each day.

We:

- Heated an antique iron over our gas stove burner and ironed a dress.
- Ground wheat kernels with rocks.
- Beat a rug with an old fashioned rug beater.
- Made cream by taking turns shaking a jar of whipping cream (place a marble in the jar and shake for about 15 minutes.)
- Baked tea cakes.
- Tried washing clothes using a washboard.
- Made a candle.
- Made a slate from black construction paper and wrote on it with chalk.
- Memorized a portion of the *New England Primer.*
- Read from *Poor Richard's Almanac.*
- Tried tin punching (remove labels from cans).
- Made a wig from white construction paper cutting strips down the sides and curling like ribbon.
- Made a quilt square and puff painted the name of a colony on it.(Each child did a mini-report on their colony and placed the quilt square in their notebook.)
- Put together the colonial houses.
- Worked on notebooks. Organized and completed unfinished assignments.

- Wrote a one page colonial newspaper.

- Wrote book reports.

- Pretended to be a town crier.

- Read the poem *Paul Revere's Ride* by Longfellow.

- Wrote with a quill pen and ink.

Now, before you say, "Ah ha, I knew you had to DO a lot of activities!" consider how quickly each activity can be completed. Each one only took about 15 minutes, was the highlight of the day and required very little preparation, thought or materials. Again, you will choose how many activities you wish to include in any unit study - it's completely up to you. Just remember, these are the things your kids like to do and will remember… and will place you in the Best Mother Hall of Fame! I like to do activities… - short easy ones. I cheat my way into the Hall of Fame!

I also read excerpts from a textbook which had valuable information about different aspects of colonial life. (Remember, this textbook is just a resource/tool like all my others.)

REVOLUTIONARY WAR UNIT STUDY

The Revolutionary War study is the next topic chronologically but IS different. Colonial Times is more about daily life in the Colonies whereas the Revolution is a time of unrest and war. THIS, is one of my favorite studies. We have included these sample unit studies to help you see what a study might comprise. Have fun and use them BUT we do offer a full guide for both of these studies if you are needing more help!

Goal: To gain a general knowledge about the American Revolution, why it came about and what was accomplished by the war. To learn about important people of the revolution.

GETTING STARTED

Length of Study -Four-six weeks

Subjects Incorporated - History, Reading (reading aloud and silent), Writing/Grammar, Geography, Hands-on activities (diagrams, etc.), Crafts, Research, Spelling/Vocabulary.

To begin your unit study on The Revolutionary War choose a main source for information. We suggest the Landmark book *The American Revolution* by Bruce Bliven. (The Landmark Series books are fast-moving, dramatic, readable, and fun.)

Next, read over the list of Objectives and Activities and decide which ones will be suitable for your study and children's ages. You could conduct this study with K-8th grades, but war is always a hard subject - you can "lighten up" and do the Yankee Doodle thing! If you plan to conduct this study over a four-week period, plan what activities you will do each week. Prepare your spelling and vocabulary list for each child (considering age), and make copies of documents from reference books plus any other handouts you will use.

Divide a sheet into two columns entitled "Famous Events" and "Famous People."

Compile a list of items you will need such as construction paper, books, etc. Check the library for items you can check out including audio tapes, books, etc.

Prepare three notebook sheets. Label the first "People," the second "Places" and the third sheet "Things." OR New England, Middle, Southern listing people and colonies in the correct slots as you learn filling in as your study progresses.

Example:

- **People:** Nathan Hale, Josiah Quincy (mentioned in Johnny Tremain), Abigail Adams

- **Places:** Boston, Delaware River, Fort Ticonderoga

- **Things:** Declaration of Independence, flintlock musket, The Quartering Act

NOTE: These lists are very different from filling in worksheet blanks because the children are creating their own reference sheet with information they find useful and wish to include in their individual notebooks where they can organize information.

LEARNING OBJECTIVES AND CONNECTED ACTIVITIES

- Learn about the original 13 colonies New England, Middle, Southern and outline on U.S. map.

- Write an essay explaining what motivated our founding fathers and what character traits they possessed.

- Make a mural picturing famous people of the Revolutionary War. Who did what and why? Draw your own pictures or use old textbooks.

- List dates, events and reasons for the war.

- Make a Revolutionary War Wall Timeline. (Copy information onto 8 1/2x11 for notebook.)

- Study the ships used during the war. Make a diagram labeling parts of the ship.

- Learn about everyday life during the period. List vocations, important towns, ports, etc.

- Report on an important event such as Paul Revere's ride, the Boston Tea Party, or The Stamp Act.

- Look at a copy of Constitution and try writing with a feather pen.

- Pretend to be a Founding Father. Write and give a speech. (Maybe you'll be the next Patrick Henry!)

- Study the life of Ben Franklin. Read "Poor Richard's Almanac." Try writing an anecdote.

- Study cooking of that era and try some recipes.

- Look up Scriptures about freedom and liberty in the Bible. Use these verses for handwriting practice.

- Study the life of George Washington with an eye to his character. Read his "Rules of Decent Behavior" or a biography about his life.

- Have older children read historical fiction novels for silent/independent reading.

- Make a British and American Flag (copy, draw your own, or use construction paper). Research the different flags (Union Jack, etc.)

- Have the children write a biographical sketch of one famous person.

- Sing some patriotic songs such as "Yankee Doodle" and "The Star Spangled Banner." Research the story behind the songs.

- Compile a report on an important event or aspect of the war. Use the pictures from the Dover educational coloring books to enhance the report.

- Compare the Revolutionary War with different wars found in the Old Testament.

- Look up Scriptures about freedom and liberty in the Bible use it for handwriting practice.

- Make a vocabulary and spelling word list for each child (considering age) for their notebook.

ACTIVITIES FOR EARLY LEARNERS

- Make Yankee Doodle Hats.

- Cook macaroni for lunch.

- Make flags for England and the Colonies.

- Read aloud *Sam the Minuteman* by Nathaniel Benchley.

- Visit the seafood section of the grocery store, and show the children a real lobster. (Colonists called the soldiers "Lobster Backs" because of their red coats.)

- Find Britain and America on a map. Point out the 13 colonies, the surrounding areas, and the Atlantic Ocean.

- Talk about how muskets had to be loaded and fired as compared to our present day guns.

- Make a fife and drum (use a coffee can and cover with construction paper and shoelaces).

- Check out a book on Betsy Ross from the Juvenile section of the library. Give children scraps of cloth along with a needle (with large hole and blunt tip) and thread to make their own original U.S. flag.

- Hold an Independence Day celebration at the end of the study. Make red, white and blue cupcakes.

BOOKS, MATERIALS AND RESOURCES

The American Revolution (Landmark Books) by Bruce Bliven, Jr.

Johnny Tremain by Esther Forbes (a MUST read for this topic)

My Brother Sam is Dead by James Lincoln Collier and Christopher Collier

Sam the Minuteman and George the Drummer Boy both by Nathaniel Benchley

Carry On, Mr. Bowditch by Jean Lee Latham (post revolution, but a MUST read)

Will You Sign Here, John Hancock? by Jean Fritz

The Fighting Ground by Avi

The Price of Liberty by Wayne Whipple (republished by Mantle Ministries)

What People Wore by Douglas Gorsline - 1,800 black and white illustrations of historical costumes (Dover)

Turning Back the Pages of Time by Kathy Keller. This is an American History literature guide.

Historical Cookbooks by Patricia Mitchell (Foodways Publications) Cookbooks written about every historical event in U.S. history. Includes lots of recipes and information surrounding the time periods.

Take Your Hat Off When the Flag Goes By - Audio tape of patriotic songs by BRITE - **CHECK AVAILABILITY**.

American Family of the Early Republic - paper dolls (Dover)

Uniforms of the American Revolution (Dover)

The Story of the American Revolution (Dover coloring book)

The Declaration of Independence and the Constitution

WORLD GEOGRAPHY UNIT STUDY

Plan to study World Geography by studying each of the seven continents spread out over a whole school year. It actually took us two years studying one or two days a week. This schedule has worked well for my children as they have enjoyed having a break from whatever other unit we are studying on Fridays to study "The World." We wanted our study to encompass more than geography, so along with learning the names and locations of countries, rivers, deserts, and mountains, we studied such things as money, religions, customs, industry and resources, homes, dress, and mission work.

Week #1 - North America   **Week #5** - Australia

Week #2 - South America   **Week #6** - Antarctica

Week #3 - Europe   **Week #7** - Asia

Week #4 - Africa

Activities:

- Study countries by continents learning capitals, topography, climate, culture, about the language, government, etc.

- Choose one country from each continent and do a mini-report.

- Make passports.

- Each child should choose a couple of books or biographies about people from different lands or that are set in a different country (i.e., *Heidi* by Johanna Spyri, *Hans Brinker and the Silver Skates* by Mary Maps Dodge, a biography about David Livingstone, *Amos Fortune-Freeman* by Elizabeth Yates).

- Research and write about an important historical event and the country where it happened.

- Invite another family or two to join in a co-op and have a banquet using costumes and food from different countries.

- Become familiar with maps and map terminology (equator, meridian, International Dateline, longitude, etc. Make a list of geography terms. Add new vocabulary words as you go.

- Make a mural using cuttings from old National Geographic magazines showing different cultures. Make collages on regular sized paper to include in the notebook.

- Prepare an oral presentation about a country telling about their religions, food, dress, etc.

- Learn some songs from different countries.

- Write an essay on the United Nations (its good and bad points).

- Have your little ones create their own flag for a pretend country, name the people & draw pictures and make a "My Country Book" OR write a book about an already existing country.

- Learn current events from a few countries. Watch the news and read the newspaper.

- Plan to do lots of art and crafts from around the world.

Resources:

The following list includes books we have found valuable; however, you do not need them ALL:

A World Atlas, Globe & World Map

Encyclopedias (books or CD-Rom for computer)

Round the World Cookbook (Usborne)

Passport to Adventure - activity book of children from around the world (reproducible). Available through Steward Ship.

Round the World Songbook (Usborne)

Wee Sing Around the World audio tape

National Geographic magazines

Where in the World is Carmen San Diego (board game or computer game)

Kids Multicultural Art Book by Alexandra M. Terzian

You Can Change the World (Operation World for kids) by Jill Johnstone

A Quick Look at This World - a hands-on study (a notebook resource which shows you how to conduct a world geography study continent by continent). Available through Steward Ship.

NOTE: You'll need to use the library to get books about people and places around the world.

Plans:

- Make a list of spelling & vocabulary words using geography terms.
- Decide which continent you'll start with then take a trip to the library and find some good books to use during your study.
- Choose a read-aloud title to fit with the continent/countries you start with.
- Order books, make copies, organize your plans into days and weeks.
- Starting with basic geography, teach the seven continents and oceans marking on your notebook size ma.
- Learn about as many countries and islands and their locations as possible.
- Have each child pick a famous explorer to study.

BIRTH OF CHRIST UNIT STUDY

Week #1 - Prophesy about the Coming of a Savior

Week #2 - The Birth of Christ

Week #3 - What Does the Great Gift Mean to Us?

Week #4 - Focusing on Giving to Others

Resources:

The Bible as your MAIN source (Matthew & Luke)

Celebrate With Joy by Sondra Burnett (order through Steward Ship)

Advent Foretold by Gary & Wanda Sanseri

The Tale of Three Trees retold by Angela Hunt

The Miracle of Johnathan Toomay by Susan Wojciechowski

Jotham's Journey: A Storybook for Advent by Arnold Ytreeide (Also Barholomew's

Passage and Tabitha's Travels - wonderful stories to read at Christmas time)

Adornaments - Twelve colorful, cardboard ornaments each with a "name" of Jesus to read and "adore" Him

Activities:

Miscellaneous ideas for activities to do at random times through out your study.

- Read all gospel accounts then choose one to use for making Scripture cards.

- Pick a needy family to minister to during the holidays, invite them for dinner, make them a gift (food basket, etc.), and have children give them the Scripture cards.

- Have young children make their own "Story of Christmas" book while listening to the Bible story or Christmas music. Draw pictures or use stickers using, Scriptures as captions.

- Research the origin of Christmas Carols.

- Write out the words to a carol like a poem (in stanzas) and recite it for family.

- Write a paper about St. Nicholas (children will understand where Santa Claus came from).

- Pick a country and study their Christmas beliefs, traditions, food, decorations, etc.

- If your family writes an annual Christmas letter, ask the children to help.

- Have children write out Luke 2:1-20 for handwriting practice.

- Keep Christmas cards in a basket on your dinner table, pick a person each day to pray for. Continue to pray even after Christmas time.

- For family reading time, read *The Tale of Three Trees* by Angela Elwell Hunt
- *Celebrate With Joy*, (written by homeschooling mother, Sondra Burnett) offers many ways to help keep the focus on Christ and is full of great family ideas including crafts, the advent wreath, devotionals, etc. (Available through Steward Ship.)

We don't usually do a unit study during the month of December because there are so many distractions that time of year. Instead, we try to focus on other people, visiting and doing things we never take the time to do. This particular topic, The Birth of Christ, would be a perfect time and topic for this time of year and you can take it a little easier and not do so many of your academics.

Planning Sheets

Samples

Forms

High School

Sample Bubble Diagram

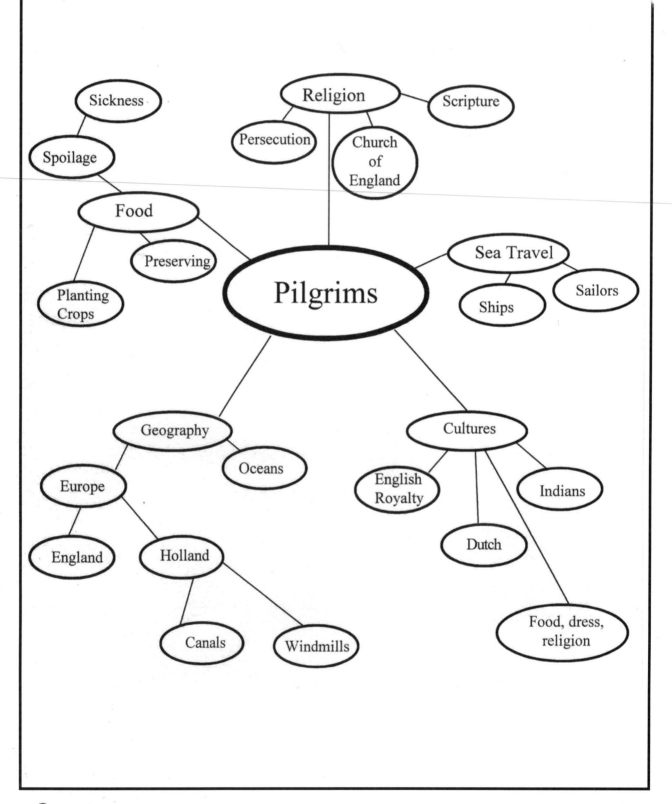

The "Big Picture" Plan

Future Topics to Study:

_____   _____   _____

_____   _____   _____

_____   _____   _____

_____   _____   _____

Topics for this year:

September _____   October _____   November _____

December _____   January _____   February _____

March _____   April _____   May _____

June _____   July _____   August _____

Possible Co-op Units:

_____   _____   _____

Families to Co-op With:

_____   _____   _____

Considering Child's Interests:

Child: _____   Child: _____   Child: _____

Interest: _____   Interest: _____   Interest: _____

Type of Unit: _____

	Sept.	Oct.	Nov.	Dec.	Jan.	Feb.	Mar.	April	May	June	July	August
History												
Science												
Literature												
Geography												
Character												
Arts												
Other												

Brainstorming My Plans

Transfer ideas from Bubble diagram to this sheet

Topic: _____

Sub-Topic: _____   Sub -sub topics: _____

_____   _____

Sub-Topic: _____   Sub -sub topics: _____

_____   _____

Sub-Topic: _____   Sub -sub topics: _____

_____   _____

Sub-Topic: _____   Sub -sub topics: _____

_____   _____

Subject areas topics fit into:

History _____

_____

Science _____

_____

Geography_____

_____

Literature _____

_____

Language Arts _____

_____

Art _____

Music _____

Character _____

_____

Other _____

_____

I find my ideas too broad. Now I will pare these topics down to what I wish to study. Areas:

_____

_____

_____

_____

_____

_____

_____

					Monday
					Tuesday
					Wednesday
					Thursday
					Friday

Map out your annual plans on a calendar

September	January	May
October	February	June
November	March	July
December	April	August

Week # _____ Main Focus: _____ Topic: _____
Monday: _____
_____
Tuesday: _____
_____
Wednesday:_____
_____
Thursday: _____
_____
Friday: _____
_____

Week # _____ Main Focus: _____ Topic: _____
Monday: _____
_____
Tuesday: _____
_____
Wednesday:_____
_____
Thursday: _____
_____
Friday: _____
_____

Week # _____ Main Focus: _____ Topic: _____
Monday: _____
_____
Tuesday: _____
_____
Wednesday:_____
_____
Thursday: _____
_____
Friday: _____
_____

Week # _____ Main Focus: _____ Topic: _____
Monday: _____
_____
Tuesday: _____
_____
Wednesday:_____
_____
Thursday: _____
_____
Friday: _____
_____

Use for more detailed or specific daily plans

Topic _____   Date _____

Areas to cover each week:

Week # 1	Week #2	Week #3	Week #4

Four week planning sheet

The Planning Grid

Topic _____

Sub -Topics	Areas to Study	Books / Resources	Activities

In this book, we have included several different styles of planning sheets for your consideration. The more you do unit studies, the easier planning will become and you will find a planning style to fit your needs. Below is another "Planning Sheet" option.

Topic - *Pilgrims*

Sub -Topics	Areas to Study	Resources	Activities
Religion	Persecution Religion in England The King's army Meeting in secret	Stories of the Pilgrims from Christian Liberty Press	Look up Scriptures to compare the Pilgrim's persecution to 12 disciples hiding in the upper room
Food	1) What is food like in Holland? 2) Preparing for the voyage 3) Spoilage 4) Going hungry 5) No stores in New World 6) Learning to plant crops 7) Running out of supplies	If You Sailed on the Mayflower	Try making hardtack Sample or make beef jerky Conduct experiment to learn about food spoilage Corn planting experiment
Geography	Life in England Travel from England to Holland - culture of the dutch - windmills- canals Voyage to New World Plymouth Plantation - Indian Culture What life was like on board ship	Squanto...Friend to the Pilgrims Stories of the Pilgrims The Mayflower Pilgrims The Plymouth Settlement (William Bradford's diary) Sarah Morton's Day If You Sailed...	Locate countries and travels on world map Put together a windmill model - study how windmills work- draw pictures of dutch people, tulips, wooden shoes, brightly colored dress etc. Look at pictures of cross section in "If You Sailed..." Keep a daily journal Use a compass Rope tying
Sea Travel	Sailors disliked pilgrims Present dangers Cramped and smelly quarters Length of voyage		
Cultures	England, Holland, Indian Type of government Type of housing Language	Use Encyclopedia	Indian Sign Language Build a Teepee

Topic:	Co-op Yes ☐ No ☐

Book List (books at home)	Library book list:

Books to order: Order from:	Read Aloud Title:

Books to borrow: Borrow from:	Unit Study Guide or Curriculum:

Activities and projects:

Subject   Activity

Subject   Activity

Subject   Activity

Subject   Activity

Subject   Activity

Subject   Activity

Subject   Activity

Field Trips to:

Topic:	Co-op Yes ☐ No ☐

Book List (books at home)	Library book list:
Books to order: Order from:	Read Aloud Title:
Books to borrow: Borrow from:	Unit Study Guide or Curriculum:

Activities and projects:

Subject   Activity

Subject   Activity

Subject   Activity

Subject   Activity

Subject   Activity

Subject   Activity

Subject   Activity

Field Trips to:

Topic: *The Pony Express*	Co-op Yes ☐ No ☒

Book List (books at home)	Library book list:
The Pony Express - from Cornerstones of Freedom series	*The Sweetwater Run*

Books to order:	*Pony Express by Steven Kroll*	Read Aloud Title:	*Riders of the Pony Express by Ralph Moody*
Order from:	*Scholastic Book Club*		

Books to borrow:	*Heading West Activity Book*	Unit Study Guide or Curriculum:	*Creating from scratch*
Borrow from:	*Sheila Martin*		

Activities and projects: *(NOTE: the example below might include work a student would do over a period of several days)*

Subject	Activity
Writing	*Write essay on "How the Doughnut Came to Be"*
History	*Make a Pony Express timeline (include ship, stagecoach, & telegraph)*
Geography	*Make maps to show topography and include pony express trail landmarks*
Art	*Make a wanted poster requesting pony express riders*
Bible	*Read 11 Cor. 3: 1-3. Discuss how our lives are like letters people read*
Crafts	*Make a mail pouch*
Handwriting	*List the names of pony express riders and stations*
History	*Research Samuel Morse and the Morse Code. Write out a message in code for a friend to decode. Try tapping it using dots and dashes.*

Field Trips to: *Take a trip to the post office.*

Supply List:	Spelling Words:	Ideas:
Brown fabric for making mail pouches	horse rider transcontinental plateau plains Indians danger orphan stagecoach overland Missouri stations progress telegraph gold rush post office saddle prairies mountains	Kids can start a stamp collection Make maps to show sea, stagecoach, and pony express routes Teach how to write letters (also parts of a letter) Research durability of breeds of horses used
U.S. maps		
3 1/2" binders for notebooks		
Recipe for making doughnuts		

Other related activities: *Go into the Gold Rush - visit historic Coloma and try gold panning*

Child's silent reading titles:

Child: *Brooke*   Book: *Pony Express / Kroll*

Child: *Tyson*   Book: *Buffalo Bill / Beal*

Child: Book:

Date of study: *May 1-15*

Length of study: *Two weeks*

Resources or materials: *Article on Pony Express from National Geographic*

United States Postage Stamp coloring book
Story of California Gold Rush coloring book

With my materials laid out on the table, often I will plan a unit study in just a couple of hours, by jotting down plans using a plain piece of paper like this:

Topic - Pony Express
Time frame - two weeks mini unit (May)

Ideas for Assignment Sheets
Writing Activities -
essay on "How the doughnut came to be", a description of how the telegraph works, a list of the pony express stations, write different types of letters

Art Activities -
Make a "Wanted" poster (asking for riders), color pictures from educational coloring books, sketch picture of horse and rider, obtain a copy of Frederick Remington's "Coming and Going of the Pony Express" and study it, make a mail pouch, design a postage stamp.

Supplies: brown fabric for making mail pouches
Black line U.S. Maps (reproduce)
Doughnut recipe

Geography -
Map mail ship route around tip of So. America, make map of transcontinental telegraph, map out mail stagecoach route, map out pony express trail

Activities to do in a group -
Make a wall timeline
Work on mail pouches
Go on field trip to Post Office
Read aloud time
Work on stamp collections
Tap out a message in "morse code"

Books to Use -
The Pony Express (Cornerstones of Freedom series)
The Sweetwater Run (juvenile)
Riders of the Pony Express (Read Aloud)
Pony Express by Steven Kroll
Heading West Activity Book

Spelling words:
horse, rider, plateau, plains, Indians, danger, orphan, station, telegraph, stagecoach, saddle, mountains, post office progress, Missouri

Sample "Birds" Study Assignment Sheet

Bible
- ❑ Read and color pictures from Birds coloring book
- ❑ Look up Bible verses relating to Birds
- ❑ List birds mentioned in the Bible
- ❑ Memorize a Scripture about birds (Matt. 6:26-27, 33-34 and Psalm 17:8)

Writing
- ❑ Write bird watching observations in bird diary
- ❑ Write instructions for how to make a bird house / do a mini report
- ❑ Write a poem
- ❑ Write a composition describing your favorite bird
- ❑ Describe how airplanes and birds are alike

Research
- ❑ Find out why the eagle was used as America's national bird. Write your findings and include a picture of the seal of the President
- ❑ Look up something about birds on the internet
- ❑ Birds are classified as AVES. Find out what other animals are grouped as.

Geography
- ❑ Classify and alphabetize birds by habitat (grasslands, lakes, marshes etc.)
- ❑ Make a map showing migration patterns
- ❑ Read about the 50 state birds. Fill in a black line copy of a U.S. map with names of state birds

Hands-On Activities
- ❑ Work on Quick Look fact sheets
- ❑ Work on topic, information and posters for oral presentation

Worksheets / Notebooks
- ❑ Make a sheet listing in 2 columns which birds are helpful and which are harmful
- ❑ Make a paper showing the largest and smallest bird. Label with names and include pictures.
- ❑ Make a diagram showing parts of a bird. Another parts of a feather, a bird skeleton, and life cycle.
- ❑ Fill out worksheets for beaks and feet
- ❑ Color pictures from Dover for notebooks.
- ❑ Make a sheet showing the breakdown of: classes, families, genus, species etc.

Language Arts
- ❑ Do your silent reading daily
- ❑ Read and memorize a poem
- ❑ Study your spelling words / look up vocabulary words

Art
- ❑ Draw or sketch a picture of a bird

Sample Assignment Sheet   *Kally (Age 7)*   Topic - Pony Express

Bible
❑ Listen to Mom read a "letter" from the New Testament
❑ Think of a messenger from a Bible story. Have Mom or Dad read you the story from the Bible.

Handwriting
❑ List the names of some of the pony express riders or copy a list Mom writes.

Writing
❑ Copy a sentence about Buffalo Bill Cody.
❑ Draw a picture of a pony express rider as he rides through and grabs a doughnut. Ask Mom to write a paragraph as you tell her "How the Doughnut Came to Be."
❑ Write a sentence in Morse Code and put into your notebook.
❑ Write a letter and send to a friend.
❑ Discuss the meaning of the word "transcontinental."
❑ Write the name of the messenger you named in your Bible story and narrate the story.

Arts & Crafts
❑ Draw a picture of: a type of horse used for pony express, Chimney Rock, a pony express station etc.
❑ Make a Wanted Poster and draw a picture of a horse and rider.
   Have Mom write in the request for riders to join the pony express.
❑ Make a mail pouch.
❑ Using the National Geographic article on The Pony Express. Copy photos of riders and other pictures to make a pony express art gallery or collage.
❑ Design your own postage stamp.
❑ Make a mini stamp collection for your notebook.
❑ Design a cover for your Pony Express Notebook.

Research
❑ Find out what kind of horses riders used and look at pictures of them.
❑ Find a picture of Samuel Morse to put in your notebook.

History
❑ Make a Pony Express timeline.

Geography
❑ Make a U.S. map showing the stagecoach route, the pony express route and another one for the telegraph.

Spelling
❑ Learn to spell three words. Learn the meaning of two new words.

Activity
❑ Obtain a copy of "The Morse Code" and try tapping a message out using the dots and dashes.
Write a message for another person to decode.

Sample Assignment Sheet   *Brooke (Age 9)*   Topic - Pony Express

Bible
- ❑ The New Testament is filled with letters written to the churches. Find one and write out a "salutation."
- ❑ With help, look up "Messenger" in a Bible concordance. Name one messenger from the Bible.

Handwriting
- ❑ Find the names of as many pony express riders as you can find, place in list form and alphabetize list.
- ❑ List the names of some of the well known pony express stations along the trail.

Writing
- ❑ Take dictation (or copying) from the book "Buffalo Bill Cody."
- ❑ Pretending you are a pony express rider, write 1) a description of what you would see along the trail or 2) something exciting that happened to you.
- ❑ Write a description of the telegraph, how it functions and explain how "Morse Code" works.
- ❑ Using "The Write Source 2000," learn the parts of a letter and how to write a one. Send one copy of your letter through the mail and place another copy of your letter in your notebook.
- ❑ Write a paragraph on: "The Pony Express and the History of the Post Office," also "How the Doughnut Came to Be."
- ❑ Learn the meaning of the word "transcontinental" and write the definition.
- ❑ Write the name of the messenger you looked up in the Bible. Include some details about the story.

Arts & Crafts
- ❑ Draw a picture of: a type of horse used for pony express, Chimney Rock, a pony express station etc
- ❑ Make a Wanted Poster: (draw a picture of a horse and rider and write in request for pony express riders.)
- ❑ Using a piece of brown fabric, leather or some other material, make a pony express mail pouch.
- ❑ Using the National Geographic article on the Pony Express, copy or cut photos of riders and other things to make a pony express art gallery or collage. Label pictures.
- ❑ Design your own postage stamp.
- ❑ Start your own "mini" stamp collection for your notebook.

Research
- ❑ Research the types of horses used to ride in the pony express and include pictures and descriptions of the different types of horses for your notebook.
- ❑ Find out who Samuel Morse was (try to find a picture of him to put in your notebook and write a short paper about him.)

History
- ❑ Make a Pony Express timeline (both a WALL timeline and a notebook timeline.)

Geography
- ❑ Make a 3 maps showing: 1) the route the ships took around South America, 2) the stagecoach route 3) the pony express route.
- ❑ Make a map showing the route of the transcontinental telegraph.

Spelling
- ❑ Study your Pony Express spelling words. Learn the meaning of 4 words and write out definitions.

Activity
- ❑ Obtain a copy of "The Morse Code" and try tapping a message out using the dots and dashes. Write a message for another person to decode.

Save all your work and put into the correct sections of your notebook.

Sample Assignment Sheet   *Whitney (Age 12)*   Topic - Pony Express

Bible
- ❑ The New Testament is filled with letters to the churches. Find one, read it to your family and discuss.
- ❑ Find a passage that shows a time when a messenger delivered a message.
- ❑ Writing letters is a way to communicate. Look up II Cor. 3:1-3 and explain what this means.

Handwriting
- ❑ Find the names of as many pony express riders as you can. List their names and some of the stations.
- ❑ Write out the passage above, in cursive.

Writing
- ❑ Take dictation from the book "Buffalo Bill Cody."
- ❑ Write a description, pretending you are a rider, what you would see along the trail or
       of something that happened to you.
- ❑ Write a description of the telegraph, how it works and what Morse Code is.
- ❑ Using "The Write Source 2000," learn how to write 3 kinds of letters. (letter of inquiry, request,
       complaint, or a friendly letter) Include samples of each in your notebook . Send a friendly letter to someone.
- ❑ Write a paper "The Pony Express and the History of the Post Office" also "The History of the Doughnut."
- ❑ Write a definition of the word "transcontinental." Give example of other transcontinentals.

Arts & Crafts
- ❑ Draw a picture of: a type of horse used for pony express, Chimney Rock, a pony express station etc.
- ❑ Make a Wanted Poster, drawing a picture of a horse and rider (write in request for pony express riders).
- ❑ Make a mail pouch.
- ❑ Using the National Geographic article on the Pony Express (and other resources) , cut out or copy photos of riders
       and other things and make a pony express art gallery or collage.
- ❑ Design your own postage stamp.
- ❑ Make a mini stamp collection for your notebook.

Research
- ❑ Research the types of horses used to ride in the Pony Express and include pictures and descriptions of horses.
- ❑ Research Samuel Morse and the beginning of the Morse Code. Write a one page essay about him
       and try to include a picture. Put this assignment in your notebook.
- ❑ Print something from the computer/internet about the pony express, read, give an oral report, then
       include in your notebook.

History
- ❑ Make a timeline showing the events leading up to the pony express, when it started, ended, and other
       events connected with it.

Geography
- ❑ Make a map showing the ship route around South America, the stagecoach route, and the pony express route.
       Show how many miles for each route.
- ❑ Mark the pony express stations on a map (there are many!)
- ❑ Make a map showing the transcontinental telegraph.
- ❑ Make a topography map of the U.S. showing mountain ranges, The Great Plains, and other Pony Express
       landmarks (like Chimney Rock in Nebraska).

Spelling
- ❑ Study your spelling words - make a vocabulary words list and define words.

Activity
- ❑ Obtain a copy of "The Morse Code" and try tapping a message out using the dots and dashes.
       Write a message for another person to decode.

© Jennifer Steward (from "Everything You Need to Know About Homeschool Unit Studies")

Students place assignment sheet in the front of their notebook and try to complete all assignments by the end of the unit.

Assignment Sheet

Student _____ Unit _____

Subject _____

☐

☐

☐

Subject _____

☐

☐

☐

Subject _____

☐

☐

☐

Subject _____

☐

☐

☐

Subject _____

☐

☐

☐

Subject _____

☐

☐

☐

Activities To Do During Together Time:

Work on notebooks / paste stickers and fill in fact sheets
Daily bird watching / write observations
Take photos - identify and add to notebook
Make a bird house   Make a bird observation tent
Memorize scripture about birds   Blow out and decorate an egg
Cooking (chicken, turkey, cornish game hens, eggs)
Learn homonym prey / pray, sow / sew, fowl / foul etc.
Learn about areas: homes, food, species, feathers, flight, beaks, feet,
habitats, and all the details about birds (Using source books)
Read Aloud - A Cote of Many Colors by Janette Oke

Activities To Do in Co-op:

Tissue Art   Work on presentations, posters
Learn a song   Watch a video   Feed Ducks
Field trips - Ostrich Farm, Sacramento Zoo, Conservation Nature Trail
Older students read book to younger   Make a nest

Activities Children Can Do on Their Own - *See Assignment Sheet*

Vocabulary Words (spelling words for older students)

gliding   soaring   broods habitat   fledgling   chickadee
migration   preening   aerodynamic

Spelling Words

feathers   seeds   worms   beak   prey
hatch   egg   web   migrate   fly
soar   nature   marsh   habitat   glide
lake   fertilize warmth   bird   upstroke
observe   nest   wings   classify   species
downstroke

Things to Include Notebooks / Reports

When doing unit studies, your "notebook" will actually become a full report.
Here is a list of ideas for sheets you can create and put in your notebook / report.

History Topics - About Time Maps

Charts & Graphs
Pictures or photos depicting events
Famous quotes or speeches
Diagrams (labeling parts)
Geographical items - flags of country, map of country
Create newspaper article or copy a real (historical) one
Maps showing routes of exploration
Timeline of specific topic (timeline of Columbus' life
or timeline of inventions etc.)
Copies of pictures of ships, inventions, people
Mind Maps (sort of like picture timelines)

Biographical Reports - About People

A copy or photo of the person
Your "Original" artwork
A picture of their work (piece of art, book, invention)
Coat of Arms
Reports about people can include maps or murals
showing pictures of country where person is from
Book reports of biographies read (oral or written)
Provide examples of actual items that pertain to the
person or his work (Gutenburg, movable type - printed
material)

Geography - Around the world

Make passports
How holidays are celebrated (use pictures -
cuttings from magazines)
Words to songs   World costume
Maps
Recipes from cooking experiments
Diagrams including longitude & latitude
Pictures of people, cultures, customs, food, money
Continent Maps (show resources and industries)
Information on current events

Other Ideas:

_____
_____
_____
_____

Science Topics - God's World

Experiments that you did or that can be done
Charts & Graphs
Diagrams (labeled)
Statistic sheets
Oral book reports or presentations
Biographical sketch of scientist
Pictures of items in topic (insects, clouds, plants)
Sheet listing Scriptures that pertain to topic
Famous people related to topic
Stories or creative writing
Original artwork
Comparisons
Lists
Observations
How-To instructions

Literature Reports

Pictures relating to characters
Copy or picture of book read
About the author
Timeline of events in book
Original artwork
Other works by same author
Map showing setting
Related Scripture, quotes etc.
Favorite character sketch

Other Ideas:

_____
_____
_____
_____
_____
_____
_____
_____

The study of _____

Student's name _____

Date of study _____

Read Aloud title: _____

Books used during study: Author / Publisher

_____   _____

_____   _____

_____   _____

_____   _____

_____   _____

_____   _____

Resources used: _____

_____

_____

_____

Describe projects:_____

_____

_____

_____

Field trips taken: _____

_____

Music or Art connected with this study: _____

_____

Other information about this study: _____

_____

_____

Student's notebook record sheet.

The study of _Birds_

Student's name _Whitney Steward_

Date of study _October 1997_

Read Aloud title: _A Cote of Many Colors_ by Janette Oke

Books used during study: Author / Publisher

Eyewitness Birds

Backyard Birds

Ornithology   Usborne

Stormbird   by Elisia McCuteleon

State Birds colorbook   Dover Publications

Resources used: _Birds of the Bible (Lutheran Laymen's League), All the Birds of No. America / Field Guide, 48 Favorite Bird Stickers (Dover Pub.)_

Describe projects: _We built a bird house and a feeder stand._
We cooked Ostrich Kabobs

Field trips taken: _The Sacramento Zoo, The Lazy Faye Ostrich Farm_

Music or Art connected with this study: _We listened to a tape of songbirds_

Other information about this study: _We did a co-op for this study with the Klein Family. We went to a park and built bird nests. Also observed the ducks_

Student's notebook record sheet.

Student's notebook record sheet

Monthly Record Keeping Sheet

Year _____ Month _____ Student _____

Unit Study Topic: _____

Books Used : _____

_____

_____

Other Resources Used: _____

_____

_____

History : _____

Science: _____

Math: _____

Grammar: _____

Spelling / Vocabulary: _____

Handwriting: _____

Writing: _____

_____

Bible: _____

Silent Reading: _____

Read Aloud Title: _____

Narration: _____

Dictation: _____

Computer: _____

Music: _____

Art: _____

P.E. _____

Field Trips: _____

Other Academically Related Activities: _____

_____

Monthly Record Keeping Sheet

Year __1997__ Month __October__ Student __Whitney Steward__
Unit Study Topic: __BIRDS__

Books Used : __Ornithology (Usborne), All the Birds of No. America__
__Field Guide, Children's Guide to Birds by Jony Johnson,__
__A Cote' of many Colors__

Other Resources Used: __48 Favorite Birds Stickers, Fact Sheets,__
__Birds of the Bible color book__

History : __Read biography of James Audubon by Landmark__
__Books__
Science: __Explore aspects: homes/habitats, food, migration, flight,__
__beaks, feet, types, classes, feathers, bones, courting, nests eggs__
Math: __Math-U-See - Daily Lessons__

Grammar: __Edit writing 3x each week . Work from__
__The Great Editing Adventure 1x each week.__
Spelling / Vocabulary: __Study spelling words. Written test__
__twice. 5-10 New vocabulary words (taken from read aloud__
Handwriting: __copy poems from the book "Birdwatch", dictatic__
__bird story / rewrite in good penmanship. Luke 12:23-24__
Writing: __Fact sheets, bird watching observations, wrote a__
__poem, journal writing, writing letters to missionairies,__
__worked on my notebook__
Bible: __Look up all birds mentioned in Bible, Listed them,__
__memorize Luke 12:23-24__
Silent Reading: __Stormbird by Elisia McCuteLeon__
Read Aloud Title: __A Cote of Many Colors by Janette Oke__
Narration: __Once a week from read aloud__
Dictation: __Twice a week (8x total) from read aloud__
Computer: __Typing practice 2 x each week (Typing Tutor)__
Music: __Daily piano practice (20 min) Songbirds tape__
Art: __Sketch birds, tissue paper art activity__
P.E. __Ride bikes 30 min. 3 x each week__
Field Trips: __Sacramento Zoo, Ostrich Farm__
Other Academically Related Activities: __I compiled a complete__
__notebook and completed all activities and assignments__
__on my assignment sheet.__

Book
Report

Title of Book _____

Author: _____

Main Character : _____

Type of Book: _____   Date Read: _____

Number of Pages: _____   Rate book from 1-10 _____

Describe the book to help others determine if they wish to read it -

_____

_____

_____

_____

_____

_____

_____

_____

_____

_____

Who was your favorite character? _____ Why? _____

_____

What was your favorite part? _____

_____

Where did story take place? _____

Reading List

Title of Book _____ Date read _____ Comments _____ _____	Title of Book _____ Date read _____ Comments _____ _____
Title of Book _____ Date read _____ Comments _____ _____	Title of Book _____ Date read _____ Comments _____ _____
Title of Book _____ Date read _____ Comments _____ _____	Title of Book _____ Date read _____ Comments _____ _____
Title of Book _____ Date read _____ Comments _____ _____	Title of Book _____ Date read _____ Comments _____ _____
Title of Book _____ Date read _____ Comments _____ _____	Title of Book _____ Date read _____ Comments _____ _____
Title of Book _____ Date read _____ Comments _____ _____	Title of Book _____ Date read _____ Comments _____ _____
Title of Book _____ Date read _____ Comments _____ _____	Title of Book _____ Date read _____ Comments _____ _____